HOUSTON LEGENDS

"Like, Rome, Houston was not built in one day. It took many years and the special talents of generations of visionaries and builders. In his book, *Houston Legends*, Hank Moore has captured the unique entrepreneurial spirit that has made our City great."

—**Fred Hofheinz**, Mayor of Houston, 1974-1978.

"Hank Moore is a thought leader. Cognizant of the past, he weaves the accomplishments of others into dynamic strategies. I've worked with him and admire his writings."

—**George P. Mitchell**, Chairman of Mitchell Energy & Development. Developer of The Woodlands and downtown renovation in Galveston.

"Hank Moore truly embodies the concept of the Renaissance Man, from his worldly connections and involvement to his almost eerie sense of business acumen, in forecasting trends and patterns of commerce. To those of us who deal in the often delicate balance of customer and company, it is blessing to have, in Hank Moore, a resource we can depend on for fair, statesmanlike and balanced observation. I count him as a valued business friend."

—**Dan Parsons**, President, The Better Business Bureau of Metropolitan Houston & South Texas.

"Hank Moore is a local Houston icon! He has been the adviser to many leaders in our great state and nation. His book looks to be a grand story telling of what has made Houston so different and great! "

—**Martha Wong**, educator. Former member of the Texas Legislature. Former member of the Houston City Council.

"Every book that Hank Moore writes is a keeper. That's because of his thought leadership and ability to target what is paramount. *Houston Legends* is not only required reading, it is blessed reading for those of us who are Houstonians and those around the world who wish they were. Hank Moore brings out the grits and guts of these pioneers like nobody else could. You will be recommending this book to your friends."

—**Anthony Pizzitola** MBA, CFM, CBCP, MBCI, Quality Assurance Manager - Jones Lang LaSalle.

"Hank Moore knows more people than a person who just got elected as President of the United States, and more importantly he knows how to bring out their traits. I don't know how he does it."

—**George W. Strake Jr.**, Chairman and President of Strake Energy, Inc. Former Texas Secretary of State.

"I am pleased to endorse the great book, *Houston Legends*. People like Hank Moore and the legends he writes about are what continue to make our city better and greater. Continue your great community service for many more years. Your friend always."

—**Felix Fraga**, Neighborhood Centers, Inc. Former member of the Houston City Council. Former member of the HISD school board.

"Great cities draw upon rich histories and visionary people. I've read Hank Moore's previous books and attest that his approach to local history is world-class. Hank has long been a friend and trusted adviser."

—**Lee P. Brown**, Mayor of Houston, 1998-2004. Former chief of police in Houston, Atlanta and New York City.

"The growth of Houston was fueled by opportunity, entrepreneurial spirit and commitment to community building. My family has been proud to be a part of this legacy. Hank Moore's book skillfully details the collective contributions of many great families and citizens. I'm so glad that such an important historical perspective has been written and congratulate Hank for this mighty undertaking."

—**Judson Robinson III**, President and CEO, Houston Area Urban League. Former member of the Houston City Council.

"Hank Moore works miracles in changing stuck mindsets. He empowers knowledge from without by enthusing executives to reach within."

—**Dino Nicandros** (1998), Chairman of the Board, Conoco.

"Mr. Moore is one of the true authority figures for business and organization life. He is the only one with an Ethics Statement, which CEOs understand and appreciate."

—**Ben Love** (2009), Vice Chairman, Chase Bank.

"Hank Moore's Business Tree™ is the most original business model of the last 50 years."

—**Peter Drucker** (2002), business visionary.

"Someday, Hank Moore will write the history of the city to whose future he has mightily contributed."

—**Lyndall Wortham** (1974), community leader.

"Always ahead of the trends, Hank Moore's insights are deep, applicable beyond the obvious."

—**Lady Bird Johnson** (1993), former First Lady of the United States.

"Hank Moore provides fresh approaches to heavily complex issues. His step-by-step study of the business layers makes sense. It shows how much success one could miss by trying to take shortcuts. There cannot be a price put on that kind of expertise."

—**Roy Disney** (2000).

"How can one person with so much insight into cultural history and nostalgia be such a visionary of business and organizations? Hank Moore is one of the few who understands the connection."

—**Dick Clark** (2003), TV icon.

"Hank Moore is a million dollar idea person. He is one of the few business experts whose work directly impacts a company's book value."

—**Peter Bijur** (2007), Chairman of the Board, Texaco.

"30 minutes with Hank Moore is like 30 months with almost any other brilliant business guru. He's exceptional, unlike any other, and with a testimonial list to prove it. As a speaker, he's utterly content rich, no fluff, no 'feely-touchy' nonsense, right to the point and unashamed to tell the truth. There is nobody better. Every CEO needs him."

—**Michael Hick**, Director, Global Business Initiatives.

"I could not have wished for a better boss and mentor in my first professional job than Hank Moore. He leads by example, and taught me valuable lessons not only about business, but also professionalism and ethics that have stood me well throughout my career. Indeed, when I was in a position to mentor others, I've often repeated "Hank Moore stories" to my staff, and they've all heard of my first boss. Over time, I grew to understand more and more that Hank Moore treats others with respect, and thereby commands respect. I was privileged to be trained by this creative and brilliant thinker who gets more accomplished in a day than most do in a week."

—**Heather Covault**, Media Relations Manager,
Writer, Web Editor at Kolo, Koloist.com.

HOUSTON LEGENDS

History and Heritage
of Dynamic Global Capitol

*Back stories of companies, community
leaders and innovators in energy, medicine,
space, technology and entrepreneurship*

HANK MOORE

New York

HOUSTON LEGENDS

History and Heritage of Dynamic Global Capitol

Back stories of companies, community leaders and innovators in energy, medicine, space, technology and entrepreneurship

Published in New York, New York, by Morgan James Publishing. Morgan James and The Entrepreneurial Publisher are trademarks of Morgan James, LLC.
www.MorganJamesPublishing.com

The Morgan James Speakers Group can bring authors to your live event. For more information or to book an event visit The Morgan James Speakers Group at
www.TheMorganJamesSpeakersGroup.com.

A **free** eBook edition is available
with the purchase of this print book.

CLEARLY PRINT YOUR NAME ABOVE IN UPPER CASE

Instructions to claim your free eBook edition:
1. Download the BitLit app for Android or iOS
2. Write your name in **UPPER CASE** on the line
3. Use the BitLit app to submit a photo
4. Download your eBook to any device

ISBN 978-1-63047-468-3 paperback
ISBN 978-1-63047-469-0 eBook
ISBN 978-1-63047-470-6 hardcover
Library of Congress Control Number:
2014918264

Cover Design by:
Rachel Lopez
www.r2cdesign.com

Interior Design by:
Bonnie Bushman
bonnie@caboodlegraphics.com

In an effort to support local communities, raise awareness and funds, Morgan James Publishing donates a percentage of all book sales for the life of each book to Habitat for Humanity Peninsula and Greater Williamsburg.

Get involved today, visit
www.MorganJamesBuilds.com

Habitat
for Humanity®
Peninsula and
Greater Williamsburg
Building Partner

Dedicated to Joan Wilhelm.

TABLE OF CONTENTS

PREFACE

Many of the names in this book have never appeared in a history book or in a business book. They should have been recognized and saluted. Thus came this look at Houston. I chose representative industries and community service niches as snapshots of a wider photo album. Not every name and fact is in here, but this business focused look gives perspective to modern life.

I am a business guru at the national and international levels. My other books are about business, save one on Hollywood (which is big business). This book is a nostalgic stroll down memory lane in Houston, with small doses of business advice thrown in. The purpose is to recall and remember our heritage of business, entrepreneurship and the will to achieve even more.

In researching for this book, I studied dozens of others. Most were picture books and dwelled in the old days from community settlement and emerging society perspectives. It was nice to read about the fight for Texas independence and see pictures of all the old homes that used to be located downtown. This book looks at specters of business, commerce, distribution, consumption and opportunity, which typify Houston's dynamic growth. Hopefully, this history compliments those books full of old pictures.

I started visiting Houston in the early 1950's. I had an aunt, uncle and cousins that lived here. Houston was so much bigger and more cosmopolitan than the little town that I lived in (Austin). Today, I see Houston as a collection of communities, economic engines and entrepreneurial opportunities. I work all over the world and finally got the opportunity to write a hometown book.

ACKNOWLEDGEMENTS

Acknowledgements to:

Sharon Connally Ammann, Jess Bailey, Jim Bardwell, Cyndi Barnett, Robert Battle, Jennifer Bayer, John Beddow, Jodi Bernstein, Judy Blake, Angela Blanchard, Patty Block, Bo Brackendorff, Tom Britton, Robert Brooks, Lee P. Brown, Johnny Carrabba, Tony Chase, Cary Clayborn, Ernie Cockrell, Keena Collins, Rob Cook, Heather Covault, Dirk Cummins, Hector & Arleigh DeLeon, Michael & Jenna Devers, David Dickey, Chuck Finnell, Beverly Gaston, Martin Gaston, Douglas Gehrman, Mary Gibbs, Carl Glaw, Diane Payton Gomez, George Greanias, Darcee Grice, Claire Hart-Palumbo, Phillip Hatfield, Joe Heller, Irene Helsinger, Royce Heslep, Michael Hick, Mary Higginbotham, Paul Hobby, Leisa Holland-Nelson, Richard Huebner, Mitch Jeffrey, Tom Kennedy, Soulat Khan, Jon King, Ken Klingensmith, Dan Krohn, Kirby Lammers, Rich Latimer, Nancy Lauterbach, Torre Lee, Steve & Barbara Levine, Mike Linares, Alex Lopez Negrete, Karen Love, Jackie Lyles, Aymeric Martinola, Dennis McCuistion, Brandi McDonald, Helen McDonald, Eugene Mikle, Julie Moore, Larry Moore,

Sue Moraska, Rob Mosbacher, Dr. Angela Mosley, Bill Moyers, Dennis Murphree, David Pace, Dan Parsons, Howard Partridge, Bill Pellerin, Skip Piatkowski, Anthony Pizzitola, Gordon Quan, Doug Quinn, Judson Robinson III, Donna Rooney, Mike Rosen, Robert Rowland, Grant Sadler, Bill Sherrill, Bill Spitz, Clay Spitz, Joan Spitz, Jonathon Spitz, Lee Spitz, Nelson Spitz, Doris St. Cyr, Maggie Steber, Rod Steinbrook, Gail Stolzenburg, George Strake, Jane Moore Taylor, Pam Terry, Charlie & Laura Thorp, Rich Tiller, Frank Todaro, James & Carolyn Todd, Linda Toyota, Kathie Turner, Louie Werderich, Kathryn Crawford Wheat, Kathy Whitmire, Laura Wilhelm, Sara Wilhelm, Robert Willeby, Melissa Williams, Beth Wolff, R.D. Yoder, John Younker.

Special remembrances to:

Some of the Houston legends in this book whom I knew and worked with: Red Adair, Nancy Ames, Dan Ammerman, Mary Kay Ash, Alan Bean, Allen Becker, Lloyd Bentsen, Garvin Berry, Jeff Bezos, Sarah Campbell Blaffer, Jack Blanton, Paul Boesch, Dr. J. Don Boney, Ed Brandon, Buddy Brock, George R. Brown, Barbara Bush, George H.W. Bush, Earl Campbell, Rod Canion, Phil Carroll, Leonel Castillo, John Chase, Dr. Paul Chu, Ed Clark, Roger Clemens, Seymour Cohen, John Connally, Nellie Connally, Dr. Denton Cooley, Walter Cronkite, Howard Creekmore, Jim Crowther, Bob Cruikshank, Walt Cunningham, Dr. Michael DeBakey, Dominique de Menil, Clyde Drexler, Dr. Red Duke, James A. Elkins, Roky Erickson, Harold Farb, Farrah Fawcett, A.J. Foyt, Felix Fraga, Joe Gaston, Ed Gerlach, Mickey Gilley, John Glenn, David Gockley, Dick Gottlieb, Dr. Norman Hackerman, Michel T. Halbouty, Roy Head, John Hill, Gerald Hines, Oveta Culp Hobby, William P. Hobby Jr., Gary Hoffman, Dr. Phillip G. Hoffman, Fred Hofheinz, Judge Roy Hofheinz, Ima Hogg, Michael Holthouse, Molly Ivins, Don Janicek, Leon Jaworski, Lady Bird Johnson, Lyndon B. Johnson, Richard J.V. Johnson, George Jones, Jay Jones, Janis Joplin, Barbara Jordan, Larry Kane, Tom Katz, Jim Ketelsen, Bob Lanier, Ninfa Laurenzo, Melanie Lawson, William Lawson, Johnny Lee, Mickey Leland, Carl Lewis, Dr. Charles A. LeMaistre, Leo Linbeck, Sonny Look, Ben Love, James A. Lovell, Adie Marks, Anita Martini, Peter Marzio, Carroll Masterson, Harris Masterson, Glenn McCarthy, John Mecom, Ray Miller, Walter Mischer, Cynthia Woods Mitchell, George Mitchell, Huey Meaux, Bill Nash, Don Nelson, Dino Nicandros, Hakeem Ojajuwon,

Hanni Orton, Stewart Orton, John O'Quinn, Nancy Owens, Dr. Rod Paige, Page Parkes, Marcella Perry, Bum Phillips, Andre Previn, Dan Rather, Mary Lou Retton, Leo Reynosa, Don Robey, Judson Robinson Jr., Sylvan Rodriguez, Kenny Rogers, Larry Sachnowitz, Robeert Sakowitz, Wally Schirra, Kenneth Schnitzer, Eddy Scurlock, Marc Shapiro, Dudley Sharp, Alan Shepard, Allan Shivers, Jaclyn Smith, Steve Smith, Ron Stone, Albert Thomas, B.J. Thomas, Rudy Tomjanovich, Jack Valenti, Nina Vance, Dave Ward, Ellen Weingarten, Neva West, Mark White, Harold Wiesenthal, Martha Wong, Gus Wortham, Lyndall Wortham, Bill Young, Frank Young and Marvin Zindler.

Acknowledgements for historical research:

Houston Public Library, Houston Metropolitan Research Center, Fondren Library at Rice University, Johnson Presidential Library, Texas State Library, Texas State Historical Association, the Ray Miller books, other published histories, websites of community service organizations, newspaper files, public records, public domain resources.

Acknowledgements to these organizations:

Leadership Houston
Silver Fox Advisors.
Better Business Bureau
Greater Houston Partnership
Asian Chamber of Commerce
Hispanic Chamber of Commerce
Houston Citizens Chamber of Commerce
Houston Area Urban League
Anti-Defamation League of America
Jewish Community Center
River Oaks Country Club
Houston Garden Club, Forum of Civics
Houston Polo Club
Harris County Historical Society
Houston Public Library
Houston Forum

World Affairs Council

Rotary Club and its Houston area chapters

Neighborhood Centers, Inc., and its affiliate Sheltering Arms

The University of Texas

The University of Houston

Rice University

Texas Southern University

Houston Baptist University

The University of St. Thomas

Houston Community College

United Way of the Texas Gulf Coast, United Way of America

Greater Houston Partnership

Chapter 1

BUILDING FOR GENERATIONS

H ouston represents many things to many people. This is where we live and work, where we are educated and entertained, where culture and community pride are stimulated and where we learn some lessons in living together with others.

Houston is a growth community. It has seen industries emerge and mature. It boasts generations of healthy families. It encompasses lifestyles, cultures and opportunity that no other world-class city can match.

Yet, when you look at Houston, it is a collection of neighborhoods, business districts and quality lifestyles. Houston embodies many growing communities, the confluence being an international hub for this nation. Creative partnerships account for Houston's documented growth.

As the city lives the 21st Century, we celebrate the historical, utilize state-of-the art technology and reflect changing social needs will always be at the forefront of the future. With a sense of pride, reflection and optimism for the future,

Houston's business is dedicated to identifying, meeting and serving every need of our community.

Houston is a collection of neighborhoods, cultures and families. Communities which grow and prosper will analyze and serve the needs of present generations. While honoring the heritage, we carefully plan for the future. Whether in the global sense or on the blocks on which we live, layers of generations comprise our essence.

Every community is a collection of lifestyles, inspired through the structures in which they take place are centers of synergy.

Houston leaders are contributing to the quality of life and encompass the needs and activities of Houstonians.

Growing and Collaborating

The spirit of the early pioneers took shape in structures and lifestyles attributed to business. Stephen Fuller Austin was the first land developer to bring settlers to Texas. The initial group was 300 families.

Austin had complete civil and military authority over his colonists until 1828, subject to rather nominal supervision by the officials at San Antonio. He allowed them to elect militia officers and local officials, corresponding to justices of the peace in the United States. To assure the uniformity of court procedure, he drew up forms and a simple civil and criminal code. As lieutenant colonel of militia, he planned and sometimes led campaigns against Indians. To meet current costs, Austin's only resource was to assess fees against the colonists.

Austin wrote shortly before his death that his wealth was prospective, consisting of the uncertain value of land acquired as compensation for his services as impresario. Besides bringing the colonists to Texas, Austin strove to produce and maintain conditions conducive to their prosperous development.

Aware of the importance of external trade, Austin consistently urged the establishment of ports and the temporary legalization of coasting trade in foreign ships. He believed that coastal trade would establish ties of mutual interest between the colonists and Mexico and enable Mexico to balance imports from England by exporting Texas cotton. Congress legalized the port of Galveston after a survey of the pass by Austin in 1825. As a result, external trade was confined to the United States.

Austin began the Anglo-American colonization of Texas under conditions more difficult in some respects than those that confronted founders of the English colonies on the Atlantic coast. He saw the wilderness transformed into a relatively advanced and populous state, and fundamentally it was his unremitting labor, perseverance, and foresight. His aim was to promote and safeguard the welfare of Texas.

John R. Harris was a New York native who platted the town of Harrisburg, a maritime trading post, in 1824. He built a home and store and in 1829 began assembling a steam sawmill in partnership with others. He died of yellow fever, while in New Orleans on business, leaving his brothers to resolve the inheritance of the town. Houston absorbed Harrisburg in 1926,

Brothers Augustus Allen and John Kirby Allen came to the area in 1836, having entered Texas four years earlier. They were transplanted New Yorkers, with a surveyor named Gail Borden. In 1836, the Allen brothers tried to purchase the town but found that the price was too high. They found a suitable plot of land further up the coastal prairie at the intersection of White Oak Bayou and Buffalo Bayou. The city was founded and named after Texas hero Sam Houston. The city was incorporated in 1839.

By the time of the Civil War, the population was 6,000. By 1900, the population was 44,000. In 1940, Houston ranked as the nation's 27th largest city. By the late 1980's, it had become the fourth largest city.

Prior to 1900, Houston's development centered around cotton, railroads and timber. With cotton reigning as king, textile mills all over the world received and processed the commodity. Middlemen such as William Marsh Rice shipped the "white gold" to northeastern and British textile mills. Rice University, founded in 1912, was named for him.

By 1900, Galveston and Waco were the two largest cities in Texas because they were the dominant cotton producing centers. In 1900, a hurricane wiped out Galveston, killing 6,000 people. Houston's port, though 50 miles inland, picked up the shipping business. The cotton, timber and cattle shipping town evolved into a major port. The conversion of the marshy Buffalo Bayou into the Houston Ship Channel precipitated rapid industrial growth.

Paul Bremond was the primary lumber figure. He dreamed of linking Houston to the Piney Woods with a timber-hauling railroad. The line that he built was by

1890 part of a network that made transportation by the bayou important. Thus, the motto "Houston, Where 17 Railroads Meet the Sea." The early red brick Cotton Exchange building still stands at the corner of Travis at Franklin.

Houston's building activity was brisk and reflected the spirit of early settlers, pioneers, business leaders and community participants. The early leaders of Houston set high standards of behavior that have been followed enthusiastically others over the years.

The earliest bankers included Thomas Bagby, T.W. House and Benjamin Shepherd, all names reflected on streets today.

The city was organized in response to specific needs. Its history is one of addressing and meeting other emerging needs and innovation. In 1900, a hurricane wiped out Galveston, killing 6,000 people. This removed Galveston as a rival to Houston. It spurred the construction of the Port of Houston, which opened in 1914.

Meanwhile, oil was discovered at the Spindletop field, near Beaumont, in 1901. More oil was discovered at Humble in 1904. With Houston becoming a boom town, abundant growth occurred. The limitless economic opportunity fueled the city as an energy provider to the nation. With the outbreak of war in 1917, the heightened need for fuel assured Houston's prosperity and continued expansion. By 1920, the population was 138,000, and Houston was known as "the Magnolia City."

The new Houston became home to industrial and commercial enterprises. Howard Hughes Sr. founded Hughes Tool Company. The Anderson Clayton Company, one of the nation's largest cotton firms, opened headquarters in "the Bayou City." Energy corporations formed in Houston, including Texaco in 1908, Gulf in 1916, Humble in 1917 and Sinclair in 1918.

New sources of wealth created elite business leaders, including lumberman and builder Jesse Jones, Humble co-founder Ross Sterling, lumberman and oilman John Henry Kirby and Texaco founder J.S. Cullinan.

Everywhere that you look in Houston, you see the fingerprints of business. This includes downtown, the Medical Center, the universities and colleges, the Galleria, NASA, Greenway Plaza, entertainment and sports facilities, airports, churches, and schools. As business and industry were challenged to perform at their highest standards, the entire community has benefited exponentially. In the minds of innovators and those who have followed, we care, we achieve, and we look for ways to get better at what we do.

As a result, Houston has experienced several eras of planned, sustained growth. We're more than a boom or a trend. When reading this history of Houston, you will find the legacy of business on almost every page. Orderly growth has been achieved by mastering technology, business standards and adapting to changing community dynamics. Entrepreneurs have embraced innovation, creativity, safety and commitment to quality.

The best indicator of progress made is to periodically re-examine our best work, celebrate the teamwork involved and then re-apply the winning ingredients toward the next phase of growth. Because our community has mastered the fine art of collaboration, we have many great successes to recognize and admire. Houston Legends are symbolic of the mission and actual practices of community leaders, bringing the best minds and resources into successful business partnerships.

Every facet of business plays a part in facilitating orderly community growth. As our communities prosper, so do our member firms. Collectively, we make artistic, technical, procedural and economic differences in the greater Houston area.

As our city progresses through the 21st Century, we celebrate the historical, utilize state-of-the-art technology and continually seek to improve the quality of life. Strategies which address and reflect changing social needs will always be at the forefront of the future.

Time Capsule

The year was 1923. Houston was nearing its century mark as a growth-oriented city, well into its fifth generation of residents.

Milk and ice were still being delivered to homes in wagons. Regular gasoline was pumped into model-T Fords at four cents per gallon. Windup Victrolas played jazz music for the Roaring 20's. It was an era of homemade bread, band concerts in outdoor gazebos and ice cream socials. Houston had two high schools and not yet enough traffic to warrant highways.

In 1923, the population of Houston was about 70,000. Calvin Coolidge was President, and Oscar Holcombe was Mayor. Downtown was primarily dominated by homes. There were some magnificent commercial structures, including the new Rice Hotel. Trolley cars took citizens out to the far edges of town, the recently annexed Heights and the brand new Medical Center, built on the site of a lumber mill across the country road from Rice University.

In 1923, tracts of land in the new River Oaks subdivision were selling for less than $2,000. A major building under construction was the Museum of Fine Arts...a renovation to that same museum is one of tonight's Apex Award winners.

Around town, you still saw horse-drawn carriages and other vestiges of Houston's bygone days. Citizens were learning more about each other—through newspapers. Telephones hung on the wall and had to be cranked. Houston still had not yet had its first radio station sign onto the airwaves.

The industrial age was just beginning to spawn economic growth opportunities. Houston was ahead of the curve, usually has been and still is.

Downtown Houston, circa 1918, when streetcars were the primary source of public transportation.

U.S. President Franklin D. Roosevelt (left), conferring with Houston's Jesse Jones. Following the Depression, Mr. Jones was an advisor to the government on economic and business matters.

Chapter 2
REAL ESTATE, CONSTRUCTION AND BUILDING

P rofessional builders and contractors, rather than the owners themselves, constructed Houston's first houses. These houses, with glass window panes, wooden floors and brick chimneys were more tightly sealed and better insulated than the earlier cabins.

Housing types and size varied within the city, in contrast to the early settlers' basic requirements. Many years ago, it was common to have multiple generations in family dwellings. Some early residents augmented their incomes by taking in boarders. Many of the new immigrants and workers lived in the hotels.

The first capitol building for the Republic of Texas was built in 1837 on what later became the 900 block of Texas Avenue. After serving as the state capitol for two years, the building became a series of hotels until it was demolished in 1881. It was replaced by the Capitol Hotel, which was razed to make room for the Rice

Hotel. The Rice opened in 1913 and closed in the 1970's. In 1998, the building was renovated into luxury lofts.

The city was divided into wards, geographic boundaries that were common in the early 19th Century. Houston had six wards, each electing two aldermen to the Houston City Council. The election of the Mayor of Houston was citywide. The wards came together at the intersection of Congress and Main streets.

The first ward housed the city's market house and produce industry facilities. The second ward included the courthouse and warehouses, where lawyers and merchants resided. The third was southeast, where businesspeople, craftsmen and professionals resided. The fourth ward was the central portion of the city. Freed slaves developed Freedmen's Town in the fourth ward. The fifth ward was added in the 1860's and the sixth ward in the 1870's to accommodate the city's growth.

The ward system was abolished in the early 1904. The city changed to a commission form of government. Residents still identify certain communities, especially those part of the city since incorporation, as being "wards" of the city.

The Houston Club, established in 1894, was the oldest social club in Houston, with a 118-year history. In 1954, the Houston Club moved to the 811 Rusk building in Downtown Houston. Members included business leaders, cultural leaders, consuls general, doctors, entrepreneurs, governors, mayors and presidents.

The original Binz Building was Houston's first skyscraper in 1898. It had six stories. For citizens, riding up and down its elevator was a fun pastime. The building was named for Jacob S. Binz, one of many industrious German immigrants in the business scene. A new Binz Building was constructed in 1951, followed by the current structure in 1982. In the 19th Century, homes in Houston were centered in and near the downtown era. After 1900, two fine home areas emerged: Westmoreland Place and Courtlandt Place. The forerunners of River Oaks, they housed the rich and powerful.

Westmoreland Place was built in Victorian times, created in 1902. According to the National Register nomination, the Westmoreland Historic District encompasses Houston's first planned, elite residential neighborhood. Westmoreland Place was developed by the South End Land Company as a "private place" neighborhood. It contained an eclectic mixture of Late Victorian and early 20th Century house types of both large and moderate size.

A major characteristic of Westmoreland houses is glass front doors with transom and sidelights. Many houses had large entrance halls, frequently off center, containing a staircase with Colonial or Craftsman motif balustrades. Many early Westmoreland house had stables or garages with staff quarters above on the rear property line. These sometimes emulated the architecture, materials and detailing of the main house.

Courtlandt Place was one of Houston's earliest elite residential subdivisions. The residential enclave began in 1906, when the Courtlandt Improvement Company purchased the land and laid out the subdivision on the southern edge of the city. The first houses were built in 1909. Gateways at the end of the central boulevard limited access to residents only, while deed restrictions stipulated land use, minimum cost and house size. Courtlandt Place served as a model for Montrose in 1910. Early residents were the old elite of Houston. The district was admitted to the National Register of Historic Places in 1979 and received a Texas historical marker in 1989.

The Warwick Hotel was opened in 1926 as an upscale apartment building. In the 1960's it was purchased by oilman John Mecom. It was upgraded by furnishings, including wall panels owned by Napoleon's sister. When it was re-launched as a hotel, guests reveled to the gold-plated Rolls Royce on the ballroom dance floor, filled with presents for the guests. The Mecom fountain, facing the Warwick, is an icon along Main Street.

Legends Who Built the City

AmREIT Inc. headquartered in Houston, Texas is a full service, vertically integrated and self-administered real estate investment trust, founded in 1993 by H. Kerr Taylor. It owns, operates, acquires and selectively develops and redevelops neighborhood and community shopping centers located in high-traffic, densely populated, affluent areas with significant barriers to entry. AmREIT's portfolio consists of 29 retail properties in Houston, Dallas, San Antonio, Austin and Atlanta. In addition, AmREIT manages and has varying minority ownership interests in eight advised funds, which operate 18 properties.

George Rufus Brown, businessman, civil engineer and philanthropist, was born in Belton, Texas, on May 12, 1898. He joined the U.S. Marines in the final months of World War I and later worked briefly as a mining engineer in Butte,

Montana. After being injured in a mining accident, he returned to Texas to join a small construction firm founded by his brother, Herman Brown. The firm later became Brown and Root, Incorporated, after Herman's brother-in-law, Dan Root, a prosperous cotton farmer, made an investment in the firm.

The paving of dirt roads and building of steel bridges for municipal and county governments led the firm to successful joint bids to construct the Marshall Ford (now Mansfield) Dam on the Colorado River. In 1940, the company won a $90 million joint bid to build the Naval Air Station in Corpus Christi. By the late 1950's, Brown and Root was one of the largest engineering and construction companies in the world. In the 1960's and 1970's the firm completed jobs world-wide, including Guam, Spain, the United Kingdom, Iran and the Persian Gulf.

In 1942, the brothers formed the Brown Shipbuilding Company on the Houston Ship Channel, which built 359 ships during World War II, employed 25,000 people and was awarded a presidential citation. After the war, the Browns and a group of investors purchased the Big Inch and Little Inch pipelines and founded Texas Eastern Transmission Corporation. After Herman's death in 1962, George became president of the company. Later that year, the corporation was sold to the Halliburton Company. Brown served as a director of the Halliburton Company, Armco Steel Corporation, Louisiana Land and Exploration Company, International Telephone and Telegraph Corporation, Trans-World Airlines, Southland Paper Company, First City Bancorporation and Highland Oil Company.

George R. Brown served on important commissions for presidents Truman, Eisenhower, Kennedy and Johnson, and was appointed to commissions for the state of Texas, from the 1930's under Governor James Allred up to the 1970's under Governor Dolph Briscoe. He was a well-known friend and visible supporter of Lyndon B. Johnson throughout his political career. He was the recipient of many honors during his lifetime, including Awards from Rice University, Colorado School of Mines, Southwestern University and the University of Texas. He received several awards in construction and engineering, including the John Fritz Medal in 1977 from the five national engineering societies and the American Petroleum Institute Gold Medal. Brown served as chairman of the board of trustees of Rice University for 15 of his 25 years of service on the board.

In 1951, the Brown brothers and their wives established the Brown Foundation, through which they pursued a strong and generous interest in philanthropy.

The foundation had granted more than $400 million to charitable institutions, primarily in higher education and the arts.

John Saunders Chase Jr. was the first licensed African-American architect in the state of Texas. He was also the first African-American to serve on the U.S. Commission of Fine Arts, which reviewed the design for the United States. Upon graduation from UT, Chase moved to Houston and started his own firm. In 1963, he built the Riverside National Bank, the first black-owned bank in Texas. In 1971, he and 12 others founded the National Organization of Minority Architects (NOMA).

Randall Davis led in the development, selling and leasing of lofts in downtown Houston.

Harold Farb transformed the city's landscape with more than 30,000 apartments. He amassed a fortune by developing reasonably priced complexes and was landlord to more than 1 million people in a career than spanned more than 50 years.

Harold entered the real estate industry through his father, who operated a drugstore and two movie houses, the Rainbow Theater and the Sunset Theater. In 1953, Harold Farb established his own real estate development business. His first project was a 20-unit complex in the Montrose area at 1811 Richmond at Woodhead. The successive complexes were much bigger. By the 1970s, Farb had become the leader of the apartment development business,

He was also the first developer to bring amenities like exercise rooms and gathering places for those in the community. He was the first to embellish landscaping around large courtyards. In 1984, Forbes magazine named Farb among the 400 richest people in America. In addition to the Carlyle, he published Ultra magazine, a lifestyle monthly aimed at high income readers.

His love of entertainment came from hanging around the theaters. Once he became a successful developer, Farb financed five albums of himself singing show tunes and built a posh supper club called the Carlyle in the early 1980's to have a place to sing standards by composers like George Gershwin and Cole Porter.

Gerald Hines was a Houston real estate developer, his reach going to 18 countries. Hines, an Indiana steelworker's son, came to Houston in 1948. He formed an engineering partnership and started a fledgling real estate business on the side, as Gerald D. Hines Interests in 1957. The early projects were warehouses and small office buildings. His first large-scale commercial development came in 1967 when Shell Oil Company hired him to construct a new headquarters building. The Galleria, Pennzoil Place, Williams Tower and 400+ others followed.

The Hines portfolio of projects underway, completed, acquired and managed for third parties includes more than 1,100 properties representing approximately 454,000,000 square feet of office, residential, mixed-use, industrial, hotel, medical, retail and sports facilities, as well as large, master-planned communities and land developments. With controlled assets valued at approximately $25.8 billion, Hines is one of the largest real estate organizations in the world.

Roy Mark Hofheinz, was born in Beaumont and at age 15 began working to support his mother. He graduated from law school at age 19. Hofheinz served in the Texas House of Representatives (1934-1936) and as Harris County judge (1936-1944). After losing the election for his third term as county judge, Hofheinz turned to advancing his career in private-sector law and business. He returned to public life in 1952, when elected Mayor of Houston.

Hofheinz returned to law and business. He and his partner, R.E. "Bob" Smith, created the Houston Sports Association, which sought to build a gigantic sports stadium under a roof. HSA received a major-league baseball franchise on the promise of building a new stadium and in 1965 the world's first domed stadium was completed. Hofheinz claimed the Astrodome was "the Eighth Wonder of the World." Though several Harris County bond issues had funded most of the $31.6 million for the stadium, the HAS held a long-term lease on the building.

The Astrodome soon became the home of the Houston Colt 45's (renamed the Houston Astros) and the Houston Oilers. Other events held in the Astrodome included the Houston Livestock Show and Rodeo, as well as Ringling Brothers and Barnum & Bailey Circus. To the Astrodomain complex, he added Astroworld and hotels. Eventually, John J. McMullen and Dave LeFevre purchased the Houston Astros. Servico Incorporated bought the hotels. Six Flags Over Texas took management of Astroworld. His son Fred Hofheinz served as Mayor of Houston from 1974-1978.

William Clifford Hogg, lawyer and businessman, son of Governor James Stephen Hogg. While studying at Southwestern University, he contemplated entering the Methodist ministry but finally decided to study law at the University of Texas, where he received his LL.B. degree in 1897. Will Hogg practiced law for a few years in San Antonio and then joined his father in the firm of Hogg, Robertson and Hogg at Austin. He later was associated with the Mercantile Trust Company in St. Louis until his father's death in 1906 made it necessary for him to take charge of the Hogg interests in Houston.

He became assistant to Joseph S. Cullinan of Texaco and was a director of such subsidiaries as Southern Trust Company, Midland Securities Company and Producers Oil Company. In 1913, Hogg, Cullinan and James L. Autry formed the Farmers Petroleum Company, the Fidelity Trust Company and the American Republics Corporation. During World War I. Hogg served in Washington as a dollar-a-year man in the special intelligence service.

After the war, Hogg Brothers was organized to handle the family properties and investments. Will Hogg promoted various altruistic projects including the Houston Civic Center and the Forum of Civics. In 1922, he sponsored development of the restricted residential River Oaks Addition in Houston. He developed the Organization for the Enlargement by the State of Texas of its Institutions of Higher Learning. He was a member of the UT Board of Regents. After his death in 1930, his will left bequests to various Texas institutions of learning and gave the bulk of his estate to UT, in support of the Hogg Foundation for Mental Health.

Bob Lanier was born to working class parents in the refinery town of Baytown in 1925. He was influenced by events and policies during the Depression who was greatly influenced by Franklin Delano Roosevelt's policies. After graduating from the UT Law School, in 1949, he joined Baker & Botts, practicing law for 10 years before switching to a business career. He worked in banking and established himself as a major Houston real estate developer, focusing upon subdivisions and apartments.

His first involvement in the public sector was as a gubernatorial appointee to the Texas Highway Commission, which he chaired, and chairman of METRO, Houston's transit authority. Lanier also was a founding member of Houston Community College. In 1991, Lanier was elected Mayor of Houston, serving until 1997. He averaged 88 percent in his re-election races, with strong support in each political party and ethnic group. As mayor, he was affectionately called "Mayor Bob" and worked with council members to build as collaborative culture in municipal government. The emphasis of his terms included diversity, improving the effectiveness of city government and improving public safety.

Lanier's recognitions included the NAACP's Texas Hero award, the Hubert Humphrey Civil Rights Award, National Auto Dealers award, Bond Market Association award, Associated General; Contractors APEX award, Urban Beautification Award from the American Horticultural Society, Texas Transportation Institute's Hall of Honor and the Houston Hall of Fame.

Leo Linbeck founded the Linbeck Group, LLC, in 1938. The company was subsequently captained by Leo Linbeck Jr. and now by Leo Linbeck III. In 1967, the company pioneered the Team Building process. In 1997, the company helped co-found the Lean Construction Institute and is one of the first builders to deploy Integrated Project Delivery.

J. W. Link was an early 20th Century land developer. He envisioned a "great residential addition" according to the neighborhood's original sales brochure. Link's planning details for the area included four wide boulevards with the best curbing and extensive landscaping. Link built his own home in Montrose, known as the Link-Lee Mansion, now part of the University of St. Thomas campus. The Montrose Line ran streetcars through the neighborhood. Link wrote: "Houston has to grow. Montrose is going to lead the procession." It grew far beyond the neighborhood Montrose was first platted in 1911. In 1926, the Plaza Apartment Hotel, Houston's first apartment hotel, opened on Montrose Boulevard, modeled after the Ritz-Carlton in New York.

During the 1960's and 1970's, Montrose was called "a uniquely Houston kind of Bohemia, a mad mix made possible by the city's no-holds-barred, laissez faire form of growth." The area includes restaurants shops, street festivals, nightclubs, cultural venues and street life. Lovett Blvd. was once "radio row," with KTRH, KLOL, KILT and KPFT. The Westheimer Colony Art Festival began in 1971 and the subsequent street fair in 1973. Folk music clubs like Anderson Fair and Sand Mountain catered to the folk scene and other venues featured psychedelic rock, blues, punk and new wave clubs like Paradise Rock Island, Omni and Numbers.

Many of the old homes have been converted to businesses and/or restaurants since 1936. Examples of Houston's historic residential architecture can be found in the bungalows and mansions off Montrose and Westheimer. Montrose boasts many thrift, vintage, second-hand and antique stores. Montrose encompasses a thriving arts district, including the Museum of Fine Arts, Contemporary Arts Museum, Menil Collection, Rothko Chapel and the Chapel of St. Basil.

Walter Max Mischer was a real estate developer and banker whose most lasting influence was in persuading the Legislature to approve creation of municipal utility districts. Municipal Utility Districts allowed developers to profitably lay subdivision streets, water and sewer systems and allow residents to pay off the debt as homes were built and sold. The results have been thousands of affordable homes. Subdivisions he had a hand in developing include Cinco Ranch, Briargrove Park, Briar Meadow, Fondren Southwest, Cypress Creek Lakes, Stablewood, River Park, Heritage Park, Oak Park Trails, The Park at Memorial Heights, The Vintage and Vintage Lakes.

Walter P. Moore and his firm, a national leader in the design of high-rise buildings and sports facilities, guided the engineering of many renowned structures, including Astroworld, The Summit, Exxon Chemical headquarters complex, Delmar Stadium, Hofheinz Pavilion, Miller Outdoor Theatre, The Astrodome, 1100 Milam Building and Rice Stadium.

Seth Irwin Morris formed an architectural partnership in Houston in 1938. Prominent structures under his creative wing included the Astrodome, Harris County Family Law Center, World Trade Center, On e and Two Shell Plaza, Pennzoil Place, Wortham Center, Houston Central Public Library, First City Bank Tower, One Allen Center and Memorial Hospital Southwest. He was 1961 president of the American Institute of Architects and named a Distinguished Alumnus of Rice University in 1981.

Kenneth Schnitzer was a third-generation Houstonian and a visionary Texas real estate developer and civic leader whose 30 commercial buildings form much of the city skyline. After a stint as a salesman for his family's Magnolia Paper Company, he began a career that produced the 71-story Wells Fargo Bank Plaza, the 50-story Enron building, Mcorp Plaza and Citicorp Center.

The 127-acre Greenway Plaza was among the nation's first large-scale, planned urban developments to emphasize greenbelts and extensive landscaping. By the 1980's, the complex had a 400-room hotel, an underground shopping mall, the Summit home of professional sports teams and a workday population exceeding 12,000 spread through 10 office towers.

The Houston Summit, built as a public-private joint venture, served as a model widely copied elsewhere. Schnitzer won a political fight to have the city build the arena, which opened in 1975, at Greenway Plaza instead of downtown. In the arena's early years, he was co-owner and managing partner of the Houston Rockets basketball team and the Aeros hockey team, both Summit tenants. The arena was later known as Compaq Center and is now known as Lakewood Church.

Kenneth Schnitzer was a founding director of Houston Proud, created to spur a rebound from the oil price collapse in the 1980's. He was founding chairman of the Houston Economic Development Council, director of the Greater Houston Partnership and director of the Greater Houston Convention and Visitors Bureau. A vacation in Mexico inspired him to create and develop a master-planned resort in Los Cabos, near the tip of Baja California, a $200 million luxury community called Villas del Mar overlooking the Sea of Cortez.

Robert Everett Smith, Houston oilman and civic leader, played semi-professional baseball for 10 years. He was an oilfield roughneck for Humble, Gulf and Texaco. He was district manager in sales for an oilfield supply firm, WKM Company, the position that led to his first entrepreneurial enterprise as a drilling contractor and producer in 1920. Smith went into partnership with Claude Hamill, established a Houston headquarters in 1925, and began to purchase land near Hobby Airport. In the 1940s he bought out Hamill's interest, including 36 oil wells.

R.E. "Bob" Smith was a regional director of Civil Defense, chairman of Houston Housing Authority and president of the Petroleum Club. His Jamaica Corporation developed Jamaica Beach, Tiki Island and other Galveston subdivision. He was a partner to Roy Hofheinz on the Astrodome project. By 1964, Smith owned more land than any other person in Harris County, over 11,000 acres, where he raised Santa Gertrudis, Brahman, shorthorn, and Hereford cattle, as well as thoroughbreds and quarter horses. His success in oil, real estate, and cattle ranching led to an estimated fortune of $500 million.

Tom Tellepsen founded Tellepsen Builders in 1909. The company's first notable project was the Miller Outdoor Theatre in 1922, followed by the Rice University Chemistry Building in 1923. In 1925, the company began work on Houston's first 10-story hotel at Texas Avenue & La Branch. The company constructed the Palmer Memorial Episcopal Church in 1927 and the Episcopal Church of the Redeemer in 1932. Tom's son, Howard Tellepsen, became president of the Tellepsen Construction Company in 1940. The firm was awarded many projects that have become Houston landmarks, such as Ellington Field, Annunciation Greek Orthodox Cathedral, Texas Children's Hospital, St. Luke's Episcopal Hospital, the Falcon Dam and the Melrose Building. The company was involved with the construction of the Shamrock Hotel. Howard Tellepsen Jr. succeeded his father as CEO of Tellepsen Builders.

Weingarten Realty Co., founded in 1948, spun from the grocery store chain that had been founded in 1902. The firm owns and leases shopping centers, becoming a publicly traded company in 1985.

Beth Wolff is president of Beth Wolff Realtors. She served as president of the Houston Association for Realtors. She has been appointed to city commissions by Houston Mayors Kathy Whitmire, Bob Lanier, Bill White, Lee Brown and Annise Parker. She was involved with the first house built by Houston Habitat for Humanity, the convention center hotel, Quality of Life Coalition and oversight chair for Opportunity Houston. I met Beth in 1987, when she picked me to be in Leadership Houston. In 2013, she was named a Houston Legend.

Welcome W. Wilson Jr. has a real estate development firm specializing in single-tenant office buildings and industrial properties with warehouse and manufacturing facilities. He has extensive experience in industrial development, residential subdividing, office buildings and retail centers. In 2011, he was appointed to the University of Houston System Board of Regents by Governor Rick Perry. He is a director of River Oaks Financial Group and chairman of the board for Southwest Houston Redevelopment Authority.

Metropolitan Area Communities

Alief began in 1861, when land was claimed. It was sold in 1893 to Francis Meston who planned to engineer a community, named the Dairy, Texas. The first two settlers were Dr. John S. Magee and his wife, Alief Ozelda Magee. She applied to open the first post office in 1895, and it was named "Alief" in her honor to avoid confusion with mail intended for the similarly named town of Daisy, Texas. The site of the post office, which was operated from her home, was given a Texas State Historical Marker in 1990. The town was officially renamed Alief in 1917. The community was annexed by the City of Houston in 1977.

Alvin was settled in the mid-19th century when bull ranches were established. The Santa Fe Railroad expanded, and a settlement was established along the railroad. It was named Morgan by residents in honor of Santa Fe employee Alvin Morgan. When it discovered that the name Morgan was already taken, the town named itself after Morgan's first name. Alvin incorporated in 1893, making it the oldest incorporated settlement in Brazoria County. The Nolan Ryan Baseball Museum is in the Nolan Ryan Foundation and Exhibit Center on the campus of Alvin Community College.

Baytown began to be settled as early as 1822. One of its first residents was Nathaniel Lynch, who set up a ferry crossing at the junction of the San Jacinto River and Buffalo Bayou. The ferry service that he started is still in operation today, now known as the Lynchburg Ferry. Other early residents included William Scott, one of Stephen F. Austin's original settlers, and Ashbel Smith, who owned a plantation in the area.

The city now known as Baytown was originally three separate towns. Goose Creek was named for the bayou where Canadian geese wintered and whose name is still reflected in the area's Goose Creek CISD, whose establishment dates back to 1850. With the discovery of an oil field, the communities of Pelly and East Baytown developed as boomtowns. The three were merged in 1948 as Baytown. In 1916, Humble Oil and Refining Company built the first offshore drilling operation and later built the Baytown Refinery, which would become one of the largest Exxon refineries in the world. Steel manufacturing in Baytown began in 1970 when United States Steel opened the Texas Works near the city, now operating as JSW Steel USA, Inc.

Beaumont was first settled in 1824 by Noah and Nancy Tevis, who organized a farm on the west bank of Neches River. A small community grew around the farm, which was named Tevis Bluff. In 1835, the land of Tevises and the nearby community of Santa Anna (50 acres) was purchased by Henry Millard, Joseph Pulsifer and Thomas B. Huling, who platted a town named after Jefferson Beaumont, Millard's brother-in law. Beaumont became a town on Dec. 16, 1838. Entrepreneurship made Beaumont thrive, including real estate, transportation expansion, retail sales, railroads, construction, lumber sales and communications.

The Beaumont Rice Mill, founded in 1892 by Joseph Eloi Broussard, was the first commercial rice mill in Texas. Oil was discovered at nearby Spindletop on Jan. 10, 1901, the first major oil field and one of the largest in American history. The city became a major center for shipbuilding during World War II. Oil is, and has always been, a major export of the city, and a major contributor to the national GDP.

Bellaire was founded in 1908 by William Wright Baldwin, who was the president of the South End Land Company. Bellaire was founded on what was part of William Marsh Rice's 9,449-acre ranch. Baldwin started Bellaire in the middle of "Westmoreland Farms" to serve as a residential neighborhood and an agricultural trading center. South End Land Company advertised to farmers in the Midwestern United States. Baldwin stated that the town was named "Bellaire" or "Good Air" for its breezes". Bellaire may have been named after Bellaire, Ohio, a town served by one of Baldwin's rail lines. Bellaire was incorporated as a city with a general charter in 1918, 10 years after its founding.

Bryan is named for an original settler. The area was part of a land grant to Moses Austin by Spain. His son, Stephen F. Austin helped bring settlers to the area, among them his nephew, William Joel Bryan. The town of Bryan was founded in 1821 and grew when the Houston & Texas Central Railroad arrived in 1860. In 1871, the City of Bryan became incorporated. In nearby College Station, Texas A&M College opened in 1876. In 1910, the town built an interurban railroad to College Station Texas. In 1913, the first Jewish place of worship, Temple Freda synagogue, was opened. In 2006, the Texas A&M University System announced the Texas A&M Health Science Center campus to be built in Bryan

Channelview was given its name since it is located on the northeastern curve of the Houston Ship Channel. The site of Channelview was home to Lorenzo de Zavala, one of the founding fathers of the Republic of Texas. During World War II the area south of Market to the Ship Channel, and what is now DeZavala St. to the tollway, was part of the U.S. Army Ordnance Depot.

Clear Lake City sits on land developed by James Marion West, a businessman with interests in ranching, lumber and oil. His main ranch property and the site of his home was near the shores of Clear Lake and Clear Creek. Humble Oil purchased the property from West in 1938 after oil was discovered. When plans were made to establish the Johnson Space Center in the area, Humble Oil's venture, Friendswood Development Company, made plans to establish a residential development. The Clear Lake City Community Association was established in 1963. Clear Lake City was annexed by the city of Houston in 1977. The eastern portion iwas annexed by the city of Pasadena.

Conroe was named after lumberman Isaac Conroe, who founded a sawmill there in 1881. The city benefited from the lumber and oil industries. Originally named "Conroe's Switch" it had an influx of residents in the late 19th century due to the lumber demands on the piney wood forest of the area. It was incorporated in 1904. During the 1930s', due to oil profits, the city boasted more millionaires per capita than any other U.S. city. Elvis Presley performed at the Conroe High School football field on August 24, 1955.

Cypress was populated by the Atakapa and Akokisa Indian tribes, joined in the 1840's by German settlers. The German heritage is reflected in such street names as Huffmeister and Telge Roads. General Sam Houston and his Texas Army camped in the area on March 22, 1836, just before the Battle of San Jacinto. The area is also called Cy-Fair for Cypress-Fairbanks, This comes from when the Big Cypress School and Fairbanks High School combined in the 1930's to form Cy-Fair High School and the Cypress-Fairbanks Independent School District. Large residential and commercial development began in the 1980's transformed the once rural area into one of the Houston area's largest suburban communities. In 2008, the Cypress Historical Society was formed as a non-profit corporation.

Deer Park was founded in 1892 by Simeon Henry West, a farmer and adventurer from Illinois. He named the town for the deer that roamed the Gulf plains. The subdivision was established in 1893 and was the site of a Galveston, Harrisburg and San Antonio Railway station. A Deer Park post office was established in 1893, discontinued in 1919 and re-established in 1930. Shell Oil Company built a new refinery in 1928. The citizens of Deer Park voted to incorporate in 1948.

Deer Park bills itself as the "Birthplace of Texas," being near the site of the Battle of San Jacinto, where Texas won its independence from Mexico. The final battle of the Texas Revolution took place on April 21, 1836. General Santa Anna was captured at Vince's Bayou. The San Jacinto Monument is a 567-foot column located between Deer Park and La Porte. The monument began construction in 1936, which was the 100th anniversary of the battle. It was completed and dedicated on April 21, 1939. The San Jacinto Museum of History is located inside the monument, and focuses on Texas culture and heritage. The San Jacinto Battlefield was designated a National Historic Landmark on in 1960 and is listed on the National Register of Historic Places. The monument was renovated in 1983 and was the scene of the Texas Sesquicentennial Celebration in 1986. It was designated a Historic Civil Engineering Landmark in 1992.

Anchored across the road from the San Jacinto Monument is the Battleship Texas. The USS Texas (BB-35) was launched in 1912 and commissioned in 1914. It saw service in World War I and World War II (one of six ships to have that distinction). It was decommissioned in 1948, having earned a total of five battle stars for service in World War II and was turned into a museum ship. It was the first battleship declared to be a National Historic Landmark.

Dickinson is located on a tract of land granted to John Dickinson in 1824, and named after him. A settlement had been established in this area on Dickinson Bayou before 1850. The Galveston, Houston and Henderson Railroad was built directly through Dickinson, used during the Civil War to successfully retake Galveston. The Dickinson Land and Improvement Association was organized in the 1890's by Fred M. Nichols and others. It marketed to potential farmers with claims of the soil's suitability for food crops, and to socialites with the creation of the Dickinson Picnic Grounds and other attractions. By 1911, the Galveston–Houston Electric Railway had three stops in Dickinson.

Friendswood was founded in 1895 by members of the Religious Society of Friends (Quakers). The city has a total area of 20.9 square miles. In 2007, CNN/ Money Magazine rated Friendswood as one of "America's Best Places to Live."

Galveston Bay was settled by the Karankawa and Atakapan tribes, particularly the Akokisa, who lived throughout the Gulf coast region. Spanish explorers such as the Rivas-Iriarte expedition and José Antonio de Evia charted the bay and gave it its name. The pirate Jean Lafitte established a short-lived kingdom based in Galveston in the 19th Century with bases and hide-outs around the bay and around Clear Lake. Lafitte was forced to leave in 1821 by the U.S. Navy. Following its declaration of independence from Spain, Mexico moved to colonize its northern territory of Texas by offering land grants to settlers both from within Mexico and from the nearby United States. The colony established by Stephen F. Austin and the Galveston Bay and Texas Land Company of New York rapidly began a wave of settlement around the bay.

Hempstead was organized in 1856 by Dr. Richard R. Peebles and James W. McDade to sell lots in the newly established community. In 1858, the Houston & Texas Central Railway was extended to Hempstead, causing the community to become a distribution center between the Gulf Coast and the interior of Texas.

Hempstead is famous for its watermelon crop, holding an annual Watermelon Festival each July.

The Houston Heights was created in 1891 by Oscar Martin Carter and other investors. The Omaha and South Texas Land Company purchased 1,756 acres of land and established infrastructure, including alleys, parks, schools, streets and utilities. The Heights was a streetcar suburb of Houston, which attracted people who did not wish to live in the dense city. It had its own municipality until the City of Houston annexed the Heights in 1919.

Hitchcock was created as a station of the railroad between Galveston and Houston in 1873 and around the turn of the 20th Century became a vegetable shipping center. The settlement's economy crashed in the 1930s after insect plagues in the surrounding areas, and the area stayed impoverished until the establishment of the Camp Wallace anti-aircraft training base and the Hitchcock Naval Air Station at the beginning of World War II. Hitchcock was incorporated in 1960 and today serves as a suburb of Galveston and NASA workers.

Humble was first settled by Joseph Dunman in 1828. A ferry was built over the San Jacinto River, and the area of Humble became a center for commercial activity due to the region's large oil industry. The city got its name from one of the original residents, Pleasant Smith Humble, who opened the first post office in his home and later served as justice of the peace. In 1883, he operated a fruit stand. In 1885, he was a wood dealer, and in 1900 as attorney at law. Humble became an oil boomtown in the early 20th century when oil was first produced there. ,Railroad linkage was established in 1904, and shortly thereafter the first tank car of oil was shipped out of Humble's oil field. By 1905 the Humble oilfield was the largest producing field in Texas. Nearby, Houston Intercontinental Airport opened in 1969 and put Humble into suburban community status.

Huntsville began in 1836, when Pleasant and Ephraim Gray opened a trading post. Ephraim Gray became first postmaster in 1837, naming it after his former home town, Huntsville in Madison County, Alabama. Huntsville became the home of Sam Houston, who served as President of the Republic of Texas, Governor of the State of Texas, Governor of Tennessee, U.S. Senator and Tennessee congressman. Located in Huntsville are two of Houston's homes, his grave and the Sam Houston Memorial Museum. Houston's life in Huntsville is also commemorated by his namesake Sam Houston State University and the statue, "Tribute to Courage" by artist David Adickes.

Jersey Village was where Clark W. Henry operated F&M Dairy and raised Jersey cattle. Henry and LeRoy Kennedy began developing the community in 1954, with the first houses along Jersey Drive. The community was incorporated in 1956. In 1972, Leonard Rauch gave Jersey Village a city hall building, still used for the fire department and public works departments.

Katy was known as Cane Island, named for the creek that still runs through the area. The trail from Harrisburg to San Antonio known as the San Felipe Road ran through it. In 1845, James J. Crawford received a land grant that included this area. 30 years later Crawford, John Sills and freed slaves Thomas and Mary Robinson were the only recorded residents of Cane Island. In 1893 the Missouri–Kansas–Texas Railroad started laying rails through Cane Island. In 1895, James Oliver Thomas platted a town and in 1896 the town of Katy was named through Thomas's post office application. The name was based on appreciation for the MKT Railroad. Katy later became known for rice farming, with the first concrete rice driers in the state of Texas were built there in 1944. The City of Katy was incorporated as a municipality in 1945.

Kingwood was created in 1970 as a joint venture between the Friendswood Development Company and King Ranch, the name derived from the partnership. Foster Lumber Company originally owned some of the land since 1892, which they sold to the joint venture in 1967. Kingwood has maintained the slogan "The Livable Forest."

La Marque was settled as Highlands and Buttermilk Station. It was renamed in the 1890's when residents learned of another mainland community of the same name. Madam St. Ambrose, postmistress, chose the new name, which in French means "the mark." During the Civil War, the town was known as Buttermilk Station after the soldiers bought buttermilk on the trip between Galveston and Houston. By 1914, the community had been reached by four railroads, a railroad station and general store. It is a residential community for employees at chemical plants in the La Marque-Texas City area, as well as the Galveston Island Medical Center.

La Porte was founded in 1892 as a speculative real estate venture. A 22-acre public space known as Sylvan Grove was reserved by the waterfront. The area soon added amenities bathhouses, boating piers and a Victorian hotel with a dance pavilion. La Porte quickly became the most popular tourist destination in the Houston area. Sylvan Grove Park was acquired in 1896 by Adoue & Lobit and renamed Sylvan Beach. Cottage retreats were built around the waterfront. During the 1920's and 1930's, Sylvan Beach Amusement Park became a top destination, with beauty contests and band concerts starring Guy Lombardo, the Dorsey Brothers, Phil Harris and Benny Goodman. A boardwalk, amusement rides and other attractions were added. The nearby Bay Ridge community contained beachfront summer homes in neighboring Morgan's Point built by wealthy Houstonians. The San Jacinto Monument, in the unincorporated area of La Porte, commemorates the battle for Texas independence. La Porte was the home of Barbours Cut Terminal, operated by the Port of Houston.

League City was settled on the former site of the Karankawa Indian village. Three families, the Butlers, Cowarts and Perkinses, are considered to be founding families of the city. The first resident of the town proper, George W. Butler, arrived from Louisiana in 1873 and settled at the junction of Clear Creek and Chigger Bayou. J. C. League acquired the land from a man named Muldoon and laid out his town site along the Galveston, Houston & Henderson Railroad. It has grown into the largest city in Galveston County. In 2013, the financial website NerdWallet named League City the best city in Texas for people looking for jobs.

Liberty is the third oldest city in the state, established in 1831 on the banks of the Trinity River and incorporated in 1837. It is in a major oil and gas production area served primarily by the Union Pacific Railroad. Liberty served as a shipping point for plantations along the Trinity, lumber operations and shipments from farmers. By 1840, James Taylor White, in cooperation with Jones & Co., an English firm, had built what was probably the first meat packing plant in Texas on the banks of the Trinity River in Liberty, marked also by Historical marker. Texas heroes William B. Travis, Sam Houston and David Burnet practiced law in Liberty. Oil discoveries in 1903 at the Batson-Old oilfield in neighboring Hardin County made Liberty, the nearest train stop, a boomtown. Three cotton gins, a gristmill and cigar factory were operating in Liberty around 1910. During World War II, a camp for German prisoners of war operated at the Liberty fairgrounds. The city also has only true un-cracked replica of the Liberty Bell, dedicated by actor John Wayne in 1960 in association with Sally and Nadine Woods fight against muscular dystrophy. The Sam Houston Regional Library and Research

Center opened in 1977 and serves as both a museum and depository for thousands of historical documents.

Missouri City goes back to 1853, when the Buffalo Bayou, Brazos and Colorado Railway began operating its first 20 miles from Harrisburg (now Houston) to Stafford's Point (now Stafford). It was the first railroad in Texas and the first standard gauge railroad west of the Mississippi River. It continued westward until, in 1883, it linked with its eastward counterpart, completing the Sunset Route from Los Angeles to New Orleans. In 1890, two real estate investors, R.M. Cash and L.E. Luckle, purchased four square miles of land directly on the route of the BBB&C, only a mile and a half from its first stop at Stafford's Point. They advertised the property as "a land of genial sunshine and eternal summer" in St. Louis, Missouri, and its surrounding areas. Three years later, W.R. McElroy purchased 80 acres nearby and, in effort to promote jointly with Cash and Luckle in St. Louis, he named it Missouri City. The settlement was registered in Texas in 1894, and incorporated in 1956. The city was first made over by Fondren Park near US 90A in the early 1960s, followed by Quail Valley, Lake Olympia, Riverstone and Sienna Plantation.

Orange was originally Green Bluff in 1830, named for a man named Reason Green, a Sabine River boatman. In 1840, the town was renamed Madison in honor of President James Madison. To resolve confusion with another Texas community called Madisonville, the town was renamed Orange and incorporated in 1858. The town grew due to sawmills and immigrants. The harbor leading into the Port of Orange was dredged in 1914 to accommodate large ships. The U.S. Navy Department selected Orange as one of eight locations where it would store reserve vessels. The chemical industry continues as a leading source of revenue to the area.

Pasadena was founded in 1893 by John H. Burnett. He named the area after Pasadena, California, because of the perceived lush vegetation. Burnett was involved in both construction and promotion of railroads and knew their impact on the value of property. He established the nearby towns of Deepwater and Genoa, later to be incorporated into Pasadena and Houston. The 1900 hurricane heavily damaged Pasadena. The city received Galveston refugees who relocated to the mainland following the catastrophe. Donations by the Red Cross, including millions of strawberry plants to Gulf Coast farmers, helped revive the community. This and the subsequent establishment of a major strawberry farm in the area by

Texaco founder Joseph S. Cullinan made Pasadena a major fruit producer for many years afterward. Rice farmers from Japan settled in the community, further diversifying the agriculture. Champion Coated Paper Company of Ohio opened a paper mill in 1937. Pasadena incorporated in 1928. Petroleum, heavy industry, high-tech businesses related to NASA and Bayport shipping terminal contributed to the city's economic base. The Pasadena Volunteer Fire Department is the largest all-volunteer municipal fire department in the U.S.

Pearland had humble beginnings near a siding switch on the Gulf, Colorado and Santa Fe Railway in 1882. When a post office was established in 1893, the community was originally named Mark Belt. In 1894, the plat was filed with the Brazoria County courthouse by Witold von Zychlinski,. The area had many fruits harvested by residents. Zychlinski saw the pear trees and decided that Pearland would make a good name for the community. Pearland was promoted by its developers (Allison & Richey Land Company) as an "agricultural Eden." The Galveston hurricanes of 1900 and destroyed most of the fruit trees and slowed growth for a time, but agriculture rebounded. Oil was discovered nearby in 1934, which led to the development of the Hastings Oilfield. By 1990, Pearland city limits had extended into Harris County, and home developers grew the area into the suburban community that it is now.

Port Arthur was settled as Aurora in 1837, and by 1840 promoters led by Almanzon Huston were advertising town lots. The area came to be known as Sparks after John Sparks and his family moved to the shores of Sabine Lake near Aurora. The Eastern Texas Railroad, completed between Sabine Pass and Beaumont just before the outbreak of the Civil War, passed by Sparks. By 1895, Aurora was a ghost town, and the abandoned community became Port Arthur, incorporated in 1898. The city was once the center of the largest oil refinery network in the world. The Port of Port Arthur opened in 1899.

Santa Fe was established in 1877, when the Gulf, Colorado and Santa Fe Railway was built through the western part of Galveston county. By the turn of the century, three small, unincorporated towns had formed along the railway: Alta Loma, Arcadia and Algoa. The Santa Fe Independent School District, named after the railway, was established shortly afterward to serve the area.

South Houston was founded as Dumont in 1907 by C.S. Woods of the Western Land Company. In 1913, it was incorporated as the city of South Houston.

Elephants belonging to former South Houston mayor George Christy, a circus owner, assisted the construction of Spencer Highway.

Southside Place opened in 1925. Edlo L. Crain, the developer, placed a pool and a park in a subdivision to attract residents to the town. The first section to open was south of the park. It was in close proximity to Bellaire Boulevard and the streetcar line, which was nicknamed the Toonerville Trolley. In 1926, development of the second section of Southside Place began. The site of Southside Place previously housed the Harris County Poor Farm. Southside Place incorporated in 1931.

Spring was originally inhabited by the Orcoquiza Native Americans. In 1838, William Pierpont placed a trading post on Spring Creek. By the mid-1840s many German immigrants, including Gus Bayer and Carl Wunsche, moved to the area and began farming. People from Louisiana and other states settled in Spring, where the main cash crops were sugar cane, cotton and vegetables. In 1871, the International and Great Northern Railroad opened. In 1901–1903 the International-Great Northern Railroad opened, connecting Spring to Fort Worth. Spring became a switchyard with 200 rail workers and 14 track yards. The Spring State Bank opened in 1912. In the 1970's Houston's suburbs expand in the Spring area. The Old Town Spring Association formed in 1980 to promote the shopping area of the restored houses, becoming a tourist area.

Stafford is in both Fort Bend and Harris Counties. William Stafford established a plantation with a cane mill and a horse-powered cotton gin in 1830. In 1836, during the Texas Revolution, soldiers under General Santa Anna stopped at Stafford's plantation and ordered it to be burned. He rebuilt and lived there until his 1840 death. A settlement called Stafford's Point built around the plantation, becoming a town in 1853, when the Buffalo Bayou, Brazos and Colorado Railway began stopping at Stafford's Point. Stafford incorporated as a city in 1956.

Sugar Land was founded as a sugar plantation and incorporated in 1959. Sugar Land is home to the headquarters of Imperial Sugar and the company's main sugar refinery and distribution center was once located in this city. Recognizing this heritage, the Imperial Sugar crown logo can be seen in the city seal and logo.

Texas City was founded when three duck hunters in 1891 noted that a location along Galveston Bay, known locally as Shoal Point, had the potential to become a major port. Shoal Point had existed since the 1830s, when veterans of the Texas

Revolution were awarded land. The duck hunters were three brothers from Duluth, Minnesota, Benjamin, Henry and Jacob Myers, formed the Myers Brothers syndicate and sold 10,000 acres of Galveston Bay Frontage, including Shoal Point, renaming the area Texas City.

Tomball was first settled in 1838, where immigrants found an open, fertile land that received adequate rainfall, ideal for farming and raising cattle. In 1906, the area started booming. Railroad line engineers often noticed that the Tomball area was on the boundary between the low hills of Texas and the flat coastal plains of the Gulf, making it an ideal location for a train stop. The railroad could load more cargo on each car, because the topography gently sloped toward the Galveston ports and provided an easier downhill coast. Thomas Henry Ball was an attorney for the Trinity and Brazos Valley Railroad and convinced the railroad to run the line right through downtown Tomball. Soon after, people came in droves to this new train stop. Hotels, boarding houses, saloons and mercantile stores all sprung up. In 1907, the town was officially named Tom Ball, later to be shortened to one word, honoring Mr. Ball. Tomball became incorporated in 1933.

Webster was founded in 1879 by James W. Webster. It was marketed as a colony for settlers from England. Railroads such as the Missouri, Kansas & Texas were built through the area. Farmers raised pears and other produce. In 1903, with Rice emerging as an important cash crop. A farming consultant (Seito Saibara) was invited to come to Texas and teach rice production. Dairies and livestock ranches developed. Petroleum was discovered at the Webster-Friendswood Oilfield in the 1930's. Webster was incorporated in 1958, when it was announced that NASA would build nearby. Webster is a thriving bedroom community closely tied to the Clear Lake Area and its high-tech industry.

West University Place was developed in 1917 by Ben Hooper, a former governor of the state of Tennessee. The name West University Place originated from its proximity to Rice University. In the 1920's, Lillian Nicholson, an English major at Rice, lived with a friend whose father was a city planner. The city planner asked Nicholson and her friend to name the streets of WUP. Nicholson took names from her English literature book and gave to streets. Some are named for authors, such as Geoffrey Chaucer, John Dryden and William Shakespeare. One of them, Weslayan Road, is a misspelling of "Wesleyan." The city incorporated in 1924 because Houston was reluctant to extend power lines that far from the city center.

The Woodlands was founded by George P. Mitchell in 1974, managed by The Woodlands Corporation as an extension of Mitchell Energy & Development. He planned to establish a conference center, hotels, office parks, retail malls, schools, large distribution centers and golf courses. The name was chosen by his wife, Cynthia Woods Mitchell, who is further discussed in Chapter 13.

Yet another traffic jam in downtown Houston, this one in 1938.

Chapter 3
ENERGY LEGENDS

Houston's opportunities have literally burst from the earth. Leadership in the field of energy meant people of determination and vision, who saw in "black gold" the way of life that we now enjoy.

The dean of the oil industry was Joseph Stephen Cullinan. He went into court in Beaumont in the wild and lawless days of Spindletop in 1901. He demanded and got the right in advance to kill any marauder who might oppose his charge to clean up and quiet down in the skyrocketing boomtown.

In 1901, oil was discovered at the Spindletop field, near Beaumont. In 1903, two young men met at an overcrowded boarding house in Beaumont. They were William Stamps Farish and Robert E. Blaffer. Farish had come to inspect Spindletop for an uncle in England. Blaffer had started in the coal business. He came to Beaumont to buy oil for the Southern Pacific Railroad locomotives.

In 1904, Farish and Blaffer joined forces to form a drilling partnership. The next year, they moved to Houston to concentrate on the nearby Humble field where oil had been discovered in 1904. In the early years, they were so short of operating money that they lived in a shack in the fields. Blaffer put up his gold watch as security to guarantee payment of a drilling crew's wages. By 1908, they had become comfortably established.

Harry Wiess was the only Beaumont native. His father and grandfather were in the lumber business. He was 16 when Spindletop exploded in his hometown. His father (a one-time steamship captain) saw the potential and formed two small oil companies. Harry Wiess was the last of the first crop of oil giants to survive who came to know the vast benefits of energy from the constant addition of knowledge through chemistry, physics and other sciences that are now applied to every product.

In 1911, Farish, Blaffer and Wiess joined forces with Ross Sterling and Walter Fondren in founding the Humble Oil & Refining Company. Other founding directors included Frank Sterling, Charles B. Goddard, Lobel A. Carlton and Jesse Jones.

Humble became one of the giants in the industry through association with Standard Oil Company of New Jersey. Humble Oil became known as Enco in the west and Esso in the east, later renamed Exxon and now known as ExxonMobil Corporation.

In 1904, oil was discovered at Humble. In 1902, Texaco was founded. In 1916, Gulf Oil was founded. In 1917, Phillips Petroleum was founded. In 1918, Sinclair Oil was founded.

T.J. Donoghue brought oil strategy, understanding and tolerance that aided it over many a political rough spot. The fathers of oil conservation were Underwood Nazro of Gulf Oil and W.S. Farish of Humble Oil & Refining Co. There were the great salesmen of oil, such as John W. Gates. Howard Hughes Sr. and W.B. Sharp Sr. saw ways to aid in the search for, capture and utilization of oil. The result was the creation of a vast new manufacturing industry: oil tools and supplies.

Oil was difficult to transport on land. So, the pipeline was invented. Oil was difficult to transport by sea. Thus, the tank-ship was invented. Oil was difficult dangerous to refine. The most complex machinery was created to handle oil and gas safely, surely and cheaply.

Oil has grown even harder to find. Even airplane equipment is used to map huge underground areas for prospective oil bearing formations, while drilling in even the rough waters in the Gulf of Mexico and the Pacific Ocean.

Into the shoes of the pioneers of energy stepped such wildcatters as H.L. Hunt, Hugh Roy Cullen, George Strake, Glenn McCarthy and Sid Richardson. To them, the sky was not too high nor the earth too deep to hide oil from them.

The Gulf Oil Corporation was an expansion of the J. M. Guffey Petroleum Company, organized in May 1901, and which acquired the interests of Anthony F. Lucas and John A. Galey in the Spindletop Oilfield. In this company, organized to exploit the new oil discovery, Guffey's partners included A. W. Mellon, R. B. Mellon, James H. Reed, William Flinn, J. D. Callery, T. H. Given and Joshua Rhodes. They organized the Gulf Refining Company of Texas for the purpose of refining and marketing the crude oil produced by the Guffey company, and a refinery was built at Port Arthur.

Dwindling production at Spindletop made necessary searches in new directions. Gulf built a 400-mile pipeline from Port Arthur to the Glenn Pool field in Oklahoma, which had been discovered in 1906, and began refining Oklahoma crude in September 1907. During the next 20 years Gulf expanded its production operations into nearly all of the major oilfields in the United States, Mexico and Venezuela. Gulf was characterized by integration from production of crude to retailing of refinery products. In 1929, Gulf expanded the retail business. The dramatic increase in demand for oil during World War II further fueled the company's expansion.

In 1951, Gulf completed one of the world's largest catalytic cracking units in Port Arthur and built plants for manufacturing ethylene and isooctyl alcohol, developing its petrochemicals division. In the 1950s, Gulf joined with B. F. Goodrich Company to form a new company, Gulf-Goodrich Chemicals, Incorporated, through which Gulf maintained an important position in the manufacture of synthetic rubber from petroleum-derived materials. In 1956, it acquired Warren Petroleum Corporation and increased its interest in British American Oil Company. Gulf was a 55% participant in Kuwait Oil Company.

In 1983, Thomas Boone Pickens's Mesa Petroleum Corporation, following an unsuccessful attempt to acquire General American Oil Company, began to buy up shares of Gulf Oil. After Mesa had gained control of 11% of Gulf stock, Pickens engaged in a proxy fight for control of the company. Gulf executives invited takeover offers from other companies. On March 5, 1984, the Gulf board voted to sell the company to Chevron (Standard Oil of California) for

$13.2 billion. Gulf operations were merged into Chevron in what was the largest corporate merger to date.

Innovations and Expansions

The chief goal was to reach for riches. In 1921, they scoured South Texas reserves. In 1926, the West Texas oil industry was launched. In 1929 came the huge discoveries in Conroe's Cookfield Belt and the Frio sands of the Gulf Coast. On the flood of oil lived three out of five people in those production areas. Oil and chemical industries stabilized the economy of the Golden Triangle.

In 1926, natural gas was piped into Houston for the first time. It came from a field in Refugio. Up to that point, only manufactured gas had been available.

In January 1930, a young engineer opened a small office in a walk-up apartment house on Polk Avenue, as the only representative for a small radical type of service to the oil industry. He was Roger Henquet. The new company was Schlumberger Well Surveying Corporation. In 1930, the U.S. Schlumberger presence consisted of Henquet, one helper and one truck unit. The first Henquet tracking service contrasts with the corporation that grew. The company that he introduced to Houston oil operators is now spread all over the world and is one of the largest oil service organizations.

Since World War II, the state's chemical industry has boomed and grown until it is the largest manufacturing employer in Texas. The industry is a complex mixture of companies which produce chemical raw materials, basic chemicals, petrochemicals, agricultural chemicals, plastics, synthetic rubber, metals, drugs and household chemicals.

Shell Oil moved its corporate headquarters from New York City to Houston in 1971. The campaign leading up to that momentous relocation has its roots years earlier.

I had served on the HemisFair committee. HemisFair was a World's Fair, held from April-October, 1968, in San Antonio, Texas. Its objectives were to promote travel and tourism for the state, to promote the LBJ diversity agenda and to encourage corporate relocations to Texas. Downtown San Antonio was given a makeover, with the Riverwalk re-routed. A conscious effort was made to direct major conferences and conventions to San Antonio.

On the corporate front, campaigns were launched. Shell Oil was one of the preferred corporations in the master strategy. A management study for Shell tended to favor Houston as the site. As part of the effort, the Texas Legislature finally adopted Liquor by the Drink, an exhibition of the forward thrust of the state, not to mention the revenue enhancement for state coffers. Shell Oil felt that the business-friendly climate was right, not to mention having their offices nearer to their operations. Developer Gerald Hines built One Shell Plaza downtown. The Shell Oil relocation was one of the biggest corporate moves in history.

The expansion of Houston's energy sector is exemplified in the various growth strategies of its corporations. For example, in 1985, Atlantic Richfield (guided by president Bob Gower) lumped its Houston refinery and its Channelview chemical complex together to form Lyondell Petrochemical Company. Subsequently, Lyondell reached Fortune 500 status within five years. In 1987, the Sterling Group (Gordon A. Cain, chairman) in 1987 completed a rollup of several Houston area plants, including Dupont's Chocolate Bayou facility.

The history of Houston industry is dotted with the work and accomplishments of many dynamic legends.

Energy Legends

Jack Sawtelle Blanton was raised in Houston, where his father was general manager of the chamber of commerce. Blanton went to work in 1950 for Eddy C. Scurlock at Scurlock Oil Company in the Division Order Department. He rose through the company ranks to become its president in 1958 and CEO-chairman in 1983, after the company was sold to Ashland Oil. He retired from his position in 1988 to become the president of Eddy Refining Company.

Blanton served as the chairman of the board of Houston Endowment Inc. He served on the boards of the Methodist Hospital Healthcare System, Texas Medical Center, Houston Zoo and Jesse H. Jones School of Management at Rice University. From 1985–1991, he was a Regent of the University of Texas, serving as chairman from 1987–1989. During the oil and real estate crises of the 1980's, he served as chairman of the Greater Houston Chamber of Commerce, where he notably helped resolve conflict with effective communication and good working relations. In 1997, the University of Texas at Austin renamed its art museum the Blanton

Museum of Art in his honor after receiving a $12 million donation from Houston Endowment Inc.

George Herbert Walker Bush, upon graduating from Yale University, moved his family to West Texas in 1948 and entered the oil business, becoming a millionaire by the age of 40. He started as a sales clerk for Dresser Industries. In 1951, Bush opened the Bush-Overbey Oil Development company and in 1953 co-founded the Zapata Petroleum Corporation, which drilled in the Permian Basin. He was named president of the Zapata Offshore Company, a subsidiary which specialized in offshore drilling, in 1954. The subsidiary became independent in 1958, so Bush moved the company from Midland to Houston. He continued serving as president of the company until 1964 and chairman until 1966.

Bush was elected to Congress in 1966, becoming the first Republican to represent Houston. The district included Tanglewood, where the Bush family lived. He served on the House Ways and Means Committee and was elected to a second term in the House of Representatives Congress. In 1971, Bush was appointed to serve as the U.S. Ambassador to the United Nations by President Richard Nixon. In 1976 was appointed director of the Central Intelligence Agency by President Gerald Ford. He was director of the Council on Foreign Relations from 1977-1979.

Back in Houston, Bush taught at Rice University's Jones School of Business. He chaired the executive committee at First International Bank. I met him in 1979 on the organizing committee of The Forum Club. I later worked with him on the Thousand Points of Light program.

He served as Vice President of the U.S. from 1981-1989, then President of the U.S. from 1989-1993. Foreign policy accented the Bush presidency. Military operations were conducted in Panama and the Persian Gulf. The Berlin Wall fell in 1989, and the Soviet Union dissolved in 1991. The Bush Presidential Library was dedicated in 1997, located at Texas A&M University. George W. Bush (his eldest son) served as Governor of Texas (1995–2000) and as President of the United States (2001–2009). Jeb Bush (his second son) served as Governor of Florida (1999–2007).

Hugh Roy Cullen started working for a cotton broker at the age of 16. He later went into that business for himself and also dealt in real estate. He moved to Houston in 1911 and entered the oil business in 1918. He made major discoveries at Pierce Junction, Blue Ridge, Rabb's Ridge, Humble and the O'Connor field.

Cullen owned half of the South Texas Petroleum Company and later formed the Quintana Petroleum Company. He took an active interest in politics and states' rights. He promoted W. Lee O'Daniel for governor in 1938 and 1940 and for senator in 1941. Although Cullen aided the Dixiecrat movement in 1948, he normally supported Republican candidates, particularly Dwight D. Eisenhower in 1952.

Cullen gave more than $11 million each to his favorite projects, the University of Houston and Houston hospitals. In 1947, he established the $160 million Cullen Foundation to provide for continual aid to education and medicine. By 1955, he had given away an estimated 90% of his fortune. Cullen served in many capacities during his career, including chairman of the board of regents of the University of Houston, vice president of the Texas World Fair Commission in 1939 and director of the Boy Scouts of America. He received honorary degrees from the University of Pittsburgh in 1936, Baylor University in 1945 and the University of Houston in 1947. He was an honorary member of the American Hospital Association and a member of the Sons of the Republic of Texas. Cullen died in Houston on July 4, 1957.

Joseph Stephen Cullinan began working in the Pennsylvania oilfields at age 14 and learned to perform virtually every task associated with oil production. In 1882 he joined Standard Oil, and he eventually held several managerial positions in that company. When oil was discovered in Corsicana, Texas, in 1894, local developers invited him to advise them on production and marketing techniques. He organized the J. S. Cullinan Company, which later became Magnolia Petroleum Company.

Among the contributions that Cullinan made to the Corsicana oil industry were the introduction of oil as a fuel for locomotives, the use of natural gas for lighting and heating and the utilization of oil to settle dust on the city's streets. South of Corsicana, he constructed a refinery that began operation in 1899 and was the first such facility west of the Mississippi River. In 1899 he was instrumental in persuading the Texas legislature to enact the state's first petroleum conservation statute.

Cullinan moved his operations to Beaumont after the Spindletop discovery. There he founded the Texas Company (later Texaco) in 1902. When he moved his operations and the Texaco headquarters to Houston in 1905, Cullinan established the city as the focal point of the oil industry in the Southwest. He remained active in the industry after his resignation as president of Texaco. Eventually, he founded 10 companies involved in the exploration, production, refining and marketing of Texas petroleum and was instrumental in developing oil deposits in the Sour Lake, Humble and East Texas oilfields.

Cullinan served as president of the Houston Chamber of Commerce from 1913-1919 and supported the development of the Houston Ship Channel. He also constructed the North Side Belt Railway around the city in 1922. During World War I, he was a special advisor to the Food Administration under President Herbert Hoover. He was a patron of the Museum of Fine Arts, the Houston Symphony Orchestra and Houston Negro Hospital. From 1928-1933, he was chairman of the Mount Rushmore National Memorial Committee. Cullinan died of pneumonia while visiting his friend Herbert Hoover in Palo Alto, California, on March 11, 1937.

Walter William Fondren, oil operator and philanthropist, learned how to drill water wells in Arkansas, a skill he later used in drilling for oil. He came to Texas and became a farm laborer. In 1897, he gave up farming to work as a roughneck in the Corsicana oilfield, and by 1901 he was a skilled rotary driller, an expert on drilling equipment and an independent operator in the newly discovered Spindletop oilfield near Beaumont.

Fondren moved from field to field as new oil pools were discovered, and by 1905 he was operating under his own name and through a dozen companies and partnerships. He purchased stock in the firm that became Texaco, an investment that became worth millions. To avoid dependence on others for transportation and marketing, Fondren became vice president of the Coleman Oil Company, a marketer of crude oil.

In 1911, with Ross Sterling and others, he organized the Humble Oil & Refining Company. Fondren served as director of the firm and as vice president in charge of drilling and production in the Gulf Coast division from 1913 until his retirement in 1933. From its beginnings in the Humble oilfield, the company was highly successful. Company activities included acquiring, exploring, and developing oilfields in Texas, Oklahoma, Louisiana, and Arkansas; the company also refined oil, transported crude oil, and distributed refined products. Its properties included a number of refineries, more than 1,000 producing wells, and 1,200 miles of pipeline.

After his retirement, he established the Fondren Oil Company. In 1934, he accepted the post of district director of the Houston office of the Federal Housing Administration. With his wife, he gave the Fondren Library to Southern Methodist University and also gave the university endowment funds to support the Fondren Lectures In Religious Thought and a scholarship. For many years, he was a director of the Houston YMCA, and at the time of his death he was vice president of the National Bank of Commerce in Houston. Fondren died in San Antonio on January 5, 1939. In an effort to implement their combined wish to benefit institutions of higher learning, his wife established the Fondren Library at Rice University, which opened in 1949, and bestowed major gifts on the Methodist Hospital of Houston, Southwestern University, Scarritt College in Nashville, TN, and other health and education facilities.

Michel T. Halbouty was born in Beaumont Texas and joined the Glenn H. McCarthy Interests in 1935, as Vice President of Operations and Chief Geologist and Petroleum Engineer. He opened his office as Consulting Geologist and Petroleum Engineer in 1937. He was the first independent to explore in Alaska, and the first independent to discover a gas field in Alaska. He operated in an area with thye majors where no other independent dared to venture. He also explored in many frontier areas where others feared to tread. He became universally known as the most adventuresome of the wildcatters.

Halbouty's delivered numerous speeches and lectures to scientific and lay groups all over the world on subjects pertinent to the oil industry, geology, and geophysics and/or engineering. Many of his scientific articles gained worldwide recognition and are used in university and college classrooms worldwide as required reading for geology and engineering students. An innumerable amount of his papers were translated worldwide into German, French and Spanish, as well as other languages. He also authored several books, as well as edited numerous scientific publications. He was a consummate reader of the earth sciences and contributed significantly to the literature. He was the subject of three books, as well as hundreds of profile articles published in newspapers and magazines.

John Hofmeister is one of the energy industry's current top authorities. He has participated in the inner workings of multiple industries for 40 years. He retired as president of Shell Oil Company in 2008 to found and head the nationwide non-profit group, Citizens for Affordable Energy. This public policy education organization promotes sound energy security solutions for the nation, including a range of affordable energy supplies, efficiency improvements, essential infrastructure, sustainable environmental policies, and public education on energy issues. His global corporate experiences across a wide range of both energy-consuming and energy-producing companies have led him to consider environmental security in the 21st century differently from mainstream practice.

In 1978, I had an office on the 12th floor of the 2100 Travis building. In the office next door was a gentleman of distinction. I got to know him and talk about old times in the energy industry. He was Glenn H. McCarthy, an independent oil operator, known as "King of the Wildcatters." He was a bombastic, Irishman best known for building the famous Shamrock Hotel, indulging in fist-fights at his Cork Club and being the model for Edna Faber's Texas oilman Jett Rink in her novel, "Giant" (portrayed in the movie by James Dean).

Glenn McCarthy was born in Beaumont and began working as a water-boy at the age of eight in the oilfields, where his father, Will McCarthy, worked, earning 50 cents a day. In 1917, Will McCarthy moved his family to Houston's Fifth Ward while he sought out to establish the family fortune in wildcat drilling near the city. Glenn graduated from San Jacinto High School and later attended Tulane and Rice University.

McCarthy decided to leave college and enter the oil business. He first discovered oil at Anahuac. Between 1932 and 1942 McCarthy struck oil 38 times. This included the discovery of 11 new oilfields in Texas. In 1949, spent $21 million building the Shamrock Hotel in Houston. The opening of the hotel took place on Saint Patrick's Day. McCarthy rented an entire train, to transport movie stars from Los Angeles to Houston. 3,000 people were invited to the party that cost $1 million.

McCarthy was estimated to be worth $200 million by 1950. At this time he had 400+ gas and oil wells in Texas and was president of the United States Petroleum Association. His friends included Howard Hughes, John Wayne and Natalie Wood.

McCarthy owned several companies including the McCarthy Oil and Gas Company, the Beaumont Gas Company, the Houston Export Company, KXYZ

Radio, the McCarthy Chemical Company, the McCarthy International Tube Company. He also owned two banks, 14 newspapers, a magazine and a movie production company. He was also the chairman of Eastern Airlines.

In his later years, Glenn McCarthy lived a low-profile life in a two-story house near La Porte and died in 1988. His activities with the Shamrock Hilton Hotel and the Cork Club are detailed in Chapter 9.

Leonard F. McCollum attended the University of Texas to become a journalist, but a required geology course changed his fate. He went on to obtain a B.S. in geology and began his career as a staff geologist with Humble Oil & Refining Company. He became president of Carter Oil Company and was recruited by Continental Oil Company (Conoco), in 1947. He led Conoco into innovative fields of foreign exploration, natural gas processing, fertilizers, detergents and plastics. He served on the Conoco boards for 20 years, retiring as CEO in 1967. McCollum established new divisions of research and development, market research, and a planning and coordinating department.

McCollum was encouraged by family friend Dr. Michael DeBakey, to get involved in service to the medical field. He was chairman of the Baylor College of Medicine and chairman of the People-to-People Health Foundation, whose floating hospital ship HOPE offers free healthcare all over the world.

Rob Mosbacher is president of Mosbacher Energy Company. He served as chairman of the Greater Houston Partnership. His father served as energy secretary for President George H.W. Bush.

Constantine S. "Dino" Nicandros was the president and chief executive officer of Conoco Inc. from 1987-1995. He served as vice chairman of the board of Conoco's parent, E. I. Du Pont de Nemours and Company, from 1991-1996. Born in Port Said, Egypt, of Greek parents, Nicandros was a graduate of Ecole Des Hautes Etudes Commerciales in Paris, France. He held a law degree and a doctorate diploma in economics from the University of Paris and an M.B.A. from the Harvard School of Business Administration.

Joining Conoco in 1957 in Houston as a research associate in the planning department, he advanced through several positions and chaired the merger committee when Conoco merged with DuPont in 1981. He served on the board of directors of Cooper Industries, Mitchell Energy Development, Frontera Resources and Chase Bank of Texas.

Nicandros served on the board of trustees of Baylor College of Medicine and was a trustee and member of the board of governors of Rice University. He served on the advisory board of the Texas Center for Superconductivity at the University of Houston and on the board of the Greater Houston Partnership. He was a board member of the Houston Grand Opera, the Museum of Fine, Houston Ballet Foundation and Houston Forum. Nicandros was chairman of the Houston Symphony from 1995-1997.

Eddy Clark Scurlock went to work at a Standard Oil pipeline construction site as a kitchen assistant, then moved to Houston, where he bought a gas station. In 1936, Scurlock borrowed money and formed Scurlock Oil Company. A decade later, he bought a Houston refinery and renamed it Eddy Refining Company. He chartered the charitable Scurlock Foundation in 1954. It has benefited the Methodist Hospital System, Institute of Religion, Lon Morris College and many other institutions.

Ross Sterling was born on a farm near Anahuac, Texas, and only went as far in school as fourth-grade. In 1903, Ross Sterling operated a feed store, when oil beckoned. He became one of the most successful Texans of his generation, becoming a wealthy oilman, banker, newspaper publisher and Governor of Texas (1931-1933). Sterling was a principal founder of the Humble Oil & Refining Company, which eventually became the largest division of the ExxonMobil Corporation, as well as an owner of The Houston Post.

George William Strake, pioneer oilman and philanthropist, was born in St. Louis, served in the U.S. Army Air Corps in World War I and worked in the oil industry in Mexico from 1919-1925. In 1927, Strake moved to the Houston area and, as an independent oilman, leased land near Conroe. His 8,500 acres of South Texas Development Company land was the largest block of land leased up to that time for oil exploration.

After drilling many dry wells, he struck oil in December, 1931. Other wells followed, which proved Conroe to be the third largest oilfield in the United States. His oil operations spread into coastal and West Texas, New Mexico, Oklahoma, the southern states, Michigan and Nebraska. His oil fortune was estimated to be between $100 million and $200 million.

In addition to his oil interests, Strake was a director of the Mercantile-Commerce Bank and Trust Company in St. Louis, chairman of the board and president of the Aluminum Products Company in Houston and founder of the Houston Tribune. In 1937 he represented the governor and the state of Texas at the United States presidential inauguration. During World War II, he served on the citizens' committee for Houston-Harris County civil defense and as Texas' representative for Belgian war relief.

Strake gave much of his oil fortune to educational institutions, civic organizations and charities. He served on the national executive board of the Boy Scouts of America and donated several thousand acres near Conroe to the scouts, named Camp Strake. He became a founding benefactor of the St. Joseph Hospital Foundation, also contributing to the University of St. Thomas, Strake Jesuit College Preparatory School, the University of Notre Dame, Our Lady of the Lake College and the Institute of Chinese Culture in Washington.

Strake received four papal honors between 1937 and 1950, including two of the Vatican's highest honors for a layman, the Order of St. Sylvester and the Order of Malta. The National Conference of Christians and Jews, in which he served as a member of the national board, honored him in 1950 for outstanding contributions to business, civic, and religious affairs.

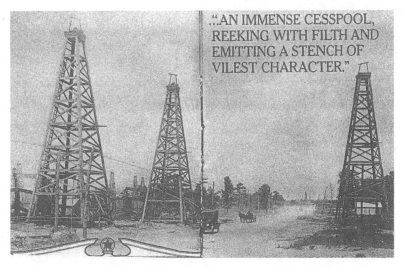

".:.AN IMMENSE CESSPOOL, REEKING WITH FILTH AND EMITTING A STENCH OF VILEST CHARACTER."

Drilling for oil in Texas boom towns in the early 20th Century.

Chapter 4
ENTREPRENEURS AND INNOVATORS

E ntrepreneurial spirit typifies each era in Houston. Needs were predicted and met with business services of the era.

In the early days, most residents were self-sufficient, with their own vegetable gardens, fruit trees, poultry yards and pastures for animals to graze, in close proximity to their homes. In the 1840's, private enterprise and city government began regulating domestic services. Butchers had to be licensed, with their trade restricted to the City Market.

Because there was no refrigeration, visits to the City Market were necessarily daily. Food products were sold from rented stalls, while farmers from the country sold their produce in the town square. There were ice wagons, and their product sold for three cents per pound. The next entrepreneurs operated delivery wagons, from whom home owners purchased dry goods, luxury foods and ingredients for cooking. This practice and the City Market grew into the need for retail stores, many of which are detailed in Chapter 6.

Houston's easy access to the Gulf of Mexico encouraged the importing of many goods that were once made at home. By 1940, Charles Power and other Houston merchants were importing ready-made clothing, household goods and luxury fabrics directly from France and England. Clothing could be custom-ordered from tailors and merchants in New Orleans or New York.

The growth of the baking and finance industries is directly attributable to this era. Merchandise stores made direct credit arrangement. Some had cotton commission departments. Several merchants and manufacturers had banking interests as sidelines. One of these was T.W. House, who dealt in manufactured goods and cotton. The evolution of full-time bankers and the dynamic institutions that they led are discussed in Chapter 5.

Quantities of imports depended upon transportation and access. Local tailors emerged. In 1853, Houston's first railroad, the Buffalo Bayou, Brazos & Colorado Railroad, began operations. By 1960, C.W. Hurley & Company sold sewing machines locally. That 1846 invention was the first of many home appliances that would revolutionize life. Sewing circles led to factories to a fashion industry.

Houston's primary industries were cotton, cattle, imported commerce and railroads. Shipping continued to grow. The continuing market for other goods necessitated a continually growing transportation and distribution system. Buffalo Bayou was developed for ships.

One of the most innovative facilities was constructed in 1929. The Mercantile & Marine Building, below ground level was while ships brought the goods. The upper levels were where the goods were distributed. The M&M Building was Houston's first indoor shopping mall. Today, it houses the University of Houston Downtown.

The early merchants shipped cotton, cattle and other cargos to Galveston, where they were transferred to sea-worthy vessels. The wharves were dotted with factories and freight movers.

In 1870, the U.S. Congress officially declared Houston as a port and began planning the upgrade of Buffalo Bayou. Congress made its first appropriation ($10,000) for ship channel improvements. In 1874, the Houston Board of Trade & Cotton Exchange was organized. In 1875, the first grain elevator was built on the Houston Ship Channel. In 1882, Houston was one of the first cities to build a power plant.

Further development of an inland port was determined by one event, the 1900 hurricane damage to the Port of Galveston, and one reality, the availability of land in Houston where it was in short supply on Galveston Island. More land accommodated more staging and storing facilities, along with manufacturers and distributors attached to the port. In 1902, the U.S. Congress appropriated $1 million for extensive work on the Houston Ship Channel.

In 1910, a group of Houston businessmen headed by the Houston Chamber of Commerce proposed to Congress a plan to split ship channel development costs between Houston and the federal government. Congress heartily accepted the plan. In 1914, the Port of Houston opened. As late as 1915, the gang-planks were still used to load cargo into ships. The Satilla became the first deep-water ship to land at Houston's upgraded docks. The Port and Houston's global dominance are intertwined.

The 8-F Influencers

The "8-F Crowd" was a group of Houston business leaders and friends who frequently met for lunch in Suite 8-F of the Lamar Hotel in downtown Houston. Jesse Jones had built the Lamar in 1927 on the corner of Main and Lamar Streets. 8-F members played an important role in Houston's civic affairs, included building Rice University's football stadium in the 1950's and the Astrodome in the 1960's.

The core of the group included Jesse H. Jones, Herman Brown, George R. Brown, Gus Wortham, James Abercrombie, James A. Elkins Sr. and William P. Hobby, who founded successful corporations and acquired considerable wealth.

Houston's 8-F players needed the help of the powerful East Texas group, so they often invited them to join them at the Lamar, where decisions were made that shaped Texas' future and its economic course. That group included Texas Governor Allan Shivers, attorney Ed Clark, State Senator Ben Ramsey, Ottis Lock and State Senator Wardlow Lane. Their influence extended into Washington through their association with politicians such as John Nance Garner, Sam Rayburn, Lyndon Johnson, and Albert Thomas.

The 8-F power brokers are all gone today and the site of the Lamar Hotel is a parking lot. But the tales of what transpired behind the doors of Suite 8-F have become an integral part of Houston legend.

Jesse Holman Jones was born in Robertson County, Tennessee, on April 5, 1874. When he was nine, the family moved to Dallas, where his managed his brother's lumberyard. In 1895, he went to work in his uncle's firm, later manager of the company's Dallas lumberyard, then the largest. In 1898, Jones came to Houston as general manager where he remained with the company for another seven years.

Jones established his own business, the South Texas Lumber Company. He expanded into real estate, commercial buildings and banking. Within a few years, he was the largest developer in the area and responsible for most of Houston's major construction. He owned 100 buildings in Houston and built structures in Fort Worth, Dallas and New York City. He sold his lumber interests and began to concentrate on real estate and banking.

In 1908, he purchased part of the Houston Chronicle. In 1908, he organized and became chairman of the Texas Trust Company and was active in most of the banking and real estate activities of the city. By 1912, he was president of the National Bank of Commerce (later Texas Commerce Bank, and by 2008, part of Chase Bank). He made one of his few ventures into oil as an original stockholder in Humble Oil & Refining Company. As chairman of the Houston harbor board, he raised money for the Houston Ship Channel.

During World War I, President Woodrow Wilson asked Jesse Jones to become the director general of military relief for the American Red Cross. He remained in this position until he returned to Houston in 1919. He became the sole owner of the Houston Chronicle in 1926. Jones served as director of finance for the Democratic National Committee, made a $200,000 donation, and promised to build a hall. These actions were instrumental in bringing the 1928 Democratic national convention to Houston.

On the recommendation of John Nance Garner, President Herbert Hoover appointed Jones to the board of the Reconstruction Finance Corporation, a new government entity established to combat the Great Depression. President Franklin D. Roosevelt appointed Jones as chairman of the RFC, a position he held from 1933 until 1939. In this capacity, Jones became one of the most powerful men in America. He helped prevent the nationwide failure of farms, banks, railroads, and many other businesses. The RFC became the leading financial institution in America and the primary investor in the economy. The agency also facilitated a broadening of Texas industry from agriculture and oil into steel and chemicals.

In 1940, Jones was offered the post of Secretary of Commerce. With congressional approval, he was allowed to retain his post as FLA chief during the war years, when he supervised more than 30 agencies that received federal money. He died in 1956. Collections of Jones's papers and memorabilia are housed at the Barker Texas History Center, University of Texas at Austin, at the Library of Congress and Houston Endowment.

James Smither Abercrombie, oilman, Houston civic leader, and philanthropist, was born in Huntsville on July 7, 1891. In 1906, his family moved into Houston's Fourth Ward. He worked for the family's dairy business and then sought work in the Houston oil business, where they would make enough money to hire extra manpower to work at the dairy.

In 1909, Jim's cousin, Charles Abercrombie, hired him to work as a roustabout for the Goose Creek Production Company. By 1910, Jim had become a driller. Crown Petroleum hired him as field superintendent, and while working for Crown he was the first to use salt water to put out a derrick fire, a discovery he made because there was no fresh water available. Abercrombie bought several; wells and left Crown Petroleum to work on his own in South Texas and Gulf Coast oilfields. He helped his brother finance the Houston Carbonate Company, which sold carbonic gas to soda fountains, creameries and bottlers.

In 1920, he bought, with Harry Cameron, the Cameron-Davant Company, a business that sold oil-drilling supplies and parts for rigs and wells. In 1921, Monarch Oil & Refining Company gave Cameron Iron Works a contract to find a way to control the increasing gas pressure in deep wells. Repeated attempts to solve this growing problem, found in many oil wells around the world, failed. Abercrombie and Cameron developed the Type MO blowout prevention device, which led to a patent for its application to the high gas pressure.

Cameron Iron Works grew increasingly successful as additional patented inventions followed. In 1929, with Dan Harrison, he formed Harrison and Abercrombie, which invested and drilled in many oilfields in Texas and Louisiana. In 1939, Cameron Iron Works developed a list of wartime products that it could produce for the United States military to use in World War II. The military eventually moved Cameron Iron Works up from sub-contractor status to direct supplier. By 1941, the company had a contract to build K-guns and arbor bombs; this led to a 1942 contract to build .50-caliber gun barrels. Techniques developed by Cameron engineers cut production time for rifling and machining the barrels. Cameron Iron Works built the Tiny Tim rockets used in beach invasions by the navy. In 1942, President Franklin D. Roosevelt asked Harrison and Abercrombie to build an aviation gas refinery at the Old Ocean oilfield. Harrison sold his share in Harrison and Abercrombie to the Magnolia Petroleum Company.

Abercrombie bought a ranch on the Guadalupe River just a few miles east of Gonzales. This ranching operation built a feed factory for ranch animals. In 1959, Abercrombie Interests was reorganized into the J. S. Abercrombie Mineral Company, which drilled wells in Texas, Louisiana, Kuwait and Saudi Arabia. Cameron Iron Works continued to prosper.

On March 10, 1950, Abercrombie and several other prominent Houston citizens chartered Texas Children's Hospital to treat sick and critically ill children. Abercrombie gave $1 million and requested that absolutely no restrictions be made on which sick children could be admitted. He also donated all proceeds from the Pin Oak Horse Show to the hospital.

George R. Brown is reviewed in Chapter 2. James Elkins and Gus Wortham are profiled in Chapter 5. William P. Hobby is discussed in Chapter 8.

The Innovators

In 1907, the Anderson Clayton Company of Oklahoma had opened a branch office in Houston. Its founders were Frank Anderson, Monroe Dunaway Anderson, Ben Clayton and Will Clayton. They were cotton brokers and moved their operations to Houston in 1916. They became the world's biggest cotton dealers.

The two original founders needed more capital and invited banker Monroe to become a partner. Monroe moved to Houston to give his company access to larger banks and, eventually, to deep water shipping upon the completion of the Houston Ship Channel in 1914. He became the chief financial officer and, following incorporation, he was named treasurer. M.D. Anderson headed the company until he died in 1939.

In 1936, M.D. Anderson had created the charitable foundation that bears his name and funded it with about $300,000. This foundation was destined to receive $19,000,000 more after Monroe's death in 1939.

His bequest went to the Cancer Center that now bears his name. Upon taking possession of the estate from its executors, the trustees noted that the 1941 Texas

Legislature had authorized The University of Texas to establish a hospital for cancer research and treatment somewhere in the state. The Anderson Foundation agreed to match state appropriations if the hospital would be built in Houston. A site was offered in the new Texas Medical Center, another creation of the Anderson Foundation.

Howard Hughes was one of the most flamboyant and colorful entrepreneurs the world has ever known. Like his father, he enjoyed tinkering with mechanical things and as a youth built a shortwave radio set and started the Radio Relay League for amateurs. In 1919, Hughes was paralyzed for a short time by an unexplained illness, developing a lifetime phobic regard for his health.

On a visit to Harvard, his father took him on an airplane ride, an experience that stimulated a life-long love of aviation. Howard spent time with his uncle Rupert, a writer for Samuel Goldwyn's movie studios, also sparking a future career interest. Howard was attending classes at Rice Institute when his father died in 1924, the elder Hughes died. At age 18, Howard received access to a large part of the family estate and dropped out of Rice. Through the decision by a Houston judge, who had been a friend of his father's, Howard was granted legal adulthood on Dec. 26, 1924, and took control of the tool company.

After a summer of tinkering with a steam-powered car, Howard and wife Ella headed for Hollywood. Howard sought to make movies. He hired Noah Dietrich to head his movie subsidiary and Lewis Milestone as director. Hughes worked next on his epic movie "Hell's Angels," a story about air warfare in World War I. He wrote the script and directed it himself. He acquired 87 World War I airplanes, hired ace pilots, took flying lessons and obtained a pilot's license. During production, he crashed and injured his face. Since talkies had become popular, Hughes added dialogue scenes to "Hell's Angels" that included actress Jean Harlow. Released in 1930, it was the most expensive movie to that date. It was a box-office smash, making Hughes accepted by the Hollywood establishment. He went on to produce "Scarface" (1932) and "The Outlaw" (1941).

In 1932, Hughes acquired a military plane and formed the Hughes Aircraft Company as a division of Hughes Tool Company. He personally test-flew experimental planes. He set a new land-speed record of 352 miles per hour with his H-1 (the Winged Bullet). He converted a special Lockheed 14 for an around-the-world flight, studying weather patterns. He invested in military aircraft.

Hughes Aircraft won a contract to build a flying boat, the "Spruce Goose," which he flew.

In 1948, Howard Hughes purchased the movie studio RKO, and in 1955 he sold it to the General Tire Company for profit. Hughes also invested in Trans World Airlines, and in 1956 pushed the company into the jet age by purchasing 63 jets. In 1953, he founded the Hughes Medical Institute in Delaware, thus funding the Medical Center he earlier had designated as the main recipient of his will.

In 1967, Hughes began buying properties to build a business empire in Nevada. In 1970, he took over Air West. In 1972, he sold Hughes Tool Company stock to the public and renamed his holdings company Summa Corporation. This ended his role as a businessman and entrepreneur. In poor health, he went to Panama, Canada, London and Acapulco. He boarded a plane to check into a Houston hospital on April 5, 1976, but died on the way.

Howard Hughes has been the subject of many books and some movies, "The Amazing Howard Hughes" (1977), starring Tommy Lee Jones, "The Carpetbaggers" (1964) starring George Peppard, "Melvin and Howard" (1980) starring Jason Robards and Paul Le Mat, and "The Aviator" (2004) starring Leonardo DiCaprio.

George P. Mitchell was the son of a Greek goatherd who capped a career as one of the most prominent independent oilmen in the United States by unlocking immense natural gas and petroleum resources trapped in shale rock formations. He also developed planned communities and gave much support to historical preservation.

In Greece, Savvas Paraskevopoulos, tended goats before immigrating to the United States in 1901, arriving at Ellis Island and taking the paymaster's name, Mike Mitchell. He settled in Galveston and ran a succession of shoe-shining and pressing shops.

George Phydias Mitchell was born in Galveston. He worked for Amoco in the oil fields of Texas and Louisiana, before joining the Army Corps of Engineers and overseeing construction projects. After his discharge, he started an oil company with partners, including his brother, doing many of their early deals at a drugstore counter.

George Mitchell founded Mitchell Energy and Development in 1946. In 1952, defying common oil business wisdom, he bought 10,000 acres in a North Texas region near Bridgeport known as "the wildcatter's graveyard." In little more than a year, the fledgling company had drilled 13 consecutive producing development wells and placed 300,000 acres under lease.

George Mitchell began drilling shale rock formations in the Texas dirt fields where he had long pumped oil and gas. He championed new drilling and production techniques like hydraulic fracturing. Mitchell's leadership is credited for creating an unexpected natural gas boom in the United States. He combined academic training as a petroleum engineer and geologist with instinct to become an influential businessman worth $2 billion. He was a petroleum industry spokesman, then a voice for environmentally responsible economic growth.

Seeking to diversify, Mitchell bought 66,000 acres of mostly undeveloped real estate within a 50-mile radius of Houston. In 1974, he created The Woodlands, a 27,000-acre forested development 27 miles north of Houston, helped by a $50 million loan from the Department of Housing and Urban Development. Mitchell visited the Bedford Stuyvesant section of Brooklyn and the Watts section of Los Angeles when planning the project.

Mitchell sold his company to the Devon Energy Corporation for $3.5 billion in 2001. Included were results of drilling more than 10,000 wells, many of which still yielded hydrocarbons. Fracking and other unconventional techniques have doubled North American natural gas reserves to three quadrillion cubic feet, the equivalent of 500 billion barrels of oil. The same techniques worked for oil extraction.

He married Cynthia Woods in 1943. They later created the Cynthia and George Mitchell Foundation, which has given more than $400 million to a variety of causes. Mrs. Mitchell is profiled in Chapter 13.

Entrepreneurial Legends

Mary Kay Ash was born in Hot Wells, Harris County. Her mother was trained as a nurse and later became a manager of a restaurant in Houston. Ash attended Dow Elementary School and Reagan High School in Houston, graduating in 1934. Ash married and had three children. While her husband served in World War II, she sold books door-to-door. Ash worked for Stanley Home Products. Frustrated when passed over for a promotion in favor of a man that she had trained, Ash retired in 1963 and intended to write a book to assist women in business.

The book turned into a business plan for her company, and in 1963, Ash started Mary Kay Cosmetics, with a storefront operation in Dallas. The company went public in 1968 and went private again in 1985. At the time of Ash's death in 2001, Mary Kay Cosmetics had 800,000 representatives in 37 countries, with total annual sales over $200 million. Mary Kay Ash authored three books, all of which became best-sellers.

George Ballas was the inventor of the Weed Eater, a string trimmer company founded in 1971. The idea for the Weed Eater trimmer came to him from the spinning nylon bristles of an automatic car wash. He thought that he could devise a similar technique to protect the bark on trees that he was trimming around. His company was bought by Emerson Electric and merged with Poulan, which was later purchased by Electrolux. Ballas was the father of champion ballroom dancer Corky Ballas and the grandfather of "Dancing with the Stars" dancer Mark Ballas.

Jeff Bezos was born in Albuquerque, NM, and grew up in Houston, where he attended River Oaks Elementary School. As a child, Bezos spent summers at his grandfather's South Texas ranch, where he developed talents in scientific pursuits. He graduated from Princeton University and founded Amazon.com in 1994. Bezos was named Time Magazine's Person of the Year in 1999. He founded Blue Origin, a human spaceflight company, in 2000.

Anthony R. Chase, Tony serves as the Chairman and Chief Executive Officer of Chase Source LP. He is a Co-Founder of SBC Communications Inc. and serves as its Chairman. He is a Principal at Crest Investment Corp., funding and leading new business ventures. He served as the Chairman and Chief Executive Officer of Chase Radio Partners Inc. In 2013, he was named a Houston Legend.

Drypers Corporation was formed in Houston in 1987 as Veragon Corporation, though the company's roots can be traced back three years earlier to when the company's founders launched another diaper business. VMG was the brainchild of three college friends, David Pitassi, Walter Klemp and Tim Wagner, all entrepreneurs. The company's product line includes disposable diapers, disposable training pants and pre-moistened wipes.

Lupe Fraga graduated from St. Thomas High School, then Texas A&M University. Lupe was in the Corps of Cadets, served in the Army and returned to Houston. He bought a small business that took off. Tejas Office Supplies grew into a big business, and Lupe Fraga has earned a lot of honors, including having served as a member of the Board of Regents at Texas A&M.

Monte Pendleton was a leader in franchising. As CEO of Lusterock International, he franchised 100 domestic manufacturers and installers of decorative tops. As CEO of Brickstone International, he franchised 100 franchised dealers nationwide who sell and install U.S. Gypsum Sculptured Masonry. As CEO of SunX International, he franchised 500 dealers and distributors of DuPont's SunX Glass Tinting in 69 countries. He then turned his attention to mentoring entrepreneurs and small business owners through the Silver Fox Advisors. He currently chairs a business mentorship program for the rehabilitation of prison inmates returning to the workforce as entrepreneurs in commerce. He served on President Lyndon B. Johnson's Small Business Commission and was a delegate to President Bill Clinton's White House Conference on Small Business.

William Marsh Rice traveled to Texas in 1838, searching for business opportunities. He became a clerk in a general store, later becoming William M. Rice and Company. He made a fortune investing in land, real estate, lumber, railroads, cotton and other prospects in Texas and Louisiana. In 1895, he was listed in the city directories as: "Capitalist. Owner of Capitol Hotel and Capitol Hotel Annex Building and President of Houston Brick Works Company."

On Jan. 28, 1882, Rice drafted a will, instructing the executors to pay over to the trustees, the Governor and the Judge, funds from his estate for the establishment of "The William M. Rice Orphans Institute." Rice felt that the benefits of his wealth should be enjoyed by the children of the city where he made his fortune. In 1891, Rice decided that he would not establish an Orphans Institute but would found the William M. Rice Institute for the Advancement of Literature, Science and Art in Houston. Rice died in 1900, and Rice University was opened in 1912.

Farouk Shami is a Palestinian-American businessman and founder of the hair-care and spa products company. He was born in Beit Ur al-Tahta, a village near Ramallah, Palestine. He has worked for decades in the field of hair-care product development and attended cosmetology school in Arkansas. He invented the first ammonia-free hair color, after developing an allergy to the chemical that initially led doctors to encourage him to leave his profession. His company, Houston-based Farouk Systems, employs 2,000 people, and exports its line of hair and skin care products under the BioSilk, SunGlitz and Cationic Hydration Interlink (CHI) brands to 106 countries worldwide. On May 1, 2011, Shami made an appearance on NBC-TV's "Celebrity Apprentice," when show contestants were given a project in which they promoted Farouk Systems products. He appeared again in the fourth episode of "All Star Celebrity Apprentice."

Dudley Sharp was a Houston businessman who was also best friends with Howard Hughes, as their fathers were business partners in the Sharp-Hughes Tool Company in Houston. He served as Secretary of the Air Force under president Dwight D. Eisenhower. Born in Houston, he joined the Mission Manufacturing Company of Houston, holding many positions within the firm. In 1955, he was appointed as Assistant Secretary of the Air Force for Materiel. He was appointed Under Secretary of the Air Force in August 1959 and became Secretary of the Air Force on Dec. 11, 1959, serving until Jan. 20, 1961.

William Sherrill is the former Governor of the U.S. Federal Reserve Board and former Director of the U.S. Federal Deposit Insurance Corporation (FDIC). He founded the entrepreneurship program at the University of Houston, which became the model for such others across the nation. In 2013, he was named a Houston Legend.

Bill Spitz moved from New York to Texas in 1950 and founded Big State Pest Control. He grew the firm by providing superior service and treatments in residential and commercial facilities. He was national president of his professional association. After 40 years and two generations in the family business, he sold to a roll-up of home services companies. He then turned his attention to mentoring entrepreneurs and small business owners through the Silver Fox Advisors. For years, he chaired the CEO Roundtable Program for the Greater Houston Partnership.

Welcome Wilson Sr. graduated from the University of Houston in 1949 and received the Distinguished Alumnus Award in 1970. He served in the Eisenhower and Kennedy administrations as a five-state Director of Civil and Defense Mobilization, a division of the Executive Office of the President, with responsibility for what is now known as FEMA. In 1966, he was appointed as Special Ambassador to Nicaragua by President Lyndon B. Johnson. He served as a UH regent and chaired the Tier One campaign. In 2011, he was named Entrepreneur of the Year by the Houston Technology Center.

Business Narrative by the Author

Fine-tuning one's career is an admirable and necessary process. It is not torture but, indeed, is quite illuminating. Imagine going back to reflect upon all you were taught. Along the way, you reapply old knowledge, find some new nuggets and create your own philosophies.

We were taught to be our best and have strong ambition to succeed. Unfortunately, we were not taught the best methods of working with others in achieving desired goals. We became a society of highly ambitious achievers without the full roster of resources to facilitate steady success.

Those who lacked conviction or held misplaced ambitions account for the great business tragedies that profoundly affected the economy and blemished the marketplace.

Most of our energies are spent on reacting to the latest business crisis, putting out fires and placing focus upon the most minute pieces of the puzzle. That's why human beings and companies spend six times more on "band-aid surgery" each year than if they planned ahead on the front end. That's why one-third of our Gross National Product is spent each year on cleaning up mistakes.

In business, I explain to senior management in Big Picture perspectives the concepts behind the activities which the employees and consultants are conducting. For diversity, team building, sales, quality, customer service, training, technology, marketing and all the rest to be optimally successful, they must fit within a context, a plan and a corporate culture.

Will every business become Big Picture focused? No, because vested interests and human nature want to keep attention on the small pieces. Those organizations with the wider horizons and the most creative mosaic of the small pieces will stand out as the biggest successes.

The Big Picture provides leadership for progress, rather than following along. The successful organization develops and champions the tools to change. The quest is to manage change, rather than falling the victim of it. Such activities cannot be studied, or developed in-house. Branch consultants cannot or should not be utilized at this level.

Two of the giants of Houston, Jesse Jones (left) and Glenn McCarthy.

Chapter 5

BANKING AND FINANCE

Houston has been an important banking center since its founding. Banking institutions were needed but not so available. Those existing were crude and possessed little of the safety of present institutions. The manner in which many merchants handled their cash during the pioneer days was uneven at best.

The first charter for a Houston bank was granted by the Mexican government during the time before the city had a name and before the Republic of Texas had won its independence from Mexico. In 1835, Sam May Williams obtained a charter for the Bank of Commerce and Agriculture, with capital of $1 million. The State Supreme Court subsequently revoked the charter of the Williams bank. Ball, Hutchings and Company took over the bank and moved it to Galveston.

An out-of-state bank operated in Texas before this time. The R&DG Mills group (bankers and planters) had banks in Galveston, New York and New Orleans. It circulated $200,000 of its endorsed bank notes, known as "Mills money," which was the first medium of U.S. money used in Texas. R&DG Mills carried stocks of $500,000 at Brazoria and Columbia, helping to finance the Republic of Texas and the plantation owners. The R&DG wealth was placed at $5 million.

In the early days, there were few banks. Among the early pioneers, money was placed in niches in the fireplace, where a brick or stone would be removed and the space used as a wall safe. Planters did their own banking and exchange business in conjunction with planting activities. Galveston was the chief banking Center in South Texas, but all banks were privately owned, and large merchants also conducted a banking business.

The big merchandise stores made direct credit arrangements with such firms as Baring Brothers Company, Kidder, Peabody Company and Brown Brothers Merchants Company of London. Some of these had cotton commission departments, and cotton was often assigned to them directly.

About 1882, Benjamin A. Shepherd began banking in conjunction with his mercantile firm (Shepherd and Crawford). In 1854, he bought out his partner, sold the store to its manager (A.J. Burke) and opened a private bank. Then, he was the only person who was exclusively in the banking business in Texas.

Several merchants and manufacturers had banking interests as sidelines. One of these was T.W. House, who dealt in manufactured goods and cotton. As did most part-time bankers, he handled business all the way to the north of the state. Caravans consisting up to 100 covered wagons came from surrounding territories to trade, borrow, spend and deposit in Houston.

That the interior of the state was not open to travelers was seen in an advertisement by T.W. house in the April 7, 1885, issue of the Houston Daily Post. It stated that the bank, established in 1838, would make collections at all places that were "accessible" in Texas.

Other private institutions produced the earliest bankers, including W.J. Hutchins, Thomas Ennis, W.N. Rice, A.C. Crawford, D.U. Barzina, Henry Fox and Thomas M. Bagby, names reflected on streets today.

When Houston's population was just 16,000, the City Bank of Houston opened in 1870. Col. W.B. Botts was its president until 1885, when W.R. Baker (the former Houston mayor) succeeded him. In 1874, the Houston Savings Bank began taking care of the city's growing financial needs. The organizers included F.A. Rice, W.D. Cleveland, J. Waldo, M.C. Howe, Col. Botts and E. Raphael.

By 1886, both institutions closed. After the city bank suspended, there was a run on the savings bank, a feverish loss of confidence that caused the other bank to fail. After the closing of both banks, business transactions fell low in the city. Very little real estate changed hands during the panic, although losses were light because of the banks' abilities to pay debts. Although the house itself cost $8,000, the home of William Marsh Rice on two blocks at San Jacinto and Franklin Streets sold at $2,500.

Soon, Houston's need for banks was evident, causing the "Big Five" coming into existence.

The First National Bank was founded by Thomas M. Bagby. After his death, Benjamin A. Shepherd became president and merged his private bank with First National. 20 years later, the Commercial National Bank was organized. The third bank was the Houston National. Hy S. Fox became its first president. The South Texas National Bank was organized in 1890 and in 1912 took over the Commercial National Bank. The fifth bank to organize was the Union National Bank. These were called the Big Five for years.

The Lumberman's National Bank was the sixth to organize, and it became the Second National Bank. The oldest trust company was organized in 1875. The banks just mentioned were all in the 50-year class.

The National Bank of Commerce, the State Bank, the City National, the Citizens State, Federal Reserve Bank, the Guardian Trust Company, the Harrisburg National, the Merchants & Employees Industrial Bank and the San Jacinto National Bank have come later to take care of the enormous business which the city of cotton, oil, lumber, rice and "where 18 railroads meet the sea" enjoy today.

How different from the pioneering days. Houston's development was brisk and reflected the spirit of early settlers, pioneers, business leaders and community participants. The early leaders of Houston set high standards of behavior that have been followed enthusiastically others over the years.

In the 20th Century, Houston was fortunate in having strong banks directed by fiscally conservative officers and staffed by efficient personnel. Like all modern cities as they progress and develop, from its inception, Houston had bankers who were city builders.

The State Bank and Trust Company was started in 1915, later renamed the State National Bank. In 1923, the bank spent $800,000 in building a lavish structure at 412 Main Street. The rooftop penthouse was designed as a clubhouse. The building is a typical skyscraper of the early 20th century, with a distinct base of rusticated pink granite, a shaft, and a crown emphasizing the building's verticality. Between 1955 and 1964, virtually all of the banks that had once lined downtown Main Street had moved to newer buildings further south. Today, the inscription on the entrance still reads: "Frugality is the Mother of the Virtues."

When the American Bankers Association met in Houston in 1938, Bert Childs, then president of the Houston Chamber of Commerce, said in an address to the visiting bankers:

"Welcome to Houston. We have a territory that, like our city, is highly diversified in its industries and in its income. The greatest oil center in the world, we do not rely solely upon this great natural resource. We not only are a great manufacturing area, but we are the center of agricultural country with exceptionally large production. We not only have one of the nation's greatest livestock sections, but we are the fastest growing packing house center in America. We not only have a large retail volume that comes from a half of this great state, but a wholesale and jobbing trade that comes from many states. We are growing rapidly and solidly because we are a city of diversified industries and businesses.

"Houston presents a great opportunity, and along with financial opportunity, it presents for your consideration much more. It offers a haven for those who enjoy life at its finest. For here and all around us are living the kind of people that you would appreciate as neighbors. Fine homes, exceptional churches and an atmosphere of culture are added attractions. Here on the Gulf Coast of Texas is a vast territory abounding with recreation and pleasure spots galore, here in the sunshine and the warmth of mild winters, and the cool Gulf breezes that temper the lengthy summers, we have a land that offers health, happiness, progress and contentment."

His faith in the future of the city was justified. Today, the population of its metropolitan district is larger than any in the South. Houston's growth and progress compare favorably with any other city in the nation. And that these facts can be written is due largely to the wisdom, the activities and the leadership of the Houston banks.

Finance Legends

Joe L. Allbritton owns University Bank in Houston. After graduating from Baylor University, he founded San Jacinto Savings & Loan. In 15 years, he became the largest stockholder of First International Bancshares of Dallas. He sold that stock in 1973 and started buying shares of University Bankshares. He also owned Los Angeles-based Pierce National Life Insurance. He became chairman and CEO of Riggs National Bank. Allbritton is a director of the Lyndon Baines Johnson Foundation in Austin and the George Bush Presidential Foundation in College Station. In Washington, he helped establish a $6 million endowment fund for Washington's Arena Stage and serves on the federal city council.

Lloyd Millard Bentsen Jr. grew up on Arrowhead Ranch in the Rio Grande Valley, where his father was in the ranching, oil and banking businesses. He served as a B-24 pilot in the U.S. Army Air Forces and flew combat missions over Europe during World War II. In 1946, Bentsen was elected Hildago County Judge. In 1948, Bentsen was elected to serve in the U. S. House of Representatives, where he was a protégé of Speaker of the House Sam Rayburn.

In 1955, Bentsen moved his family to Houston, where he worked in the financial industry. He founded Consolidated American Life Insurance Company. He was chairman of Lincoln Consolidated Inc., a financial holdings company. In 1970, Bentsen was a candidate for the United States Senate. He won an upset victory over incumbent U.S. Sen. Ralph Yarborough in the Democratic primary and then went on to win the general election over the Republican nominee, U. S. Rep. George H.W. Bush. Senator Bentsen was re-elected in 1976, 1982 and 1988, eventually serving as chairman of the Senate Finance Committee. He was known for a pro-business stance and was a supporter of the oil and gas and real estate industries, as well as free trade.

In 1988, Massachusetts Governor Michael Dukakis won the Democratic Party nomination for the presidency. Dukakis picked Bentsen as his vice presidential running mate in the general election. In 1993, President Bill Clinton picked Bentsen to serve as Secretary of the Treasury. In 1999, he received the Presidential Medal of Freedom.

James A. Elkins moved to Houston in 1917. He served as District Attorney in the 1940's, then started a law practice with William Vinson. Elkins then partnered with J.W. Keeland in a bank that became First City National. He was also president of Harrisburg National Bank.

E.F. Gossett was president of South Texas National Bank. F.A. Heitmann served continuously on the bank's board for 58 years, making him the dean of the city's bank directors, as well as serving a term as president of the Houston Chamber of Commerce.

W.N. Greer was president of Houston Citizens Bank.

George Hamman was president of Union National Bank.

B.D. Harris was president of Second National Bank.

Deane Kanaly was a pioneer in combining financial planning and trust management firms. He was the author of "The Kanaly Concept," which embodied his vision of personal finance: accumulating income and managing it wisely. He established the Foundation for Financial Literacy, with educational programs in high schools and colleges promoting his ideas. Before founding the Kanaly Trust Co. in 1975, he was an executive at the former River Oaks Bank & Trust Co. and at the former Bank of the Southwest in Houston. He lectured at the University of Houston, Women's Institute of Houston, American Institute of Banking, Southern Methodist University and Texas Tech University.

F.M. Law was president of First National Bank.

Ben Love spent 22 years at Texas Commerce Bank, most of them as president of the bank or its parent company, Texas Commerce Bancshares. He helped revolutionize banking with practices that emphasized aggressive sales and marketing. Under his guidance, TCB expanded until it became the state's second-largest lending institution. Following mergers, TCB became JPMorgan Chase, now the largest bank in Texas. He was a fixture in Houston civic and philanthropic circles. He was the first chairman of the Greater Houston Partnership. He was active with the Texas Medical Center, leading a campaign that brought $150 million to M.D. Anderson Cancer Center and another for $200 million to the University of Texas Health Science Center for its Institute of Molecular Medicine. Love served on many boards, committees and advisory groups.

C.M. Malone was president of Guardian Trust Company.

Joe Meyer Jr. was president of Houston National Bank.

Brothers Carloss Morris and Stewart Morris worked in the title-insurance company established by their grandfather. As it grew, Stewart Title emerged as one of the Big Four in the title-insurance industry. The Morris brothers adopted a strategy of putting up their reserves to make the company the most liquid, thereby achieving the best financial rating among the Big Four. The Morris brothers served as co-CEOs of Stewart Information Services Corporation, which oversees the various title service and insurance companies that make up the family business.

Dennis Murphree heads a series of early-stage and growth-equity venture capital fund. Founded in 1987, his fund-management firm, Murphree and Company Inc., is headquartered in Houston and has additional offices in Austin, Colorado Springs and Birmingham. The firm is now one of the most active VC managers in the southern U.S. and is considered a "generalist, growth equity" firm doing a wide variety of traditional industry categories wherein new technologies or new business models can be employed to spur growth.

Murphree taught "Investment Management" to college seniors for 6 years at the University of St. Thomas in Houston and, for the last 20 years, has been on the faculty of the Jones Graduate School at Rice University where he teaches two second-year MBA classes: "Creative Entrepreneurship" and "Venture Capital".

Marcella Perry became president of the Heights Savings Association in 1962, succeeding her father, James G. Donovan. The two had founded the association in 1954.

Fayez Sarofim Sarofim was born in Egypt and immigrated to the U.S., beginning his career working for Anderson Clayton, the Houston cotton firm. In 1958, at age 30, he founded Sarofim & Co. with $100,000 from his father, a cotton grower in Egypt. He is a money manager who adheres top the philosophy of buying stock in big companies and holding on to them through good times and bad. Sarofim managed the pension funds at Mobil, General Electric, Ford, Rice University's endowment, the Museum of Fine Arts endowment and others. Forbes Magazine called him the "buy-and-hold king." Fayez Sarofim & Co., his investment and money-management firm, manages more than $40 billion in assets.

A. Dee Simpson was president of National Bank of Commerce.

Paul B. Timson was president of Houston Land and Trust Company.

J.A. Wilkins was president of State National Bank.

Gus Sessions Wortham started his career in the insurance industry in 1912, when he was hired by the Texas Fire Rating Board in Austin. In 1915 he and his father moved to Houston and co-founded an insurance agency, John L. Wortham and Son.

In 1926, Wortham, along with Houston businessmen Jesse H. Jones, James A. Elkins and John W. Link, organized American General Insurance Company, one of the first "multi-line" insurance companies in the nation. Multi-line underwriting allowed smaller companies with fewer customers to compete with insurance companies based on the east coast, which dominated the industry at that time. He served as chairman of the board and chief executive officer of American General for 50 years. The company expanded from two agents to more than 12,000, with operations in every state in the nation. American General is now a $61 billion diversified financial services company and one of the largest publicly traded companies with corporate headquarters in Houston.

Gus Wortham built civic support for cultural activities and parks through the Wortham Foundation. The Wortham Theater Center, built entirely with private donations, is home to the Houston Ballet and Houston Grand Opera. Wortham was a member of the "8-F Crowd," a group of Houston business leaders and friends who frequently met for lunch in Suite 8-F of the Lamar Hotel downtown. Along with other 8-F members, he played an role in the building of Rice University's football stadium in the 1950's and the Astrodome in the 1960's.

Wortham served two consecutive terms as president of the Houston Chamber of Commerce and was a director of Texas Commerce Bank, Texas Eastern Transmission Company, Longhorn Portland Cement Company, the Missouri Pacific Railroad, Rice University, Texas Children's Hospital and the Houston Livestock Show and Rodeo.

In addition to the Wortham Theater Center, several other public places in Houston are named for him, including Gus Wortham Park, Gus Wortham Memorial Fountain, Wortham Fountain at the Texas Medical Center, Wortham House (home of the University of Houston chancellor), Wortham IMAX Theater at the Museum of Natural Science, Wortham World of Primates at the Houston Zoo and Wortham Tower in the American General Center. He died in Houston on September 1, 1976.

John Lee Wortham was born in Woodland, Texas. With son Gus Wortham he started the John L. Wortham and Son insurance agency. He was on the Railroad Commission of Texas in 1911 and was Secretary of State for Texas in 1913.

Business Narrative by the Author

The biggest problem with business stems from the fact that management and company leadership come from one small piece of the organizational pie. Filling all management slots with financial people, for example, serves to limit the organizational strategy and focus. They all hire like-minded people and frame every business decision from their micro perspective.

The ideal executive has strong leadership skills first. He or she develops organizational vision and sets strategies. Leaders should reflect a diversity of niche focus, guaranteeing that an overall balance is achieved. Those with ideologies, strategies, process upholding and detail focus are all reflected. The best management team looks at the macro, rather than just the niche micro.

None of us was born with sophisticated, finely tuned senses and highly enlightened viewpoints for life. We muddle through, try our best and get hit in the gut several times. Thus, we learn, amass knowledge and turn most experiences into an enlightened life-like perspective that moves us "to the next tier." Such a perspective is what makes seasoned executives valuable in the business marketplace.

Many people, however, stay in the "muddling through" mode and don't acquire seasoning. They "get by" with limited scope and remain complacent in some kind of security. As their clueless increases, they sink through the following seven numbers, like they would fall into a well.

Life has a way of forcing the human condition to change. Due to circumstances, people start "cluing in." By that point, substantial career potential has been lost. Much damage cannot be recovered. Therefore, many people likely will stay on safe tracks...which will rarely ride the engine to glory.

At some point, each business leader takes ownership for our lives, careers and accomplishments. Events necessitating or inspiring this to happen could include:

- A recognition that the old methods are not working.
- Successive failures via the old ways of doing things.
- Financial failures or the monetary incentive to rapidly create or change plans of action.
- Loss of loved ones, causing one to grow up exponentially.
- Loss of one or more valued relationships, because they were not properly nurtured or were blatantly neglected.

- A pattern of blaming others for one's own problems and issues.
- There is no choice but to change the modus operandi.
- Loss of opportunities, customers, employees and market share.
- A "wake up call" of any type.

People are hard pressed to recall the exact moment when their value systems emerged. That's a steady process and a circuitous journey.

The most effective leaders accept that change is 90% positive and find reasons and rationale to embrace change. They see how change relates to themselves, realizing that the process of mastering change and turning transactions into a series of win-win propositions constitutes the real meaning of life.

Leadership is learned and synthesized daily. Knowledge is usually amassed through unexpected sources. Any person's commitment toward leadership development and continuing education must include honest examination of his-her life skills. Training, reading and pro-activity are prescribed.

*Mellie Esperson meets with Houston community leaders
about civic betterment projects in the 1920's.*

These are the early buildings of Second National Bank, Houston, Texas.
The small one-story was the first home in 1907.
Successive buildings date from 1908 and 1923.

Chapter 6

RETAIL, CUSTOMER SERVICE LEGENDS

I n 1860, John Kennedy, an Irish baker, moved into the narrow building at 813 Congress, a structure that had been built by Nathaniel Kellum in 1847. Kennedy was poor when arriving in Houston in 1842. He quickly built his own bakery, gristmill, retail store and several thousand acres. During the Civil War, Kennedy used his bakery to make food for the Confederate soldiers. The building, on the National Register for Historic Places, now houses La Carafe (owned by Carolyn Wenglar), making it the oldest bar location in Texas.

In 1900, Foley Brothers was opened by brothers Pat and James Foley. The 1,400-square-foot store located at 507 Main Street was stocked with calico, linen, lace, pins, needles and men's furnishings. In 1905, they added ready-to-wear clothing for women and children, as well as millinery.

In 1916, Foley Brothers ranked third in retail volume. In 1917, the brothers sold to George S. Cohen and George's father, Robert, a Galveston merchant. In

1922, the store became the city's largest department store. Shoes, a beauty shop, and radio sets were included.

In 1945, Federated Department Stores president Fred Lazarus Jr. came to Houston to visit his son, who was stationed at a nearby Army camp. He discovered that Foley Bros. was for sale and bought it. In 1947, now part of Federated, Foley's opened its doors at 1110 Main Street, heralded as the nation's "most modern department store." In 1951, the first official Foley's Thanksgiving Day Parade was held.

In the 1960's, branch stores opened in Sharpstown, Pasadena, Almeda-Genoa and Northwest stores soon followed. In the 1970's, branch stores opened in Memorial City, Greenspoint and Highland Mall in Austin. More stores opened in the 1980's.

In 1988, the May Company acquired Foley's. In 1993, the division in Colorado and New Mexico was consolidated with Foley's, creating a 49-store division that was the largest in the May Company. Stores continued to be added. In 2004, May's seven divisions now included Foley's, Filene's, Robinsons-May, Famous-Barr, Hecht's, Lord & Taylor and Marshall Field's. In 2006, the Foley's organization in Houston was dissolved, and the operation of its locations in Louisiana, Oklahoma and Texas were assumed by Atlanta-based Macy's South. On Sept. 9, 2006, the Foley's nameplate was replaced as part of the Macy's nationwide renaming of all former May Company locations.

Louis Sakowitz immigrated in 1890 from the Ukraine to New York. In 1897, he and his family opened a small store near the wharves on Galveston Bay. In 1902, his sons Tobe and Simon opened the first Sakowitz Brothers store in Galveston in 1902. In 1915, a violent storm ruined the stock of the Galveston store. In 1917, brother Tobias closed that store and moved with his family to Houston, where they opened an expanded Sakowitz store at Main at Preston. In 1929, the store was moved to Main at Rusk.

Originally a men's and boys' clothing store, it grew to sell women's and children's clothing and to serve as a premier fashion outlet for 75 years. Tobias married Matilda Littman of Galveston. They had two sons, both born in Galveston. Sakowitz was president and board chairman of Sakowitz Brothers. He was a member of the board of the Houston Chamber of Commerce and the United Fund. He served on the Selective Service Board from 1944-1947.

Bernard Sakowitz was the son of and began his retail career at R. H. Macy Company in New York. In 1929, he returned to Houston and the family business. He became president in 1957. Sakowitz became a significant Houston institution, with stores downtown, Gulfgate and at the Shamrock Hotel. The first Sakowitz suburban store was built in 1959 on the corner of Westheimer and Post Oak, the bellwether that led to development of Westheimer Road into a major Houston street that soon included the Galleria,. Bernard Sakowitz served on the board of directors of the Texas Medical Center, St. Luke's Episcopal Hospital, Houston Crime Commission and was director of the Houston Chamber of Commerce and the Better Business Bureau.

Bernard's son Robert Sakowitz graduated from Harvard and entered the family business in 1963, becoming president in 1975. Robert Sakowitz expanded to other cities, including Dallas, Phoenix and Midland. The chain Sakowitz never went public and was the last of the major family-owned chains of specialty stores in America. Robert is now a consultant to retailers. His sister is social leader Lynn Wyatt. His daughter is Brittany Sakowitz, an entrepreneur with a retail location and a website for stylish dress rentals.

Shopping Centers

Freeways and retail business have been connected since the beginning. Construction of the Gulf Freeway along I-45 began in 1938. The first big regional shopping center was Gulfgate, on the Gulf Freeway at the South Loop (610).

In 1957, the Texas Highway Department settled on the route for U.S. 59, known as the Southwest Freeway. That worked nicely into the strategy of developer Frank Sharp, who wanted the freeway to pass through his new Sharpstown development. The land owners donated to the highway development, and Sharp built a shopping center along the route.

Developer Kenneth Schnitzer concentrated his activity on the Greenway Plaza development in the 1960's and 1970's. It created a blend of commercial and residential buildings, with as hotel, restaurants, entertainment centers and creative landscaping.

Glenn McCarthy had once envisioned a second phase top his Shamrock Hilton Hotel, a multi-use retail facility. The concept was scrapped right after the Hilton

Hotel franchise took over the Shamrock in 1955. That abandoned concept would influence Gerald D. Hines in the late 1960s.

He developed The Galleria, which opened on November 16, 1970. The shopping center, anchored by Neiman Marcus, was modeled after the Galleria Vittorio Emanuele II in Milan, Italy. When it opened, the mall had 600,000 square feet of retail space. The original skylights graced a large, floor-level, ice rink, open year round and featured three hanging chandeliers. The development consists of a retail complex, as well as two Westin hotels. The office towers and hotels are separately owned and managed from the shopping center.

Galleria II was completed in 1976 and added 360,000 square feet of retail space, plus office space. In 1986, Galleria III opened with a new wing to the west, anchored by Macy's. Upon completion of Galleria IV in 2003, the shopping mall totaled 3 million square feet of retail space which include 375 high-end stores, such as Louis Vuitton, Gucci, Kate Spade, Ralph Lauren, Coach, Fendi, Chanel, Christofle, Yves Saint Laurent, Burberry, Versace, Prada, and Tory Burch. Forbes Magazine ranked The Galleria as one of the world's best shopping malls.

The 1970's brought the city a series of sprawling mega-centers. Homart Development Company (the real estate arm of Sears, Roebuck & Co.) built three big ones in 1974: Baybrook Mall, Deerbrook Mall and Willowbrook Mall.

The notion of a downtown shopping center was unheard of until Cadillac-Fairview Corporation open The Park in 1983. It was an office building tower, including an open mall with food court.

The next generations of shopping complexes resembled small-city downtowns, complimented by strip centers and malls. Such town centers were built in the 1990's in Sugar Land, The Woodlands and Katy.

Grocery Stores

Henry Henke came to Houston in 1872. He started a grocery store in 1882 and hired C.G. Pillot. Pillot was such a good worker that Henke made him a partner. They turned Henke's store into the first major retail grocery chain in the city. Henke & Pillot was purchased by Kroger in the 1960's.

Harris Weingarten immigrated with his family from Poland to Houston in the 1880's, where he operated a dry goods store. In 1901, he and son Joseph Weingarten, opened a grocery store downtown. In 1914, Joseph formed J.

Weingarten, Incorporated, and in 1920 opened a second store. Advertising "Better Food for Less," he pioneered in self-service and cash-and-carry shopping. His chain of stores in Texas, Arkansas, and Louisiana grew to 70 by 1967 (the year of his death.) In 1980, the corporation sold its stores to Grand Union, which resold the stores in 1984 to Safeway, Randall's and Gerland's Food Fair.

The Weingarten name disappeared from the retail grocery storefronts, but the company has remained active in owning and leasing shopping centers through the company that Joseph had founded in 1948. Weingarten Realty became a publicly traded company in 1985, headed by Stanford Alexander (one of Harris's grandsons). Today, the CEO is Drew Alexander, the third member of the Weingarten family to lead the company.

Joseph Weingarten was the first president of the Super Market Institute of America. He also served as a board member of the Texas Medical Center, Medical Research Foundation of Texas and Baylor Medical Foundation. In 1952, the National Conference of Christians and Jews in gave him a Brotherhood Award for his service. Impressed during a visit to Israel with the common greeting Shalom Aleichen ("peace be unto you"), Weingarten began a personal effort to promote world peace. He established the World Institute for World Peace Foundation, which promoted international conferences with academic and political leaders from countries including Poland, the Soviet Union, the Philippines, Canada and numerous nations of Western Europe, South America and Africa.

Lewis & Coker was a grocery store chain that began in 1903. It had Houston stores in the Westheimer, Gulfgate, Heights, Telephone Road, Medical Center and Palm Center areas. The chain went away in the 1980's.

Rice Food Market was founded on May 5, 1937, by William H. Levy. The Rice Boulevard was an unpaved dirt road, and West University Place was being developed. In 1955, William Levy's son-in-law, Alfred L. Friedlander, now Co-Chairman Emeritus, joined the business. Two years later, his son, Joel M. Levy, now Co-Chairman Emeritus, came into the family business. At its peak, the company 35 stores.

Randalls Food Markets was founded in 1966 by Robert R. Onstead, R. C. Barclay and Norman N. Frewin. It was named for Onstead's son Randall. By 1985, the company was the second largest grocer in the five-county Greater Houston area, with 42 stores. By 2001, Randalls operated 46 stores in the Houston area, 12 stores in Austin and 69 stores in the Dallas/Ft. Worth area. In 2005, Safeway took over the Randalls chain.

A. J. Gerland founded the Gerland's Food Fair chain in 1967, with the first store was in Spring Branch. Following the success of Weingarten's and Randall's supermarket chains in Houston, Gerland's added bakery and delicatessen departments to its stores in the late 1970s. Gerland's acquired stores from the defunct Weingarten grocery store chain in 1981, and five more from Appletree in 1994. Gerland's became Houston's seventh largest grocer, with 16 locations.

Sellers Bros., founded in 1921, is a chain of 12 grocery stores and five convenience stores based in Houston. Its officers are George R. Sellers, Joseph L. Sellers and John L. Sellers. When expanding, the chain typically buys existing properties. In 1998, it acquired an Appletree Market. In 2007, it acquired Davis Food City.

Jim Jamail and his sons opened a grocery store on Montrose Blvd. after World War II. The sons moved the store to Kirby Drive and offered premium priced highest quality food items.

A different kind of specialty grocery store was founded by Donald Bonham and O.C. Mendenhall. As buyers for retail chains, they visited marketplaces in Mexico and were impressed with the atmosphere. They duplicated the ambience with Fiesta stores. The first was in an old Kroger store that they acquired on Fulton Avenue. Fiesta had a Spanish flavor and stocked lots of international foods. Fiesta expanded into a successful chain and also featured tenant shops to round out the Mercado composition.

The success of Fiesta fueled The Mercado, a shopping center east of downtown just off 59-North. Curios and gifts reminiscent of open shopping courts in Mexico populated this building, funded in part by city revenue.

Other grocery stores of the past included State Street Grocery, Eagle, A&P, Ye Seekers, Hille's Place, Continental Finer Foods, A Moveable Feast and Minimax.

Specialty Retailers

In 1926, the Stelzig family founded a clothing shop that specialized in Western gear. The store was located on Preston, just off Market Square.

The Shudde Brothers store was founded in 1907 by Al Shudde, with the shop located at Travis and Preston, moving in the 1970's to their hat factory building at 905 Trinity. For generations, Shudde's specialized in cleaning and blocking hats. Their loyal customers included film stars John Wayne and Roy Rogers.

Car dealerships have carried the names of the owners, themselves becoming high-profile community leaders. These have included Bob Marco, Jay Marks, Mac Haik, Jack Roach, Mike Persia, Tommie Vaughn, Sterling McCall, Sam Montgomery, Jimmie Green, Russell & Smith, David Taylor, A.C. Collins, George DeMontrond, Fred Haas, Rollie McGinnis, Art Grindle, Earl McMillan, Bill Lee, Don McGill, Bob Lunsford, Joe Myers, Bill McDavid, Randall Reed, Bill Heard, Ron Carter and Jess Allen.

A sports celebrity opened a Chevrolet dealership on South Post Oak. He was A.J. Foyt, champion race car driver. Anthony Joseph Foyt, Jr. raced in motor-sports. His open wheel racing includes USAC Champ cars and midget cars. He raced stock cars in NASCAR and USAC. He holds the all-time USAC career wins record with 159 victories and the all-time American championship racing career wins record with 67.

A.J. Foyt was the only driver to win the Indianapolis 500 (four times), Daytona 500, 24 Hours of Daytona and the 24 Hours of Le Mans. Foyt won the International Race of Champions all-star racing series in 1976 and 1977. In the NASCAR stock car circuit, he won the 1964 Firecracker 400 and the 1972 Daytona 500. He survived three spectacular crashes and narrowly escaped a fourth with skillful driving.

Foyt's success has led to induction in numerous motor-sports halls of fame. Since his retirement from active racing, he has owned A. J. Foyt Enterprises, which has fielded teams in the CART, IRL and NASCAR.

Leopold Meyer followed his brothers into the retail business. He worked for F. S. Levy and Company, then joined Foley Brothers Dry Goods Company. In 1946, he opened Meyer Brothers, Incorporated, which grew to 10 stores by 1957. Leopold served as chairman of the board until he and his brothers sold the business to a national chain. In 1921, Meyer became president of the Houston chapter of the Retail Credit Merchant's Association and served as president of the National Retail Credit Association in 1929. He helped reorganize the Houston Retail Merchants Association in 1942. For years, Meyer was director of the Houston Livestock Show and Rodeo and for 23 years headed the Houston Horse Show Association.

Aron S. Gordon took a family-owned jewelry business and created Gordon's Jewelers, which is today a nationally known chain with offices in Houston and New York City. Under his direction, Gordon's eventually grew to 650 stores in 43 states and Puerto Rico. Gordon's was one of the first jewelry companies in the United States to extend credit to customers and to locate its stores in malls and shopping centers. Gordon supported such organizations as the March of Dimes, the Juvenile Diabetes Foundation, the DePelchin Faith Homes, the Anti-Defamation League, B'nai Brith and Texas Children's Hospital.

In 1919, J.S. "Jake" Oshman, an immigrant from Latvia, opened a store, Oshman's Dry Goods, in Richmond. In 1930, he moved to Houston by buying the stock of a bankrupted dry goods store. While he liquidated the inventory of the Richmond store, he observed that sporting goods were the fastest selling items. In 1931, he opened the first Oshman's Sporting Goods downtown. Oshman's opened locations in suburban shopping centers in Greater Houston and then in Bay City, Beaumont, Corpus Christi and Pasadena.

The company was incorporated in 1946. In 1978, Oshman's purchased the rights to the trade name of Abercrombie and Fitch from First National Bank of Chicago. As of 1987, the company operated 185 traditional stores, one Super Sports USA store and 27 Abercrombie and Fitch stores. In 2001, Gart Sports Company announced that it would buy Oshman's and merge into GSC Acquisition Corp., a wholly owned subsidiary. Today many of Oshman's stores are now Sports Authority.

In 1938, Max Gochman opened what was then called an Army-Navy surplus store, with locations in Austin and San Antonio. It grew as Academy Super Surplus stores. Today, Academy Sports + Outdoors is a sports goods discount store chain, operating 170 stores throughout Alabama, Arkansas, Florida, Georgia, Kansas, Louisiana, Mississippi, Missouri, North Carolina, Oklahoma, South Carolina, Tennessee and Texas. Academy Sports and Outdoors has its corporate offices and product distribution center in western Harris County, Texas, near Katy. For 74 years, it was a privately held company, owned by the Gochman family. In 2011, Academy Sports + Outdoors was acquired by the investment firm Kohlberg Kravis Roberts & Co.

Al's Formal Wear was established by Al Sankary in 1957 in Fort Worth, including his sister Lillian and her husband, Alan Gaylor, into the business. The store experimented with different concepts, including bridal stores, mall kiosks, manufacturing formal lines himself, uniform sourcing for the military and cleaning. The company stocks 50 styles of tuxedos for rental, including such designers as Ralph Lauren and Calvin Klein. Al's Formal Wear fills orders for weddings, high school proms, quinceaneras and other events from its distribution centers.

Al's Formal Wear is a family-owned business, with Alan Gaylor's son Stuart as company president. It has grown to 100 locations in Texas, Louisiana, Arkansas, Colorado, Mississippi and Oklahoma, including the purchase of Mr. Neat's Formalwear of Colorado.

In 1973, George Zimmer founded the Men's Wearhouse, a men's dress clothes retailer. The chain notably ran television and radio commercials featuring Zimmer, and the oft-repeated slogan, "You're going to like the way you look. I guarantee it." The company is publicly traded and has corporate offices in Houston. The company operates under the names Men's Wearhouse, K&G Superstores, Moores Clothing for Men, Twin Hill Corporate clothing and MW Cleaners. In 1997, it purchased, then liquidated, the bankrupt Kuppenheimer chain. In 2006, it acquired After Hours Formalwear, a clothier specializing in black tie formalwear, from Federated Department Stores, the parent company of department store giant Macy's. Douglas Ewert is the current CEO.

Stage Stores, Inc. is a department store company specializing mostly in retailing brand name clothing, accessories, cosmetics and footwear. It is headquartered in Houston and operates stores in small and mid-size towns and communities, primarily in Midwestern, Southeastern and Mid-Atlantic states. It was founded in 1988, with James Scarborough as Chairman and Andy Hall as President and CEO. The corporation operates 668 stores under the Bealls, Palais Royal, Peebles and Stage nameplates. A subsidiary of Stage acquired the Goody's Family Clothing name and reopened several of that chain's former stores.

Benjamin J. Rogers co-founded Texas State Optical. TSO offered optometrists and eyeglasses in the same location and sold eyeglasses at affordable prices. By the time they sold TSO in 1979, the company had more than 100 locations. During the 1950s, Rogers Brothers Investments was created, with Ben as managing partner. The company developed Gateway Shopping Center (Beaumont's first full-service shopping center) and Parkdale Mall (the first regional shopping mall between Houston and New Orleans). Baptist Hospital of Southeast Texas named its cancer treatment center The Julie and Ben Rogers Cancer Institute. Organizations he served included M.D. Anderson Hospital, St. Elizabeth Hospital, Boys Haven, Minnie Rogers Juvenile Home, Julie Rogers Theatre for the Performing Arts, Babe Didrikson Zaharias Museum, Wuthering Heights Park, Art Museum of Southeast Texas and Joseph R. Rogers Southeast Texas Community Health Clinic.

In 1962, Spec and Carolynn Jackson opened a small store (1,000 square feet), selling pints and half pints of liquor. Then they added include larger bottles of liquor and beer to the shelves. Spec's steadily grew and added more locations and expanded. In 1971, their daughter Lindy and son-in-law John Rydman joined the business upon college graduation. With the inventory of wines in 1974, the variety of brands and pricing made Spec's a retail wine center. What started as a shelf of party foods expanded into a full deli. The third generation (Lisa Rydman-Key) joined the business. Spec's now has 70 locations across the state, including service to Houston, Beaumont, Austin, Galveston, Victoria, Temple, San Antonio, Corpus Christi and Bryan-College Station. The Warehouse Store sells more than 40,000 labels and occupies 80,000 sq. feet of selling space.

Star Furniture was founded in 1912 and now has 10 stores in Texas (seven in Houston and one each in Austin, Bryan and San Antonio). The regional chain is a Berkshire Hathaway Furniture Division company and is currently ranked fourth in the nation in furniture sales.

Finger's Furniture goes back to the 1890's, when Sam and Annie Finger opened a general store in Shepherd, Texas. In 1925, Sam moved to Houston and opened a small store which would lead to the formation of the Finger Furniture Company, Inc. in 1946. Sammy Finger and his brother Aaron opened the Finger's "Magnificent Furniture Center," the largest furniture store in Houston with over 10 acres and 500 room settings. They introduced "concept rooms" and "room packages."

The Finger's store was built on the site of Buff Stadium, home to Houston's minor league baseball team. The original site of home plate was preserved and a museum was built around it. The Houston Sports Museum is a tribute to Houston sports, particularly baseball memorabilia. In 1989, Sammy's son Robert "Bobby" Finger became President and CEO of Finger Furniture Company. In 2009, Rodney S. Finger, Bobby Finger's son, acquired Finger Furniture Company, Inc.'s trademarks, including Finger Furniture and Finger's.

Gallery Furniture was opened by Jim McIngvale in 1981. new business venture began in an abandoned, un-heated, non-air conditioned model home park that was formerly occupied by a build-on-your-own-lot home building company. The company established a reputation for quality furniture on a budget and same-day delivery. The store has steadily grown in popularity.

Mattress Firm Inc. is a retailing company and mattress store chain founded in 1986 by Harry Roberts, Steve Fendrich and Paul Stork. The company is headquartered in Houston and operates 1,200 locations across 30 states nationwide, making it the largest bedding retailer.

Conn's Inc. is an electronics and appliance store chain headquartered in The Woodlands. The chain has stores in Texas, Louisiana, New Mexico, Arizona and Oklahoma. In 1890, Edward Eastham founded Eastham Plumbing and Heating Company in Beaumont. The First National Bank of Beaumont took over the company and renamed it Plumbing and Heating Inc. in 1931. The store hired Carol Washington Conn Sr. in 1933. He purchased the company one year later and changed the name to Conn Plumbing and Heating Company.

In 1937, Conn's began selling refrigerators and soon added gas ranges to its inventory. By 1940, Conn had purchased a store building at 268 Pearl Street in Beaumont. The company's second store opened in 1959 on Eleventh Street in Beaumont. C.W. Conn Jr. joined the company in 1953 and founded Conn's retail service repair and maintenance subsidiary company, Appliance Parts and Service, in 1962. In 1964 he co-founded Conn Credit Corporation, a retail credit financing services company, to provide retail credit financing services to Conn's customers.

Conn Jr. was named president and chief operating officer in 1966, serving until 1976. In 1983, Conn's first location in Houston opened. In 1994, Thomas Frank Sr. became Chairman of the Board. In 1998, the company reorganized and brought in a financial partner, The Stephens Group. In 2003, Conn's, Inc. became a publicly traded company. Today, in addition to appliances, electronics, furniture and mattresses, the company offers its customers service, distribution, financing, insurance and other related services at 67 retail locations; 57 in Texas, six in Louisiana, two in Oklahoma and three in New Mexico.

These retail stores of olden days are gone but not forgotten: Sage, Harold's in the Heights, Don's Record Shop, Crown Books, Wagner Hardware, Handy Andy, Rexall, Battlestein's, Massey's Office Supplies, Computer City, Eagle Food Centers, S.H. Kress, Tower Records, Levitz Furniture, J.J. Newberry, Border's Books, Circuit City, Variety Fair, Frost Brothers, Thom McAn, Handy Dan, Phar-Mor,

Bombay Company, Pick-N-Pay, Warner Brothers Studio Store, Gemco, Davis Food City, Tea's Nursery, The Woman's Shop, Sound Warehouse, Kaplan's Ben-Hur, Winn's, Shopper's World, Sussan Furniture, Meyer Bros. White House Store, Planet Universe and Woolworth's.

Food and Hospitality

In 1923, brothers James and Tom Papadakis opened James Coney Island, a hot dog themed restaurant. The early downtown location on Walker continues, with branch locations throughout the city. The business was family owned and operated from its inception until 1990, when it was sold to private investors.

In 1934, Doug Prince opened Prince's Hamburgers, a series of drive-in restaurants, replete with colorfully costumed carhops. For 45 years, Prince's was a popular hangout for the youth clientele. One by one, the restaurants closed, as fast-food chains began dominating the burger market. Prince's sons shifted their focus to running corporate dining rooms. In the 1990's, due to popular demand, Prince's Hamburgers returned to business in the format of 1950's nostalgic diners.

Felix Tijerina was born in Texas but knew no English when he started working as a restaurant busboy. In 1929, he opened his own Tex-Mex restaurant, The Mexican Inn. Felix's first Montrose location opened in 1937. In the heyday of the chain, there were six Felix Mexican restaurants in Houston and Beaumont. Tijernia became active in educational service activities and was a four-time national president of LULAC. The Houston Independent School District named an elementary school after Felix Tijerina. In 2008, the last restaurant closed. The Felix recipes were licensed to and are still served at El Patio Restaurant.

Leo Reynosa Sr. opened Leo's Mexican Restaurant in an old house on Shepherd Drive in 1942. His claim to fame was that, as a young man, he had ridden with Mexican revolutionary Pancho Villa. The walls of the restaurant commemorated his involvement. Leo's became a favorite of the band ZZ Top, who featured Leo's on an album cover. Leo sat inside the entry, greeting customers. He died in 1995 and his sons ran the restaurant until it closed in 2001.

There was a time in the 1950's that restaurants dotted South Main Street from downtown up to the Shamrock Hilton Hotel. That resulted in what was known as Café Society. One of my old friends was a key restaurateur in that era. He was Tom Katz and had a swank spot. Tom later had a more informal place across from the new Galleria development, known as 2-K Ice Cream Parlor. Tom headed up the restaurant associations and later crafted the food court concept for the Houston International Festival.

Through Tom, I met the flamboyant Glenn McCarthy. Glenn was an oilman who invested his riches in building a palace, the Shamrock. That 1949 hotel opening was high-profile, one of the biggest social events in the city's history and a major nationally broadcast event. Architect Frank Lloyd Wright referred to the Shamrock as "an imitation Rockefeller Center." The hotel had 18 stories and 1,100 rooms. It was managed by George Lindholm, who was recruited from the socially prominent Waldorf-Astoria Hotel in New York City.

This plotline was later dramatized in the movie "Giant." James Dean played the character that was based on McCarthy. Throughout his years, McCarthy stayed in the oil business. He operated The Cork Club in the penthouse of the same building where his offices were (2100 Travis). His career is detailed in the Energy chapter of this book.

The Shamrock was acquired by the Hilton corporation in 1955. For another 32 years, it was a prime hotel, especially catering to the Medical Center area. In 1987, the hotel was demolished, and the land was acquired by the Texas Medical Center. The Shamrock ballroom and garage still exist, known as the Hornberger Conference Center.

The Magnolia Brewing Company was out of Galveston and had a Houston production facility. The Historic Magnolia Brewery Building is listed in the National Register of Historic Places, honored with a Texas Historical Marker and became the first commercial Protected Houston Landmark. The Magnolia Ballroom has hosted many parties and special events.

Howard Hughes started a brewery in Houston, on the grounds of his Hughes Tool Company. It was called Gulf Brewing Company and produced Grand Prize Beer, which for a time was the best-selling beer in Texas. Hughes opened the brewery at the end of Prohibition, and its profits helped the tool company survive the Depression.

Grand Prize Beer was produced by the Houston Ice and Brewing Company. Howard Hughes owned the Grand Prize brewery, which was operated by the man who served as brew master at Houston Ice and Brewing before Prohibition. In 1913, while he was brew master at Houston Ice and Brewin, Belgian-Houstonian

Frantz Brogniez was awarded Grand Prize at the last International Conference of Breweries for his Southern Select Beer, beating 4,096 competing brewers. Brogniez left Houston during Prohibition, but Hughes convinced him to return to serve as brew master for the Gulf Brewing Company. Brogniez' son operated the brewery after his father's death. Grand Prize stopped brewing in 1964.

The tradition of Magnolia and Grand Prize is carried on by the Saint Arnold Brewing Company. It is a craft brewery, named for a patron saint of brewing, Saint Arnulf of Metz, founded in 1994 by Brock Wagner and Kevin Bartol. Other current breweries in the area include the Fort Bend Brewery, Buffalo Bayou Brewing, 8th Wonder Brewery, Karbach Brewery and No Label Brewery.

Cyclone Anaya, began his wrestling career at age 17, subsequently becoming the Champion of Mexico. He then came to the United States and was active on the professional wrestling circuit. Cyclone Anaya won numerous awards and thrilled the hearts of millions of fans. Here he met his wife, Carolina, a former Miss Houston. After many championship titles and five children, Cyclone and his family entered the restaurant business in Houston 40 years ago.

John Charles "Johnny" Carrabba III and his uncle, Damian Mandola, opened the first Carrabba's restaurant on Kirby Drive in 1986. The chain of Carrabba's Italian Grill contains more than 230 locations across the nation. In 2013, he was named a Houston Legend.

Tilman Fertitta is chairman, CEO and sole owner of Landry's, Inc., one of the nation's largest restaurant chains. He was a partner in the first Landry's Seafood, then helped open Joe's Crab Shack and Willie G's Seafood & Steaks. He gained controlling interests of both locations and in 1988 became sole owner of Landry's Restaurants. In 1993, he took Landry's public, the company now including The Golden Nugget Hotel and Casinos, Morton's The Steakhouse, Rainforest Cafe, Bubba Gump Shrimp Co., McCormick & Schmick's Seafood & Steaks, Saltgrass Steak House, Claim Jumper, Chart House, The Oceanaire, Mastro's Restaurants, Vic & Anthony's Steakhouse and others. He is chairman of Houston Children's Charity and serves on the Board of Regents for the University of Houston System.

Pappas Restaurants operates in more than 80 locations in Houston, Dallas, Cincinnati, Austin, San Antonio, Beaumont, Atlanta, Chicago, Denver, Albuquerque and Phoenix. The restaurants follow eight concepts, including Pappas Bros. Steakhouse, Pappadeaux Seafood Kitchen, Pappas Seafood House, Pappasito's

Cantina, Pappas Bar-B-Q, Pappas Burger and Yia Yia Marys. The company is run by brothers Christopher and Harris Pappas, who also serve as the executive team at Luby's, Inc., a cafeteria chain in several states.

H.D. Pappas emigrated from Greece in 1897 and opened restaurants in Arkansas, Tennessee and Texas. In 1945, his sons, Pete Pappas and Jim Pappas, moved to Houston where they obtained a franchise to sell beer coolers in South Texas. The brothers built the venture into a successful restaurant supply business, selling chairs, booths, refrigerators and kitchen equipment. The business was cyclical, however, and the brothers soon decided to try the restaurant field in 1967 with the opening of a Dot Coffee Shop. In 1970, Jim Pappas's son, Harris, joined the family business, soon followed by sons, Christopher and Greg.

The Pappas brothers distinguished their restaurants by offering large portions at moderate prices at restaurants with highly visible locations. The company had a competitive edge on publicly owned restaurant chains, which were under pressure to build new units in a hurry and to improve bottom lines for each quarter.

Anthony Russo's parents immigrated from Italy in 1962 and had a restaurant in New York. They opened Russo's Italian Restaurant in 1978 after moving from New York to Texas. Russo's Italian Restaurant was a fine dining establishment that used recipes passed down through generations from the Russo family members. In the early 1990's, Anthony opened his first restaurant, Anthony's Pizzeria, in Clear Lake. In 1992, he founded Russo's New York Pizzeria. The chain serves New York-style pizza as well as several different types of soups, salads, pastas, calzones and desserts. The chain has 30 locations in Texas, Tennessee, Arkansas, Florida and Oklahoma, with international locations in Dubai, Abu Dhabi and Sharjah, UAE.

After learning how many people are affected by Celiac disease and other gluten allergies and intolerance, Chef Anthony Russo spent two years developing a gluten-free pizza crust recipe out of rice flour, tapioca flour and cold-pressed extra-virgin olive oil. After achieving considerable success in the Celiac and gluten-free community for the pizza crust and menu options, Russo's began selling frozen gluten-free pizzas in six different varieties to nationwide grocers.

Some of the long-standing restaurants still in operation include:

- James Coney Island, established by James Papadakis and Tom Papadakis in 1923.

- Pizzitola's, established by John and Leila Davis in 1935.
- Molina's Cantina, established by Raul and Mary Molina in 1941.
- Whataburger, established by Harmon Dawson in Corpus Christi in 1950.
- Cleburne Cafeteria, established by Nick and Pat Mickelis in 1952.
- Demeris Barbecue, established by Billy Vlahakos and Yonny Demeris in 1964.
- Tony's, established by Tony Vallone in 1965.
- Brennan's, established by Ella Brennan and Alex Brennan-Martin in 1967.
- Ouisie's Table, established by Elouise Jones in 1973.
- Ragin Cajun, established by Ray Hay, Frankie Mandola and Luke Mandola Sr. in 1974.
- Pappas, established by Pete and Jim Pappas in 1967.
- Goode Company (barbecue, seafood and burger restaurants), established by JIm Goode and Joe Dixie in 1977.
- Rainbow Lodge, established by Donnette Hansen in 1977.
- Niko Niko's, established by Chris Fetokakis in 1977.
- Nino's and Vincent's, established by Vincent Mandola in 1977.
- Tony Mandola's, established by Tony Mandola in 1982.
- Damian's, established by Frankie Mandola in 1983.

These restaurants of olden days are gone but not forgotten: Kaphan's, Tokyo Gardens, Albritton's Cafeterias, Burger Chef, San Jacinto Inn, Renu's Thai, Felix Mexican Restaurant, Dirty's, Sonny Look's, Joe Matranga's, The Rail Head, Luther's Barbecue, Boston Sea Party, Mr. Steak, The Great Caurso, Maxim's, Dong Ting, Earl Abel's, Leo's Mexican Restaurant, Steak & Ale, Square Pan Pizza, Luke's Hamburgers, Bavarian Gardens, Victoria Station, Night Hawk, Shakey's Pizza, Fat Ernie's, Felix Mexican Restaurant, Bistro Moderne, The Bedford, Hamburgers by Gourmet, Vargo's, Bonanza Steak House, Café Annie, Village Inn Pizza, Strawberry Patch, Yakov's, Atchafalaya, Bojangle's the Velvet Hammer, La Bodega, The Metropole, Art Wren's Cafe, Bill Williams Barbecue, Alfred's, Kenny Rogers Roasters, Roy Rogers Roast Beef, Farrell's Ice Cream Parlors, Hebert's and Charlie Angelo's Fisherman's Wharf.

*V.A. Corrigan posed in the 1920's in front of his
downtown store, Houston Watch Company.*

*Doing business
on Texas Avenue,
downtown, in
the 1920's.*

Chapter 7

TIMELINE

1824 John Harris founded Harrisburg, a maritime trading post.

1832 Brothers Augustus Allen and John Kirby Allen came from New York to Texas.

1836 On April 21, General Sam Houston's Texas army won independence from Mexico in the Battle of San Jacinto.

1836 Augustus Allen and John Kirby Allen settled Houston. They paid $1.40 per acre for 6,642 acres of land near Buffalo Bayou.

1836 Allen Brothers called on Gail Borden (publisher, surveyor, and the originator of condensed milk) and Thomas H. Borden to survey and map the site. Gail Borden laid out the town's streets 80 feet wide, with the principal east-west thoroughfare (Texas Avenue) 100' feet wide.

1837 General Sam Houston, first president of the Republic of Texas, signed an act authorizing the city to incorporate. Houston was capital of the Republic from 1837-1840.

1837   The Laura was the first steamship to visit Houston.

1839   The city of Houston was incorporated.

1840   On April 4, seven businessmen formed the Houston Chamber of Commerce.

1842   The Galveston Daily News, Texas' oldest newspaper, began publication.

1846   Texas became the 28th state.

1853   Houston's first railroad, the Buffalo Bayou, Brazos & Colorado, began operations.

1858   The city paid $2,500 for land and buildings for a municipal hospital.

1861   Houston and Harris County voted to secede from the Union and join the Confederacy. During the Civil War, the closest fighting was at Galveston.

1868   The first mule drawn trolley cars appeared.

1870   Texas was re-admitted to the Union. 1870 census showed Houston's population up to 9,332.

1870   The U.S. Congress officially declared Houston as a port and began planning the upgrade of Buffalo Bayou. Congress made its first appropriation ($10,000) for ship channel improvements.

1874   The Houston Board of Trade & Cotton Exchange was organized.

1875   The first grain elevator was built on the Houston Ship Channel.

1877   Houston's first free public schools were established.

1880   The first telephone exchange was created.

1880   Houston got its first arc light.

1882   The first road was paved.

1882   Houston was one of the first cities to build a power plant.

1884   The Houston Post newspaper was founded.

1885   The University of St. Thomas was founded.

1891   The first electric streetcar appeared. By 1912, 200 streetcars changed across a dozen main lines.

1897   The first automobile arrived in town (an electric car, the result of a promotional gimmick by Montgomery Ward). Today, 2.5 million cars travel the city's streets.

1899   The first city park opened. This site (now Sam Houston Park) contains several of Houston's earliest buildings.

1900   Hurricane wiped out Galveston, killing 6,000 people.

1900 Foley's department store opened. It grew to $2 billion in sales and 60 stores.

1900 Baylor College of Medicine was founded.

1901 Oil was discovered at the Spindletop field, near Beaumont.

1901 The Houston Chronicle newspaper was founded.

1901 Weingarten's grocery stores opened.

1902 Texaco was founded.

1902 The U.S. Congress appropriated $1 million for work on the Houston Ship Channel.

1902 Sakowitz stores opened.

1904 Oil was discovered at Humble.

1905 Houston had 80 automobiles.

1907 Neighborhood Centers was founded.

1910 A group of Houston businessmen headed by the Houston Chamber of Commerce proposed to Congress a plan to split ship channel development costs between Houston and the federal government. Congress accepted the plan.

1911 The Houston Press newspaper was founded.

1912 Rice University was founded.

1912 Star Furniture opened.

1913 The Houston Symphony was founded.

1914 The Port of Houston opened.

1915 The first deep water vessel, the S.S. Satilla, called at Houston.

1916 Gulf Oil was founded.

1917 Humble Oil & Refining Company was founded.

1917 Phillips Petroleum was founded.

1918 City of Houston annexed the Heights.

1918 Sinclair Oil was founded.

1919 Oshman's Sporting Goods was founded.

1921 Houston adopted an ordinance dedicating tax money to its library system.

1923 Land sales and construction started in River Oaks.

1924 The Museum of Fine Arts of Houston (first in Texas) opened.

1926 Natural gas was piped into Houston for the first time.

1927 Finger Furniture opened.

1927   Buses replaced the electric trolley for everyday travel. Today, 1,500 buses travel the city's streets.

1927   The University of Houston was founded.

1928   The National Democratic Convention was held in Houston.

1929   The City Planning Commission recommended that Houston adopt a zoning ordinance, but found little support.

1931   The Houston Livestock Show and Rodeo was founded.

1934   The Intra-coastal Canal linked Houston to the Mississippi River navigation system.

1935   Braniff International inaugurated air service to Houston.

1941   A master plan for Houston thoroughfares included a loop system.

1943   The Texas Medical Center was founded.

1947   Texas Southern University was founded.

1947   The Alley Theatre was founded.

1947   Engineering began on the Gulf Freeway, Texas' first freeway.

1948   The Port of Houston ranked second nationally in total tonnage.

1949   The Shamrock Hotel opened to glitz and national attention.

1955   The Houston Ballet was founded.

1955   The Houston Grand Opera was founded.

1955   Houston metro area population reached 1,000,000.

1958   The U.S. Congress created the National Aeronautics and Space Administration (NASA).

1960   Houston Baptist University was founded.

1962   NASA's Manned Spacecraft Center moved to Houston.

1965   The first event held in the Astrodome.

1967   Kenneth Schnitzer began developing Greenway Plaza.

1969   Houston Intercontinental Airport opened.

1969   Houston was the first word spoken from the lunar surface.

1970   Gerald Hines opened The Galleria.

1971   Shell Oil Co. relocated corporate headquarters to Houston. More than 200 major firms moved headquarters, subsidiaries and divisions here in the 1970s.

1971   Houston Community College was founded.

1972   The University of Texas Health Science Center opened.

1973   Lone Star College System was founded.

1973   The Arab oil embargo quadrupled oil prices in 90 days, fueling Houston's 1973-1981 economic boom.

1974   The Super Bowl was played at Rice Stadium.

1978   Voters approved and funded the Metropolitan Transit Authority.

1981   Kathy Whitmire was the first woman elected Mayor of Houston.

1981   Gallery Furniture opened.

1983   Sally Ride was the first woman to fly into space.

1990   Houston hosted the 16th annual Economic Summit of Industrialized Nations, held on the Rice University campus.

1994   The Houston Rockets won the NBA finals, bringing Houston its first major sports championship. They repeated as champions in 1995.

1997   Lee Brown was the first African-American elected Mayor of Houston.

2004   The Super Bowl was played at Reliant Stadium.

Business Narrative by the Author

From history, I've learned that there's nothing more permanent than change. For everything that changes, many things remain the same. The art of living well is to meld the changeable dynamics with the constants and the traditions. The periodic reshuffling of priorities, opportunities and potential outcomes represents business planning at its best.

One learns three times more from failure than from success. By studying and reflecting upon the events of the past and the shortcomings of others, then we create strategies for meeting the challenges of the future.

In business, we must learn lessons from the corporate crises, the also-rans and the conditions which controlled the history. Some of those lessons that we could well learn came from these watershed events:

- The Civil War. This is a classic and tragic case of two sides fighting for causes and not fully understanding the other side's motivations. The South saw slavery as an economic factor and the only system of labor management they had ever known. The North saw opportunities to champion humanity issues, underlying the threat of insurgence within our own nation. Neither side fully articulated its issues, nor sought to negotiate before hostilities broke out. This war caused severe rifts in U.S. society for another 100 years.

- America's shift from an agricultural to an industrial economy.
- Prohibition. Take something away from consumers, and say that the action is in their best interest. They'll want the commodity even more. The great lengths that people went to getting their liquor fixes enabled organized crime to gain major footholds in America. The legislation that created Prohibition was wrong, and that action by a few spawned the gangster era, which became big business in America. Congress finally recounted after untellable damage was done.
- The Great Depression. Economics are a series of ebbs and flows. Failure to anticipate and to prepare for the next drop and to expect that the good times will never cease is foolhardy. Failure to exercise crisis management after the crash and to restore stability in judicious ways caused the Depression to drag on. It was a World War that finally pulled America out of its greatest economic slump. Lessons from the Great Depression should have been applied during the high-riding days of technology stocks and a stock market that over-hyped so much. The dot.com bust and corporate debacles could have been avoided if lessons from the Great Depression had been learned, updated and utilized.
- Diversity in the workplace.
- Shift from an industrial to an information economy.
- Watergate, bringing about more accountability by the public sector.
- The Dot.Com Bust. Analogies from the Great Depression to the dot.com crash were many. Too many tech companies did not feel as though corporate protocols of the older companies applied to them. Shortcuts were taken. The media unfairly crowned superficial darlings, such as Enron. Regulators had relaxed standards. Common practice in investment communities was to over-hype stock potential, without seeing who was truly at the switches of these companies. Had the scandals not triggered public outcry when they did, this chain of events could have led to another Great Depression.
- Corporate scandals, bringing about reforms, ethics and higher corporate accountability.

- Changing management styles. Customer Focused Management is the prevailing orientation, and companies must adapt.

Chapter 8

MEDIA LEGENDS

The Telegraph and Texas Register newspaper was founded in 1835 in San Felipe, TX, by Joseph Baker, Thomas Borden and Gail Borden. It moved to Harrisburg in April, 1836. The newspaper covered the fight for Texas independence, including events at the Alamo and San Jacinto. The Bordens sold to Francis Moore Jr., who became the editor. Moore subsequently was elected Mayor of Houston three times.

Many other newspapers were started, all with short lives. They included the Civilian, National Intelligencer, Daily Times, Mercantile Advertiser, Houston Gazette, True Southron, Commercial Express, Union, German Post, Sun, Evening Age, Texas Times, Record and Examiner.

In 1869, one newspaper editor called the other a "liar, coward and scoundrel." The two met in the street for a duel the next day. They exchanged several gunshots, missing each other but killing a bystander.

The Evening Post was founded in 1880. It was sold in 1884 to a group of Houston citizens, including William R. Baker. In 1885, the Houston Morning Chronicle and the Houston Evening Journal combined to create The Houston Post. In 1897, Rienzi Johnston, C.G. Palmer and Henry F. MacGregor controlled the business in trust until Roy Watson, assumed control in 1918. Watson, a Christian Scientist, banned advertisements for patent medicines, wildcat oil stock, liquor, wine, beer, and yeast. The paper soon lost advertising revenue, and Watson sold the Post in 1923 to Ross Sterling, joined with William P. Hobby to merge it with The Houston Post in 1924, forming the Houston Post-Dispatch.

In the 1930s, Sterling sold the paper to Jackson E. Josey, who represented Jesse H. Jones. Josey changed the name back to Post and operated the paper until 1939, when William P. Hobby, president of the paper since 1924, acquired a controlling interest. Among writers on the Post were W. S. Porter (O. Henry), W. C. Brann, Judd Mortimer Lewis and Marcellus E. Foster, founder of the Houston Chronicle.

The Houston Post continued to grow in prestige and circulation. As the Houston Post-Dispatch, the company created radio station KPRC in the 1920s (with the call letters standing for Post Radio Corporation). In 1949, the paper had a paid circulation of 165,667 daily and 177,913 on Sundays. By the early 1950s the Houston Post Company had acquired television station KPRC, and in January 1955 the company opened a new $4 million office building. In August 1955 Hobby became chairman of the board of directors, and his wife, Oveta Culp Hobby, became president and editor.

In 1963, the company purchased the News Publishing Company, a transaction that involved the sale of the Galveston News, Galveston Tribune and Texas City Sun. When Hobby died in 1964, the Post remained under the management of Mrs. Hobby, assisted by their son, William P. Hobby, Jr., who served as executive editor and executive vice president. In 1967, the Houston Post Company sold the Galveston area papers.

In 1969, William H. Gardner was named chief editorial writer and editor, and in the 1970s the paper again became a pioneer with its use of computer-set type. By 1975, Oveta Culp Hobby was editor and chairman of the board. William P. Hobby, Jr., was executive editor and president (and also lieutenant governor of Texas), and Edwin D. Hunter was vice president and managing editor.

In the early 1990s the paper was purchased by a Toronto newspaper, which sold it to the Media News Group and William Dean Singleton, a native of Graham, Texas. In 1991, the Post had a daily circulation of 335,000. In 1995, the Post was closed by owner Dean Singleton after 111 years of continuous publication.

The Houston Chronicle was founded in 1901. Jesse Jones bought the Chronicle in 1926. He was the most powerful political king-maker in the city's history. His city editor, M.E. Walters, served for many years as chairman of the City Planning Commission.

On Jan. 10, 1901, Marcellus E. Foster, a young reporter for the Houston Post, was assigned to cover the anticipated first oil well at the Spindletop field, near Beaumont. Foster recognized that he was witnessing an event of epic importance, so he gambled $30 (a week's pay) and bought an option on the well. A week later, he sold his option for $5,000. He returned to Houston with his new-found wealth and a dream of owning his own newspaper. Within days he had sold his friends on the idea, and they invested an additional $20,000.

On October 14, 1901, the Houston Chronicle was founded in a three-story building on Texas Avenue in the heart of downtown Houston. The Chronicle, which sold for two cents a copy, had a circulation of 4,378 at the end of its first month of publication, in a city of 44,638. Foster was a risk-taking man who was not afraid to take on the establishment when he believed Houston's best interests were not being served. And the people of Houston responded favorably. By 1904, the paper's circulation had grown so well that Foster started a Sunday edition with 44 pages of news and advertising and a revolutionary feature, four pages of comics in color.

By 1908, Houston's growth was attracting national attention and the newspaper had outgrown its modest home. Foster turned to Jesse H. Jones, a young builder and entrepreneur, who, just 12 years after coming to the Bayou City, was already regarded as a man of growing civic leadership and stature. They struck a deal under which Jones would build a 10-story plant and office building for the Chronicle at the corner of Travis and Texas and receive a part interest in the paper under a buy-sell agreement. Subsequent additions produced the granite and glass offices and printing plant that now occupy the entire block where Jones first built.

In 1922, the Ku Klux Klan reared its head. An overwhelming number of officeholders in Harris County were known to be members of the Klan. The city became engulfed in fear and hatred, a city divided. The Chronicle stood tall in the front ranks in the fight against the Klan, and Foster was the standard bearer. He wrote editorials attacking the Klan, while the Houston Post's less aggressive attitude led Klan opponents mistakenly to believe that the Post was in favor of the Klan. But Foster's stand was expensive for the Chronicle. Readership, circulation and advertising all suffered so much that the paper's department heads pleaded with the editor to soft-pedal his attacks. Foster answered angrily: "Before I do that, I'll dismantle the presses and throw the pieces into Buffalo Bayou."

As time went by, Jones believed that the newspaper would give him the opportunity to help guide the growth of Houston. Under the terms of the buy-sell agreement, Jones became the sole owner of the paper. Foster then joined the Houston Press as editor and continued his journalistic fervor until his death in 1938. After Foster's departure, C. B. Gillespie was named editor. Subsequent editors included William O. Huggins (1929-1934), George W. Cottingham (1934–48), M. E. Walter (1948–61) W. P. Steven (1961–65), Everett Collier (1965–79), P. G. Warner (1979–87) and Jack Loftis (1987-).

Under Jones's stewardship, the Chronicle became the voice and power that helped him accomplish things for the city. He built 60 buildings and gave generously of his time, finances and influence in the affairs of the city, state and nation. When he died in 1956, he and his wife, Mary Gibbs Jones, left the Houston Endowment with resources that have financed scores of living memorials to the Joneses' affection for Houston, one of them the Houston Chronicle. With the death of Jones, his nephew, John T. Jones, Jr., was named president, a position he held until his resignation in 1966. Houston Endowment president Howard J. Creekmore then assumed the role of publisher.

In 1964, the Chronicle purchased the assets of the Houston Press, its evening competition. In 1967, Creekmore named Frank E. Warren president of the paper. When Warren died suddenly in 1972, vice president Richard J. V. Johnson, who joined the paper in 1956 as a promotion-copy writer, was named president. Under his leadership the paper made its greatest gains. Beginning in 1973, Johnson began to move the Chronicle's evening circulation to morning. When the conversion was completed, there were fewer than 20,000 evening subscribers and the paper was well ahead of the Post in total circulation.

When the Houston Endowment had to divest itself of the profit-making paper under new state laws, the Chronicle was sold to the Hearst Corporation in 1987 for $415 million, at that time the highest price ever paid for an American newspaper. Johnson continued to serve as president until 1990, when he assumed the title of chairman and publisher. At that time his close associate, longtime Chronicle executive Gene McDavid, was named president.

In April 1995, the Houston Post closed its doors, and the Hearst Corporation purchased the Post's assets from the Media News Group, making the Chronicle the only major daily in Houston. On Nov. 1, 1995, the Audit Bureau of Circulations reported its circulation to be 541,478 morning daily and 743,689 Sunday. That year, the Chronicle was the ninth largest daily and Sunday newspaper in the nation.

The Houston Endowment Foundation, established by Jones, carried much of the same clout after his 1956 death. The last open connection between local politicians and the daily newspapers ended with the acquisition of the Chronicle by Hearst Corporation in 1987.

The Houston Press was founded on Sept. 25, 1911, and until its demise on March 20, 1964, it was the most colorful of the three 20th Century Houston daily newspapers. It was a Scripps-Howard newspaper and had a general reputation for exposing the seamier side of life in Houston and for keeping Houston politicians on their toes. The Press style of journalism was established by its first editor, Paul C. Edwards, and that style flourished under later editors Marcellus E. Foster, 1926–36, who had founded and edited the Houston Chronicle, and George Carmack, 1946–64.

The Press began publication on the corner of Capital at Bagby streets and in 1927 moved to Rusk at Chartres streets. In 1963, it averaged a daily circulation of 90,000 and employed over 300 persons; however, it operated at a loss during the early 1960's.

On March 20, 1964, president and publisher Ray L. Powers and editor Carmack announced to the assembled newspaper staff that they were preparing the last issue of the Press. The newspaper had been sold by Scripps-Howard to the Houston Chronicle for $4 million.

Copies of the early Texas Almanac, printed at Galveston, served as the key directories for new citizens. Since the city was usually the first Texas port of entry and received United States and foreign news before other places, it had two newspapers by 1838. The Galveston News is the first Texas newspaper still being published.

Houston Business Journal was founded in 1973 by Scripps Howard Business Journals. It was acquired by American City Business Journals in 1986. The publication has included an array of business announcements, case studies, company profiles, features and special sections.

Other newspapers include Houston Community Newspapers (multiple editions), The Houston Examiner, The Forward Times, La Voz, The Daily Court Reporter, The Houston Press (tabloid), The Greensheet, Jewish Herald-Voice, Texas Medical Center News, Galveston Daily News, Texas City Sun and the Conroe Courier.

Magazines have included Performing Arts Magazine, Houston City Magazine, Houston Woman, Out Smart, Preferred Agent, Small Business Today Magazine, The Examiner, West University Buzz and Houston Monthly.

Media, Radio

An amateur radio club was organized in 1919 for amateur builders and operators of crystal sets, with James L. Autrey as president. The first local commercial station was WEV, owned and operated by Hurlburt Still. On May 21, 1922, the Houston Post broadcast a Sunday concert from the radio plant of A. P. Daniel, 2504 Bagby Street. Later that year the Houston Conservatory of Music sent out programs over station WGAB. In 1924, the Houston Post–Dispatch absorbed a station operated by Will Horwitz and established it as KPRC, which made its debut in May 1925.

Several new stations were licensed in the next few years. KXYZ, which had first broadcast on October 20, 1930, was taken over by Jesse H. Jones in 1932, increasing its power to 1,000 watts two years later. When stations KPRC and KTRH installed one broadcasting plant for sending out waves simultaneously in 1936, the plant was the second of its kind in the world. Each station increased its power to 5,000 watts.

On March 24, 1930, KTRH began broadcasting from studios in the Rice Hotel, with the transmitter at Deepwater on the La Porte highway. The frequency was 1120 kilocycles. The station maintained direct wire circuits with the Lamar and Texas State Hotels, the Elks Club and several churches and theaters for broadcasting programs. The inaugural program on the new station featured "The Romance of

Texas," beginning with the Robert Cavalier Sieur De La Salle Expedition down to the present time, followed by a speech by Jesse Jones.

The station operated from the Rice Hotel for years until around 1970 when it moved out to Lovett Boulevard in the Montrose area. The call letters have not changed since the station moved to Houston. KTRH moved to its present frequency of 740 in 1942.

In 1947, KRCT in Baytown started on 650-AM. By the late 1950s, the station was owned by Leroy Gloger. Because a hurricane damaged the station, it moved to Pasadena and changed its call letters to KIKK. Thus, a country legend was born. Gloger later owned Channel 26 television, giving it the call letters KDOG.

KNUZ signed on in 1948. The station hired the first female account executive and the first black disc jockey. Other KNUZ firsts include a remote broadcast studio, helicopter reporting, wireless microphones, computer traffic system, full-dimensional FM antenna for KQUE and a solid state AM transmitter.

With the advent of television during the second half of the twentieth century the number of radio stations decreased, and by 1971 there was a combined total of 392 standard radio broadcasting (AM) and frequency modulation (FM) stations. During the next two decades there was an upswing, however, and by 1993, Texas had 311 AM and 420 FM radio stations with valid current operating licenses.

During the 1990's and into the 21st century a Texas-based communications company had a major impact on national and international radio markets. Clear Channel Communications, Inc., headquartered in San Antonio, traced its beginnings to 1972, when businessmen Lowry Mays and Red McCombs formed the San Antonio Broadcasting Company. They purchased then KEEZ-FM and in 1975 acquired WOAI-AM. Through the 1980s and 1990s Clear Channel purchased radio stations in San Antonio, Austin and Houston, other stations nationwide and stations in Australia, New Zealand and Mexico.

By 1998, Clear Channel owned and/or programmed 204 radio stations. In 1999, the company bought Dallas-based AMFM, Inc., thereby making Clear Channel the largest radio station operator in the nation with some 830 stations, reflecting a trend of mass consolidation in the radio industry. In 2000 Clear Channel Communications, under CEO Lowry Mays, owned or had interests in more than 1,300 stations worldwide.

In the early 2000s, satellite radio, consisting of digital signals broadcast via communications satellites, became increasingly popular throughout the United States.

Public radio began in 1950, when KUHF was founded, operating at the top of the Ezekiel Cullen Building on the University of Houston campus. College radio stations were also founded at Rice University and Texas Southern University.

Radio Reminiscences

Many of the radio station call letters stood for something. Radio stations east of the Mississippi begin with W. Radio stations west of the Mississippi begin with K. The initials K and W are abbreviations for an engineering term, kilowatts.

KPRC signified the Post Radio Corporation. KTRH represented the Texas Rice Hotel, where its studios were located. An on-air tagline said "Keep Tuned Right Here." KRBE was named for Kirby Drive, the street on which its original studios sat. KIKK represented its country music audience, "a bunch of kickers." KXYZ was named after radio station WXYZ in Detroit, which was named for station WABC in New York. KULF stood for the Gulf of Mexico. KODA was a music term, the coda. KCOH represented the City of Houston. KILE was named after Galveston Island. KMSC stood for NASA's Manned Spacecraft Center. KAJC answered to Alvin Junior College.

KILT was a reference to its owner, Gordon McLendon, known as the old Scotchman. McLendon's other two Texas stations were KLIF in Dallas (named for suburban Oak Cliff) and KTSA (meaning Texas San Antonio). KUHF means University of Houston FM. KUHT means University of Houston Television. KTSU signifies Texas Southern University. KTRU meant Texas Rice University.

The author of this book enjoyed a series of rich career experiences in radio. I started as a DJ at KTBC Radio in Austin, Texas. My mentor was Cactus Pryor, who also mentored Paul Berlin, a legend in Houston radio. My area of expertise was "golden oldies" shows, nostalgic reviews of what we used to call "golden discs, time tested for your pleasure."

When I moved to Houston in 1973, I had evolved as a business executive. Since I had done the oldies shows in Austin, I was asked to host such shows at various Houston stations, that being something that I did for fun on weekends for a few years. Along the way, I met and worked with many of the radio and TV broadcasting legends listed in this chapter. As a radio air personality, I hosted oldies shows at KULF, KLYX-KMJQ, KYST and KENR-KRBE.

I was also involved in an area that was not as glamorous as highly-rated music shows but was highly necessary to keep and renew broadcast licenses. This included producing public affairs programming, those weekend talk shows on community affairs which were required by the FCC and which influenced station profile and ultimately station resale prices. It was through this programming and public service announcements that I fell in love with non-profit organizations.

Through the experiences, I realized the important role that radio (regulated broadcasting) played in serving their causes. Family-owned radio stations always had the strongest commitments to communities and public affairs programming. They included the stations run by Lady Bird Johnson, Oveta Culp Hobby, Dickie Rosenfeld, Jay Jones, Joe Amaturo and Dave Morris.

Those of us who hosted such talk shows and interviewed community leaders were a fraternity, all committed to community stewardship. I thought back in the 1970's that these folks were legends and still do. They included Derrill Holly (KIKK, now working in Washington), Dan Parsons (KYND, now president of the Better Business Bureau), John Downey (KILT), Doug Johnson (KPRC), Art Kelly (KULF, now working in Washington), Lori Reingold (KEYH, later a producer at KTRK-TV), Scott Arthur (KQUE, now an executive with Star of Hope) and Ed Shane (KTRH, now one of the world's leading radio consultants).

The other thing that I got from those broadcasting experiences was an understanding of community stewardship, a subject which I have advised many major corporations (including 100 of the Fortune 500). Companies are now in business for altruistic reasons, but the art and skill with which they "give back" when they do signifies a richer organization. When I make recommendations on cause related marketing and corporate philanthropy, that harks back to the lessons that I learned when conducting Community Ascertainment for radio stations and public affairs programming. In the corporate world, we call that getting in better touch with our stakeholders.

Media, Television

Channel 2, KLEE-TV, signed on in 1949. It was named for the original owner, Albert Lee. The call letters changed to KPRC in 1950, when bought by The

Houston Post. KPRC scored a series of impressive firsts in the Houston TV market. It had the city's first TV weather radar, color broadcast (and first to convert entirely to color), videotape for field reporting, fully-staffed Austin news bureau and was the first Houston station to hire female and African-American air staff.

The station produced the longest running syndicated program in Texas, called "The Eyes of Texas." It was a magazine program focusing on the Texas lifestyle, running from 1969-1998. In its early years, KPRC was the dominant TV news operation in Houston. largely owing its success to its common ownership with The Houston Post newspaper. The owner is the Post-Newsweek Corporation.

Channel 11, KGUL-TV, signed on in 1953. It was licensed to Galveston, later moving to Houston as KHOU-TV. It is the CBS affiliate. The owner is Belo Communications, which also owns WFAA-TV in Dallas.

Channel 8, KUHF-TV, signed on in 1953. It was the nation's public TV station. It is the PBS affiliate.

Channel 13, KTRK-TV, signed on in 1956. It is the ABC affiliate. It is owned by ABC.

Channel 39, KHTV-TV, signed on in 1967. It is the CW affiliate.

Channel 26, KRIV-TV, signed on in 1973. It is the Fox affiliate. It is owned by Fox.

Channel 20, KTRH-TV, signed on in 1984. It is also owned by Fox.

Channel 45, KXLN-TV. It is the Univision affiliate. It is owned by Univision Communications.

Channel 47, KTMD-TV. It is the Telemundo affiliate. It is owned by NBC Universal.

Channel 49, KPXB-TV. It is the Ion affiliate. It is owned by Ion Media Networks.

Channel 57, KUBE-TV. It is owned by TTBG, LLC.

Media Legends

Wash Allen was a long-time radio personality and programming executive at KCOH Radio. He now owns and operates a radio station that broadcasts talk shows live via the internet can be heard through www.MJWJTalkRadio.com. He also manufactures a line of pecan pralines, sold through local grocery stores.

Dan Ammerman anchored on KTRK-TV for the station's original Eyewitness News broadcasts in the late 1960s and early 1970s. He also anchored the news on KULF Radio. During more than four decades in the communications business, he mastered the arts of on-screen fact and fiction and the ability to teach what he had learned to business clients in 43 countries.

After his broadcasting career, Ammerman founded a Houston-area communications firm. The Ammerman Experience which trained clients in the art of dealing with television interviews and managing crisis communications. He also appeared as an actor on many episodes of the CBS-TV dramatic series "Dallas." Ammerman played the doctor who dug the bullet out of the evil J.R. Ewing and appeared in other films and television shows.

Bill Bailey was a popular country music radio personality on KIKK and KENR Radio. He was also a popular announcer at the Houston Livestock Show and Rodeo. He was born Milton Odom Stanley but is fondly known to radio audiences as Buffalo Bill Bailey. In 1982, he was elected Constable for Harris County Precinct 8. He inherited a 17-member department that was focused on serving civil papers, dealing with landlord-tenant disputes and patrolling the streets of the eastern Harris County industrial communities of Pasadena, Deer Park, and La Porte. Bill built his department to 75 employees who are highly respected in the community and counts among his achievements initiating a program to guard the families and homes of astronauts while they are in space.

Kathleen Ballanfant is the publisher of the Village News and Southwest News, part of the Houston Community Newspapers group.

John Beddow is the publisher of the Houston Business Journal. In 2013, he was named a Houston Legend.

Paul Berlin was the dean of Houston radio, going back to when he joined KNUZ in 1948.

Paul Boesch was a professional wrestling promoter. He hosted broadcast wrestling matches, the earliest hit show on Houston's first TV station, Channel 2, and later on Channel 39. During the time of professional wrestling nationalizing in the 1980s, Boesch was a leader in the organization. The now-WWE hosted a sell-out retirement party in his honor in 1987.

Ed Brandon was a long-popular weathercaster on KTRK-TV. He started as a radio DJ in Arkansas, later at KNOW in Austin. He became a TV host and weatherman at the NBC affiliate in Austin before moving to Houston's Channel 13.

Ken Collins created the prototype for what has transpired in modern talk radio: the specialty program. He had careers in broadcasting and real estate. He created one of the first real estate magazines. He created and hosted a weekly real estate radio show, thus setting the pattern for brokered time broadcasts.

Walter Cronkite was long known as "the most trusted man in America." He was a 1933 graduate of San Jacinto High School and then studied journalism at the University of Texas at Austin.

Marge Crumbaker was the society columnist for The Houston Post.

Ike Eisenmann began his career as "Cadet Don" on Channel 13. As an actor, he appeared in Disney's "Witch Mountain" series.

Elroy Forbes was one of the most unforgettable characters that I ever met. He played the king in the annual Texas Renaissance Festival pageants. He created and published The Forbes Directory, which preceded the internet as the PDR of business networking and community activities.

Skipper Lee Frazier was DJ extraordinaire at KCOH Radio. He guided the "Mountain of Soul" sounds. He emceed and promoted concerts with James Brown, B.B. King, Wes Montgomery, The O'Jays and the Kool Jazz Festival. He managed two groups, Archie Bell and the Drells and the TSU Tornadoes. He wrote the lyrics to Archie's hit "Tighten Up." He owned two successful businesses, the Venus Motel and the James Stripling Funeral Home. He can be heard now each day at 2 p.m. on KWWJ Gospel 1360.

Joe Gaston was chief photographer at KTRK-TV in the 1950's and 1960's. He went into video production, founding the innovative company Electronic News Clipping Service with his wife Beverly. He shot and edited many corporate videos. His sons Martin and Darren continue to operate the video production business and have programmed television channels.

Dick Gottlieb was Houston's first full-time television announcer. On Channel 2, he hosted the popular programs "Matinee Theater," "Darts For Dough" and "The Dick Gottlieb Show." In 1969, Gottlieb was elected to at at-large seat on the Houston City Council.

Royce Guinn was a radio DJ at stations like KIKK and KNUZ. He operated Video One, a television production business.

Mickey Herskowitz has authored 30+ books, many jointly written with George Allen, Gene Autry, Bear Bryant, Prescott Bush, John Connally, Tom Kite and Nolan Ryan. He has ghostwritten biographies for such celebrities as Howard Cosell, Bette Davis, Marty Ingels, Shirley Jones, Mickey Mantle, Dan Rather and Gene Tierney. He wrote sports columns for the Houston Post and Chronicle and was inducted in 1997 into the Texas Baseball Hall of Fame.

Oveta Culp Hobby was the publisher of The Houston Post, whose company also owned KPRC Radio and KPRC-TV. Her husband was Texas Governor William P. Hobby. Her son is William P. Hobby Jr., who served as Lieutenant Governor of Texas.

Kay Bailey Hutchison was a reporter for KPRC-TV, Channel 2, the NBC affiliate, one of the first on-air newswomen in Texas. She took the job in 1967, upon graduation from the University of Texas Law School and was the legal and political correspondent.. She served in the Texas House of Representatives from 1973-1977. She served as State Treasurer of Texas from 1991-1993. Hutchison served in the U.S. Senate from 1993-2013.

Molly Ivins was born in Monterey, California, and raised in Houston. Her father was an oil and gas executive, and the family lived in River Oaks. In high school, she was active in the newspaper and yearbook. She interned at the Houston Chronicle, then went to Minneapolis Tribune.

In 1970, Ivins moved to Austin and became co-editor and political reporter for The Texas Observer. She gained increasing national attention through op-ed and feature stories in the New York Times and Washington Post. The Times hired her from the Observer in 1976. Best selling books and speaking appearances marked her later years.

Tom Jarriel was a retired American television news reporter who worked for the ABC network from 1964-2002. He graduated from the University of Houston and first worked as a news reporter at KPRC-TV, the NBC affiliate in Houston. He became a White House correspondent for ABC, during the administrations of U.S. Presidents Richard Nixon and Gerald Ford. In 1979, Jarriel joined the network's news-magazine "20/20" as an investigative correspondent. Jarriel anchored the 15-minute bulletins ABC aired late nights on weekends and served as substitute anchor on World News Tonight.

Richard J.V. Johnson was the long-time president of The Houston Chronicle.

Larry Kane was the TV host of a Saturday afternoon teen dance show on KTRK-TV from 1958-71 and on KPRC-TV from 1971-74. With the success of Dick Clark's "American Bandstand" on ABC-TV daily, the local affiliate wanted to perpetuate the popularity with a show featuring Houston teens dancing to the latest hit records. Harry Lieberman was studying in law school when he was asked to host the Larry Kane Show. After the show ended, he focused on a lucrative law career, while still holding a special fondness for the entertainment world and the kids who grew up with his show.

Tom Kennedy was the front-page columnist in the editorial section of The Houston Post. He has distinguished himself as a dealer of sports memorabilia, recognized nationally for expertise.

Melanie Lawson is a longtime news anchor at KTRK-TV. She is the daughter of Rev. Bill Lawson, Wheeler Avenue Baptist Church.

Earl Littman moved to Houston in 1955 and opened his advertising agency, known as Goodwin, Dannenbaum, Littman & Wingfield, Inc. Littman created the slogan, "The Badge Means You Care," which has been adopted by law enforcement forces throughout the U.S. and Canada. In 2002, Earl founded the P.O.P. Broadcasting Company, which changes the way global products and brands are marketed at retail.

Lyle Metzdorf started his own advertising agency in Houston in 1966. He is best known for work with Blue Bell Creameries. He is credited with helping Blue Bell grow from a 1% share of the Houston market to a 60% share of the national market and the third best-selling ice cream in the U.S.

Alex Lopez Negrete is the president of a nationally prominent advertising agency, Lopez Negrete Communications Inc. In 2013, he was named a Houston Legend.

Don Nelson is the tenured TV personality in Houston. He was a radio DFJ in Pittsburgh and moved to Houston in the early 1970's to host "Dialing for Dollars" on KTRK-TV. For many years, he co-hosted "Good Morning Houston" on the station, then joined the "Eyewitness News" morning show.

Virginia Mampre was program director for Houston Public Television and continues as a successful video producer-director.

Anita Martini grew up in Galveston. Her family ran the Martini Theatre. She became a sports reporter, the first woman to enter the profession. She hosted ca sports talk show at KPRC Radio and ran her own public relations firm at one time. I worked with her at KULF Radio and found her to be the best-informed sports broadcaster.

Hal McClain was a disc jockey with an easy-going personality and aw-shucks style. He was on KULF Radio and found his niche in country radio at KENR. Hal was an airplane pilot. Sadly, he was killed in 1981 while participating in a charity air show.

Maxine Mesinger was the society columnist for The Houston Chronicle.

Ray Miller was the News Director at KPRC-TV, Channel 2. Well known as a history expert, he created and hosted a hit show on Channel 2, "The Eyes of Texas." That resulted in him writing a series of "Eyes of Texas" books. After Ray retired from the station, news anchor Ron Stone took over hosting "Eyes of Texas" for many years.

Dave Morris was the general manager and majority owner of KNUZ-KQUE Radio.

Her name was Bunny, but she played a cat. Kitirik was a popular children's television character portrayed by Bunny Orsak. The show was broadcast on Houston ABC affiliate KTRK-TV from 1954-1971. The station had a contest to name the character. The winning name was Kitirik, where the letter "I" was placed between each station call letter.

Dan Rather graduated from Reagan High School and pursued journalism studies at Sam Houston State University. He began his broadcasting career at KTRH Radio and then moved to Channel 11. His coverage of Hurricane Carla in 1961 brought him to the attention of CBS News, which hired him and moved him top New York. He covered numerous beats for CBS, including chief White House correspondent. After subbing on the CBS Evening News for years, he was named the successor to Walter Cronkite. Rather took the CBS anchor chair in 1981 and remained a fixture on network news ever since.

Peter Roussel is a Houston based public relations counselor. He served as press secretary to Congressman George H.W. Bush and deputy press secretary for President Ronald Reagan.

Larry Sachnowitz was one of the most creative, innovative and insightful communicators. As president of Gulf State Advertising, he created dynamic campaigns for clients such as Sage, Star Furniture, Broadway National Bank and the University of Houston.

Bill Schadewald was the long-time editor of Houston Business Journal. A great fan of history, he set the stage for an appreciation of those who contributed to business in the region. His articles over the years helped inspire this book.

Mike Scott was a radio personality at KNUZ-KQUE Radio in Houston. At one time, he was the voice of Harrigan on KILT Radio's popular "Hudson and Harrigan Show." For many years, he operated an audio production company, Studio B, and later did voice-over work for radio commercials on a national basis.

Ed Shane had a successful career as a radio DJ in Chicago and then at Houston's KILT. He then became management at KTRH Radio. He subsequently became one of the nation's most respected broadcasting industry consultants.

Lisa Trapani Shumate is an Emmy Award-winning television veteran. She appeared for 11 years on KTRK-TV, co-hosting "Good Morning Houston" and reporting news. She was director of programming and marketing for KHOU-TV. She is currently the Executive Director and General Manager of Houston Public Media, leading the combined operations of KUHT-TV and two Public Radio stations. She is the recipient of national and regional awards for community service.

Steve Smith was the evening news anchor at KPRC-TV, then went to Pittsburgh, PA. He returned to Houston and for many years was the evening news anchor at KHOU-TV.

Ron Stone was the evening news anchor at KPRC-TV. When Ray Miller retired from the station, Ron picked up Ray's duties as host of the popular series "The Eyes of Texas." On April 12, 1989, Ron Stone and I were fellow recipients of the Savvy Award for top community leaders, bestowed at a gala at the Westin Galleria Hotel, hosted by Foley's. The emcee at that event was Melanie Lawson (listed above).

Thomas Thompson was a journalist and author. He graduated from the University of Texas in 1955 and worked as a reporter and editor at the Houston Press. He joined Life Magazine in 1961 and became an editor and staff writer. While at Life, he covered the JFK assassination and was the first writer to locate Lee Harvey Oswald's home and wife. Among his stories were coverage of the making of Sgt. Pepper's Lonely Hearts Club Band by the Beatles, in which he revealed the group's extensive drug use; an in-depth look at Frank Sinatra and his alleged Mafia ties; and the 40th and 50th birthdays of Elizabeth Taylor.

Thompson's books included Hearts (1971) about Houston surgeons Michael DeBakey and Denton Cooley. Richie: The Ultimate Tragedy Between One Decent Man and the Son He Loved (1973) was the story of a Long Island man who killed his drug-addicted son. Blood and Money (1976) was based on a true story of scandal and murder in Houston. Serpentine (1979), the story of convicted murderer Charles Sobhraj. Celebrity (1982) was on the national best-seller list for six months.

Jack Valenti ran an advertising agency in Houston, Weekly & Valenti. He was picked by President Lyndon B. Johnson to be a White House adviser. Later, for 36 years, he was president of the Motion Picture Association of America, creating the movie rating system.

Mary Jane Vandiver hosted "Happy Time," the earliest children's show on Channel 2. She was known as "Princess Mary Jane." It was first broadcast Saturdays and Sundays. When Captain Bob Russell, host of the Monday-Friday show, left, Mary Jane moved into0 his time period, and the title changed to "Happy Hollow." In later years, Vandiver hosted a daytime talk show on KHTV, Channel 39.

Dave Ward is the popular and long-time evening news anchor at KTRK-TV. His previous news position was at KNUZ Radio.

Dancie Perugini Ware is a public relations executive, long associated with George Mitchell and Galveston, her firm expanding nationally.

Bill Young was the kingpin behind "boss radio" in the 1960's. He was program director and on-air personality at KILT Radio, the top 40 giant. He guided programming, promotions and the whole package of youth oriented upbeat radio. As a distinctive voice, he left his stamp on the way that commercials were delivered, particularly those for concerts and special events. He founded Bill Young Productions, the ultimate voice-over talent production agency, producing commercials and other narratives for clients all over the world.

Paula Zahn was a news reporter at KPRC-TV early in a career that rose to anchoring network news at ABC-TV, CBS-TV, Fox News, CNN, PBS and the Discovery Channel..

Marvin Zindler was an aspiring boxer and musician, graduated from Lamar High School, attended an agricultural college and joined the U.S. Marines in 1941. Deciding against a career in his father's clothing shop, Mr. Zindler became a part-time radio disc jockey in 1943. In 1950, he joined a film production company that produced news for KPRC-TV. Two years later, he became a crime reporter and photographer, along the way undergoing his first plastic surgery, to remove a double chin and bob his nose. Then he went into law enforcement, joining the Harris County Sheriff's Department in 1962, hunting fugitives and establishing the Consumer Fraud Division.

In 1973, at the age of 51, Zindler began his career at KTRK-TV. As consumer news reporter, he exposed the Chicken Ranch, a La Grange brothel. Governor Dolph Briscoe then moved to close the Chicken Ranch, making Mr. Zindler a star. Eventually, Mr. Zindler earned $1 million a year as the KTRK celebrity news hound. The Chicken Ranch episode inspired a hit Broadway show and movie, "The Best Little Whorehouse in Texas."

Zindler was an early consumer advocate and action reporter, campaigning against scams, medical abuses and unsanitary food conditions. His regular Friday "rat and roach reports" had the KTRK coffee shop closed for violations at least three times. His signature phrase: "Slim in the ice machine." He reported on his own heart surgery, gallbladder removal, prostate cancer and quintuple bypass and, of course, his many facelifts.

I first met Marvin Zindler in 1974, in connection with charity events. In 1983, my client was Walden on Lake Houston. They wished to host a charity golf tournament. I recommended Marvin Zindler as the tourney namesake. We met with Marvin in 1983, and he asked, "What makes this event so special?" I noted that he had talked about special events where most funds raised went toward covering expenses, rather than to benefiting causes.

I said, "This one will be totally honest. 100% of the funds will go to the benefiting charities. The onus is on you to see that it happens." He smiled and then replied, "This one is too delicious to turn down." Thus began the annual Marvin Zindler Invitational Golf Tournament.

The growth of media spurred other creative services. These professional disciplines worked in tandem with the media but all became major industries. These include advertising, graphic design, marketing, branding, research, public relations, special events coordination, conferences, trade shows, media coaching, business-to-business, photography, audio production, voice-overs, video production, editing and Internet services.

Chapter 9

ARTS AND ENTERTAINMENT
LEGENDS

I ma Hogg was a philanthropist and patron of the arts and helped found the
Houston Symphony Orchestra, which played its first concert on June 21,
1913. Miss Ima served as the first vice president of the Houston Symphony
Society and became president in 1917. In 1946, she again became president of
the Houston Symphony Society, a post she held until 1956. Miss Ima is further
discussed in Chapter 13.

Initially, the orchestra was composed of 35 part-time musicians. The symphony
performed until 1918. It was reformed in 1930 and gave its first full season of
concerts the following year. In 1936, it officially became the Houston Symphony
Society. The orchestra performed in the City Auditorium and the Music Hall.

Jesse H. Jones envisioned a world class performing arts arena that would house
built to house the Houston Symphony Orchestra, Houston Grand Opera, ballet
and other cultural productions via Society for the Performing Arts. His nephew,

John T. Jones Jr., turned his uncle's dream into a reality. Jones Hall opened with a week-long cultural celebration in October 1966.

Music Directors of the Houston Symphony Orchestra have included Julien Paul Blitz (1913–1916), Paul Bergé (1916–1918), Uriel Nespoli (1931–1932), Frank St. Leger (1932–1935), Ernst Hoffmann (1936–1947), Efrem Kurtz (1948–1954), Ferenc Fricsay (1954), Leopold Stokowski (1955–1961), John Barbirolli (1961–1967), André Previn (1967–1969), Lawrence Foster (1971–1979), Sergiu Comissiona (1980–1988), Christoph Eschenbach (1988–1999), Hans Graf (2001–2013) and Andrés Orozco-Estrada (2014-).

The Houston Ballet has its origins in the Houston Ballet Academy, which was established in 1955 under the leadership of Tatiana Semenova, a former dancer with the Ballets Russes. In 1969, the foundation formed a professional ballet company under the direction of Nina Popova, also a former dancer with the Ballet Russes and the American Ballet Theatre. From 1976–2003, Ben Stevenson, a former dancer with Britain's Royal Ballet and English National Ballet, was artistic director of Houston Ballet, transforming the company from regional to international prominence.

The Houston Ballet produces 75 performances each year with a company of 51 dancers. The foundation also maintains the Ben Stevenson Academy, which trains more than half of the company's dancers. Houston Ballet holds one of the largest endowments for a dance company and is the fifth-largest professional ballet company in the U.S.

Houston Grand Opera was founded in 1955 through the joint efforts of Maestro Walter Herbert and cultural leaders Mrs. Louis G. Lobit, Edward Bing and Charles Cockrell. The inaugural season featured two operas, "Salome" and "Madame Butterfly." HGO has grown into a company of international stature that presents six to eight productions per season.

HGO serves 5 million people annually. One of the country's principal commissioners and producers of new works, HGO has introduced 43 world premieres and six American premieres since 1973. HGO has received a Tony Award, two Grammy Awards, and two Emmy Awards—the only opera company in the world to have won all three honors.

The Society for the Performing Arts was founded in 1966. It offers an eclectic mix of touring Broadway shows, dance, music and the finest artists from across the world. SPA has presented more than 1,000 performances of the world's finest music, dance, and theater events. SPA is the largest nonprofit presenting organization of its category in the Southwest.

Houston Friends of Chamber Music was founded in 1961. It presents concerts by ensembles of international renown, from legends like the Tokyo String Quartet, Emerson String Quartet and Canadian Brass to young stars such as the Ebène Quartet or Artemis Quartet. Its concerts are held at the Shepherd School of Music's Stude Concert Hall.

Da Camera of Houston was founded in 1987. It concerts by leading American and international musicians, with broad repertoire and musical styles, from chamber music to jazz. Da Camera showcases locally based musicians of national acclaim and enriching our community by enhancing the musical life of artists who choose to live here. Sarah Rothenberg serves as artistic director.

The Houston Arts Alliance is an organization that supports and promotes the arts. It distributes grants to 220 non-profit arts organizations and individual artists. It manages the city's civic art collection (450 pieces), as well as new acquisitions. HAA's Arts and Business Council of Greater Houston fosters partnerships between the arts sector and corporate community, focused on leadership and volunteerism.

The Fresh Arts Coalition includes 25 dance, theatre, literary, musical and visual arts organizations that have joined together to collectively raise awareness of the size and diversity of the arts in Houston.

Theatre

The Alley Theatre is one of the three oldest resident theatres in the U.S., a Tony Award-winning indoor theatre in downtown Houston. Nina Vance founded the Alley Theatre in 1948 in a former dance studio on Main Street. A brick corridor led from Main to the back of the studio, hence the name Alley Theatre. Patrons found a new location, an abandoned fan factory on Berry Avenue. The Alley re-opened on Feb. 8, 1949 with a production of Lillian Helman's "The Children's Hour."

In 1954, Ms. Vance brought in Albert Dekker to star in "Death of a Salesman." The Alley then became a professional Equity company. In 1958, the Alley Theatre was invited by the U.S. State Department to represent the American Regional Theatre at the Brussels World's Fair. In 1962, the Houston Endowment gifted land worth $800,000 and grants worth $2.5 million to the Alley from the Ford

Foundation for a new building at 615 Texas Avenue, which opened in 1968. The theatre grew from its modest beginnings into one of the most prestigious non-profit resident theatres in the world.

A wide variety of plays have appeared at the Alley. "Paul Zindel's The Effect of Gamma Rays on Man-in-the-Moon Marigolds" was staged in 1964 and in 1971 Zindel won the Pulitzer Prize for Drama. In 1977, Nina Vance was invited on the State Department tour of Russian theater, which led to an invitation from Nina to Galina Volchek, director of the Sovremennik Theater of Moscow, to come to Houston to produce Mikhail Roschin's play, Echelon. This marked the first time a Russian had been invited to the U.S. to recreate a play precisely as it appeared in the Soviet Union.

The theatre forged alliances with such international luminaries as Edward Albee, Vanessa Redgrave and Frank Wildhorn. Theatrical events at the Alley have included the world premieres of "Jekyll & Hyde," "The Civil War," and "Not About Nightingales" by Tennessee Williams, which moved to Broadway in 1999 and was nominated for six Tony Awards, including Best Play. In 1996, the Alley won the Regional Theatre Tony Award and has toured 40 American cities and abroad. In 2011, the Alley Theatre was awarded a Texas Medal of Arts Award by the Texas Cultural Trust, bestowed upon Texas leaders and luminaries in the arts and entertainment industry for creative excellence and exemplary talent.

In 1968, Frank Young founded Theatre Under the Stars to provide free public performances in the Miller Outdoor Theatre in Hermann Park each summer, thus deriving its name. Since then, 50 free large-scale musicals have been presented there. TUTS has grown into a year-round, professional, non-profit musical theatre production company.

Most of the productions are now staged at the Hobby Center for the Performing Arts. Theatre Under The Stars' season generally includes both self-produced shows as well as national touring productions. TUTS also offers educational programming through their training branch, the Humphreys School of Musical Theatre, education programs for children with special needs through The River and community outreach projects. Founded by Frank Young in 1968, TUTS is currently under the direction of President and CEO John C. Breckenridge.

The Ensemble Theatre was founded in 1976 by George Hawkins to preserve African-American artistic expression and entertain a diverse community. The theatre has evolved from a touring company operating from the trunk of Mr. Hawkins' car to being one of the finest historical cultural institutions. The Ensemble is one of the few professional theatres dedicated to the production of works portraying the African-American experience.

Stages Repertory Theatre was founded in 1978 in the basement of a downtown Houston brewery with a mission to "produce new work, interpret established work in new ways and nurture talent to invigorate culture for the good of the community." It produces more experimental plays in an intimate setting than any other venue. In 1985, Stages moved to its present location in the former Star Engraving building at 3201 Allen Parkway, which was designated a local historic landmark in 1986.

It is a professional Equity theatre and has garnered national recognition for its work, including coverage in The New York Times, Wall Street Journal, Variety, Vogue and American Theatre magazine. Through its Early Stages series, thousands of local children experience dramatic interpretations of classic folktales, stories from diverse world cultures, along with plays and musicals commissioned especially for young people. Its current Artistic Director is Kenn McLaughlin.

Main Street Theater was founded by Rebecca Greene Udden in 1975, offering theatergoers a varied selection of plays and musicals and to provide a venue for training, employment and exposure for our city's professional theater artists. Originally, it was housed at Autry House, the Episcopal Diocese's community center on Main Street, which is where the name began. Main Street Theater opened its 26th anniversary season with a new status as an Equity Professional Company.

The community also benefits from community theatres. Every major academic institution has a thriving theatre program.

Museums

The Museum of Fine Arts was founded in 1923. It is the oldest art museum in Texas. Its permanent collection totals 63,718 pieces in 270,000 square feet of exhibition space, placing it the sixth largest art museum in the United States. The museum's collections and programs are housed in seven facilities. The museum benefits the Houston community through programs, publications and media presentations. Each year, 1.25 million people attend the museum's programs, workshops and resource centers.

The Caroline Wiess Law Building was constructed in 1924, with the east and west wings added in 1926. The Robert Lee Blaffer Memorial Wing was designed by Kenneth Franzheim and opened in 1953. The Cullinan Hall and Brown Pavilion, designed by Ludwig Mies van der Rohe, were built in 1958 and 1974 respectively. The Audrey Jones Beck Building, designed by Rafael Moneo, opened in 2000. The Lillie and Hugh Roy Cullen Sculpture Garden, designed by artist and landscape architect Isamu Noguchi, opened in 1986.

The Glassell School of Art, founded in 1979 and designed by architect S. I. Morris, serves as the teaching wing of the MFAH, with a variety of classes, workshops and educational opportunities. The Central Administration and Glassell Junior School of Art Building, designed by Carlos Jimenez, opened in 1994.

The Bayou Bend Collection and Gardens, former home of Ima Hogg, was designed by architect John F. Staub in 1927. Miss Hogg donated the property to the MFAH in 1957, followed, in 1962, by the donation of its collection of paintings, furniture, ceramics, glass, metals and textiles. Bayou Bend opened to the public in 1966. Rienzi is the MFAH house museum for European decorative arts, donated to the MFAH by Carroll Sterling Masterson and Harris Masterson III. The residence was designed in 1952 by John F. Staub, the same architect who designed Bayou Bend. After Mr. Masterson's death, the MFAH transformed the home into a museum and opened it to the public in 1999. Peter Marzio was director of MFAH from 1982-2010.

The Contemporary Arts Museum Houston was founded in 1948 to present new art and to document its role in modern life through exhibitions, lectures and other activities. The first exhibitions were presented at various sites throughout the city. A permanent building was opened in 1950, with the present structure opened in 1972. Exhibitions are accompanied by publications and educational programs. The Museum reaches out to local, regional, national and international audiences of all ages.

The Art League Houston was founded in 1948 and incorporated as a non-profit organization in 1953. ALH cultivates awareness, appreciation, and accessibility of contemporary visual art within the community through exhibitions, the Art League School, the Texas Artist of the Year program, and outreach programming.

The Sarah Campbell Blaffer Gallery was founded in 1973, named in honor of a woman who made available to the University a collection of major artworks dating from the 15th Century to modern day. Blaffer Gallery has presented 250 exhibitions and has won several awards, including the Coming Up Taller Award as part of the President's Committee on the Arts and Humanities. The gallery exhibits national and international works as well as artwork by students. In 2010, Blaffer Gallery was renamed to Blaffer Art Museum. It serves as a resource for the study of art, art history and other related disciplines. By extending the educational and scholarly programs of the University to the community, the museum promotes learning as a continuous process.

The Menil Collection was opened in 1987 by John de Menil and Dominique de Menil. It includes their privately assembled collection of 20th Century art, including 15,000 paintings, sculptures, prints, drawings, photographs and rare books. The museum maintains an extensive collection of pop art and contemporary art from Jackson Pollock, Andy Warhol, Mark Rothko, Robert Rauschenberg, Vija Celmins and Cy Twombly, among others. Also included in the museum's permanent collection are Antiquities and works of Byzantine, Medieval and Tribal art. Two other buildings founded by the de Menils but now operating as independent foundations complete the campus: the Byzantine Fresco Chapel and the Rothko Chapel. The museum also has a library and bookstore.

The Houston Museum of Natural Science began in Houston in 1909 with the founding of the Houston Museum and Scientific Society. In 1946, a private nonprofit corporation known as the Museum of Natural History of Houston was formed to assume maintenance and operation of the collection. In 1959, a 99-year lease was negotiated with the city for a 4½-acre site on the northern edge of Hermann Park. The trustees received a gift from Burke Baker, which became the basis for building the Burke Baker Planetarium. In 1960, the museum was officially renamed Houston Museum of Natural Science.

In 1988, the museum became the nation's first affiliate site for a Challenger Center. The Wortham IMAX Theatre opened in 1989, as did the George Observatory in Brazos Bend State Park. Museum representatives serve local schools by teaching science classes and provide information to the public.

The Holocaust Museum was opened in 1996 and is located in the Houston Museum District. It is the fourth largest Holocaust memorial museum in the nation. The museum's mission is to make people aware of the dangers which prejudice, hatred and violence brought about during the Holocaust. The museum promotes understanding, remembrance and education with the goal that both students and the general population stay and become aware of the lesson of these tragic events. This lesson is that humankind must strive to live together in peace and harmony.

The Holocaust Museum contains permanent as well as temporary exhibitions. "Bearing Witness: A Community Remembers" is the testimony of Houston-area survivors. Another section is about resistance efforts, such as the Warsaw Ghetto uprising, prisoner revolts, sabotage, the partisan movement and Lyndon B. Johnson's "Operation Texas" refugee effort. At the end of this exhibition are shown two films with first-hand accounts of survivors, liberators and witnesses who moved to the Houston area after the World War II.

Theatrical and Film Stars From Houston

Debbie Allen was born in Houston, educated at Yates High School and Howard University. She debuted on Broadway in Debbie Allen had her Broadway debut in "Purlie." One of her earlier television appearances was on "Good Times." She has received two Tony Award nominations. She starred in the movie "Fame," followed by the TV series based on the hit musical, winning two Emmy Awards and one Golden Globe Award. She also taught choreography to former Los Angeles Lakers dancer-turned-singer, Paula Abdul. Her sister is actress Phylicia Rashad. In 2001, Allen was appointed by President George W. Bush to the President's Committee on the Arts and Humanities.

Wes Anderson is a film director and screenwriter. He was nominated for Academy Awards for Best Original Screenplay for The Royal Tannenbaums in 2001 and Moonrise Kingdom in 2012, and for the Academy Award for Best Animated Feature for Fantastic Mr. Fox in 2009.

Donald Barthelme was an author known for his playful, postmodernist style of short fiction. He was as a newspaper reporter for The Houston Post, managing editor of Location magazine, director of the Contemporary Arts Museum in Houston (1961–1962), co-founder of Fiction and a professor at various universities. He also was one of the original founders of the University of Houston Creative Writing Program.

Matt Bomer graduated from Klein High School in Spring and achieved national acclaim as an actor on CBS-TV's "As the World Turns." He stars on the USA Network's "White Collar."

Berkeley Breathed is a cartoonist, children's book author/illustrator, director and screenwriter. He is best known for Bloom County, a 1980's cartoon-comic strip that dealt with sociopolitical issues as understood by fanciful characters and through humorous analogies. Bloom County earned Breathed the Pulitzer Prize for editorial cartooning in 1987.

Burnie Burns is best known for his contributions in Machinima, a form of film-making that uses video game technology in its production. He created the Internet machinima series Red vs. Blue: The Blood Gulch Chronicles. Filmed using the video games Halo, Halo 2, Halo 3, Halo: Reach, and Halo 4, Red vs. Blue was acclaimed for its humor and originality. Burns also premiered P.A.N.I.C.S., a mini-series that utilizes the F.E.A.R. game engine. He has been nominated for an IAWTV award in the Best Hosted Taped Web Series category.

Jonathan Caouette is the director and editor of Tarnation (2003), an autobiographical documentary that premiered at the Sundance and Cannes film festivals and the director of All Tomorrow's Parties about the cult music festival. He directed the experimental short film All Flowers in Time and the feature documentary Walk Away Renee. The latter was produced by Agnes B and premiered at the 2011 Cannes Film Festival.

Lois Chiles was educated at the University of Texas and hit New York as a fashion model. She debuted as an actress in "The Way We Were" and appeared in other films, notably the James Bond "Moonraker" entry. In 2002, she taught a class in film acting at the University of Houston.

Lynn Collins was born in Houston and spent her formative years in Singapore and Japan. She attended the Juilliard School's Drama Division. Collins made her television debut in 1999, in an episode of Law & Order: Special Victims Unit, and went on to star onstage as Ophelia opposite Liev Schreiber in Hamlet and as Juliet in Romeo and Juliet. She gained notice playing Portia in the film The Merchant of Venice, starring opposite Al Pacino, Joseph Fiennes and Jeremy Irons.

Haylie Duff is an actress, singer, songwriter, producer and food blogger. Early dance lessons led her to a role in the Houston Metropolitan Theatre Company's production of "The Nutcracker." TV appearances have included "7th Heaven," "Love Takes Wing" and "Love Finds a Home."

Hilary Duff was a teen idol, starring in the Disney Channel's "Lizzie McGuire." Film roles have included "Cheaper By the Dozen" and "A Cinderella

Story." She recorded record albums and was active in the retail industry with clothing and fragrances.

Shelley Duvall is a graduate of Waltrip High School and began her career by appearing in a series of films for director Robert Altman. As a producer, she created the successful "Faerie Tale Theatre" series and other kid-friendly programs.

Farrah Fawcett graduated from Ray High School in Corpus Christi and attended the University of Texas at Austin, leaving in pursuit of a Hollywood career. Her co-starring role in the 1975 ABC-TV series "Charlie's Angels" advanced her to superstar status, complimented with the poster and magazine cover displays.

Sean Patrick Flanery is an actor, known for playing Connor MacManus in The Boondock Saints, Greg Stillson in The Dead Zone, Jeremy "Powder" Reed in Powder, Indiana Jones in The Young Indiana Jones Chronicles, as well as Bobby Dagen in Saw 3D. He is also known for his role as Sam Gibson on The Young and the Restless in 2011. He starred in Devil's Carnival, a short film which was screened on tour beginning in April, 2012. He graduated from Dulles High School in Sugar Land and attended the University of St. Thomas.

Bill Hicks was a stand-up comedian, social critic, satirist and musician. His material, encompassing a wide range of social issues as well as religion, politics, and philosophy, was controversial and often steeped in dark comedy. He criticized consumerism, superficiality, mediocrity and banality within the media and popular culture.

Larry Hovis was a singer and actor best known for the sitcom Hogan's Heroes. After studies at the University of Houston, Hovis sang in nightclubs. He recorded for Capitol Records. He appeared in theatre productions, then on television. He was discovered by Andy Griffith's manager and was hired to appear on the hit TV series Gomer Pyle. In 1965, Hovis was cast as Sgt. Andrew Carter in the CBS-TV show Hogan's Heroes. He also appeared in and wrote comedy bits for NBC-TV's Rowan & Martin's Laugh-In. He toured in the musical "Best Little Whorehouse in Texas" and was a writer/producer on the So You Think You Got Troubles game show. In the 1990s, Hovis taught drama at Southwest Texas State University, recently renamed Texas State University-San Marcos.

Richard Linklater is a film writer and director. He was born in Houston and educated at Sam Houston State University. His movies often take place in Texas and focus activities during a limited time frame, with great detail to characters and circumstances. His films have included "Bad News Bears," "Dazed and Confused," "Before Sunset" and "Before Midnight."

Renee O'Connor from Katy is an actress, producer and director best known for playing the role of Gabrielle on the TV series Xena: Warrior Princess. Her television career began at age 16 with commercials and minor television appearances. After the Xena series ended, O'Connor started her own film production company. She continues to attend Xena conventions.

Annette O'Toole began her career as a child performer in the 1950's on Channel 2's "Don Mahoney and Jeana Clare Show." After her family moved to Los Angeles, she appeared on "The Danny Kaye Show." After that, TV guest appearances, film roles and stage appearances in a distinguished acting career that continues to this day.

Tony Oller from Cypress is an actor and singer-songwriter, best known for his roles as Walt Moore on Gigantic, and as Daniel "Danny" Neilson on As the Bell Rings. He appeared in the films Beneath the Darkness and The Purge.

Page Parkes runs a statewide modeling, training and acting agency. Her clients include performers, corporate executives and children of all ages. She hosts boot camps on executive etiquette, leadership and mentorship for young people. Alumni of her programs over 30 years have taken leadership roles in business and community.

Jim Parsons from Spring stars as Sheldon Cooper on the CBS-TV sitcom "The Big Bang Theory." His performance is often cited as reason for the program's success. Parsons received the Television Critics Association award for the highest individual achievements in comedy, National Association of Broadcasters Television Chairman's Award for breakthrough in an art discipline, three Emmy Awards for Outstanding Lead Actor in a Comedy Series and the Golden Globe Award for Best Actor in a Television Series Musical or Comedy.

Dennis Quaid is an actor known for dramatic and comedic roles. His films included "The Right Stuff," "The Big Easy," "D.O.A.," "Day After Tomorrow," "Traffic" and "Footloose." He graduated from Bellaire High School and the University of Houston, studying dramas under Cecil Pickett. In 2012, UH bestowed a Distinguished Alumnus Award to Dennis.

Randy Quaid is an actor who burst onto the national scene in "The Last Picture Show." He was nominated for an Oscar for his role in "The Last Detail" with

Jack Nicholson. Other films include "LBJ," "Brokeback Mountain," "National Lampoon's Christmas Vacation" and "Independence Day." He is the third cousin of cowboy movie legend Gene Autry.

Phylicia Rashad is a Tony Award winning stage actress, singer and director. She graduated from Yates High School and Howard University. She appeared on the ABC-TV soap opera "One Life to Live" and in such Broadway productions as "Cat on a Hot Tin Roof" and "Raisin in the Sun." She is best known for her co-starring role on NBC-TV's "Cosby Show." She has starred in theatrical productions throughout the U.S. Her sister is Debbie Allen.

Molly Louise Shepard is a published dramatic author, off-Broadway playwright, and produced screen writer. Shepard's two-act Southern Gothic piece, "Tabula Rasa," was produced by the Judith Shakespeare Company at the Phil Bosakowski Theatre in New York City.

Anna Nicole Smith was a model, actress and television personality. She was Playboy Magazine's 1993 Playmate of the Year. She modeled for clothing companies, including Guess Jeans and Lane Bryant. Her marriage to oil tycoon J. Howard Marshall resulted in well-publicized lawsuits.

Jaclyn Smith is a 1966 graduate of Lamar High School. She sought an acting career and burst onto public fame as one of "Charlie's Angels." Since, she has continued a respected career by starring in TV movies and mini-series.

Brent Spiner is an actor, best known for his portrayal of the android Lieutenant Commander Data in the television series "Star Trek: The Next Generation" and four subsequent films. His portrayal of Data in Star Trek: First Contact and of Dr. Brackish Okun in "Independence Day," earned him a Saturn Award and nomination. He is a graduate of Bellaire High School and the University of Houston, having careers in the theatre and music.

Matt Stone is a voice actor, animator, screenwriter, TV director, producer, comedian, singer and musician. He is best known for being the co-creator of South Park along with Trey Parker, as well as co-writing the 2011 multi-Tony Award winning musical "The Book of Mormon."

Patrick Swayze was an actor, dancer, singer and songwriter. He is best known for starring in "Dirty Dancing." His mother was dance director Patsy Swayze. He studied at the Harkness and Joffrey Ballet Schools. Other film roles included "Ghost," "North and South" and "Road House."

Patsy Swayze is a film choreographer, dancer and dance director. She founded the Houston Jazz Ballet Company and owned a dance studio. For 18 years, she taught dance at the University of Houston, and her students included Debbie Allen, Randy Quaid, Jaclyn Smith and Tommy Tune. She choreographed movies such as "Urban Cowboy," which was filmed in Houston and Pasadena.

Tommy Tune was a 1957 graduate of Lamar High School. He studied dance under Patsy Swayze and made his Broadway debut in 1965's "Baker Street."

JoBeth Williams was a 1967 graduate of Jones High School and attended Brown University, hoping to become a child psychologist. She turned to acting in theatre, appeared on CBS-TV's "Guiding Light" and made her film debut in "Kramer Vs. Kramer." She has continued stage and film careers.

Chandra Wilson is an actress and director, best known as Dr. Miranda Bailey in the ABC television drama "Grey's Anatomy." She debuted at Houston's Theatre Under the Stars and attended the High School for the Performing and Visual

Miss Ima Hogg, philanthropic supporter of the arts, historical preservation and health services agencies.

Arts. She studied at the Lee Strasburg Theatre & Film Institute and made her New York stage debut in 1991. She also began to land guest spots on a variety of prime-time television shows. She made her big-screen debut in the 1993 film "Philadelphia" (starring Tom Hanks).

Renée Zellweger attended Katy High School, where she was a cheerleader, gymnast and member of the speech team. She is an accomplished film actress and won an Academy Award for Best Supporting Actress in 2003 for "Cold Mountain."

The author of this book, Hank Moore (right) is posed in 1968 with Andre Previn, then serving as conductor of the Houston Symphony Orchestra.

Chapter 10
MUSIC LEGENDS

Houston Legends have contributed mightily to the music scene of Texas, the nation and the world.

Huey P. Meaux was known as the Crazy Cajun. He was an American record producer and the owner of Sugar Hill Recording Studios. He independently recorded sessions and sold them to major record labels in the late 1950's. Three of those records were all cut at the same 1958 session: "Chantilly Lace" by The Big Bopper, "Running Bear" by Johnny Preston and "White Lightning" by George Jones. On each hit record, the other two sang background vocals.

Other Huey Meaux hits to go gold nationally included "You'll Lose A Good Thing" by Barbara Lynn, "Talk To Me" by Sunny and the Sunliners, "Big Blue Diamonds" by Gene Summers, "She's About a Mover" by the Sir Douglas Quintet and "Before the Next Teardrop Falls" and "Wasted Days and Wasted Nights" by Freddy Fender. Meaux also produced the early material of vocalists Roy Head and

B.J. Thomas. Meaiux also owned and operated three labels, including Crazy Cajun Records, Tear Drop Records and Capri Records.

The band Bubble Puppy recorded in Houston at Gold Star Studios for International Artists in 1968 and scored a national hit, "Hot Smoke & Sasafrass." International Artists signed another band, the 13th Floor Elevators, which commanded a devoted local following when they added vocalist Roky Erickson to the group. His song "You're Gonna Miss Me" became a hit. Musicologists have heralded Roky Erickson and the 13th Floor Elevators as pioneers of acid rock, but their overt drug use, also a trademark of the psychedelic culture, took its toll on the band.

Janis Joplin was raised in Port Arthur. In 1960, she was a freshman at the University of Texas in Austin. I was working as a DJ at radio station KTBC in Austin. Some of us went to the Old New Orleans Club to hear a folk singer in the Joan Baez style. She was Janis Joplin. During the set, she announced that she would next be singing the blues across town at Threadgill's. We heard her in that versatile showcase.

Joplin dropped out of UT and moved to San Francisco, joining the band Big Brother and the Holding Company. She sang an electrifying rendition of "Ball and Chain," which had also been recorded by one of Joplin's musical mentors, Houston recording artist Big Mama Thornton. Their performance at the Monterey Pop Festival in 1967 earned her and the band national acclaim. Rock critics praised Joplin as a great white blues singer.

Joplin returned to UT-Austin in November 1969 for a reunion concert in Gregory Gym. She died less than a year later from an accidental heroine overdose. Her posthumous single, "Me and Bobby McGee," written by fellow Texan Kris Kristofferson, reached Number 1 on the charts. Threadgill's still has a tribute wall to Joplin.

In the early 1970s, rock and blues merged in the sounds of brothers Johnny and Edgar Winter. They grew up in the Beaumont area and worked the Houston club scene before national acclaim.

ZZ Top was the state's most successful rock act of the 1970s. They started as Moving Sidewalks in Houston. As ZZ Top, they built a strong following with their Southern-influenced, guitar-driven rock. Their third album, "Tres Hombres," went platinum on the strength of the hit single "La Grange." Throughout the following decades, their popularity has continued. ZZ Top was inducted into the Rock and Roll Hall of Fame in 2004.

Beyoncé Giselle Knowles is one of the world's current superstars. She was born in 1981 in Houston and performed in singing and dancing competitions as a child. She rose to fame in the 1990s as lead singer of R&B girl-group Destiny's Child. Managed by her father, Mathew Knowles, the group became one of the world's best-selling girl groups of all time.

Beyoncé released her debut solo album in 2003, selling 11 million copies, earning five Grammy Awards and featuring two number-one singles, "Crazy in Love" and "Baby Boy." After disbanding Destiny's Child in 2005, she released her second solo album, including the hits "Irreplaceable" and "Beautiful Liar." She ventured into acting, with a Golden Globe-nominated performance in "Dreamgirls" (2006), and starring roles in "The Pink Panther" (2006) and "Obsessed" (2009). Her portrayal of Etta James in "Cadillac Records" (2008) influenced her third album. Other records are critically acclaimed, and she remains an all-time crowd pleaser in concert.

Duke-Peacock Records

Duke and Peacock were Houston based record labels that were influential in rhythm and blues, gospel, and soul music. Houston businessman and nightclub owner Don Robey had become the personal manager of Clarence Gatemouth Brown in 1947 and felt that Brown's label was not supporting him. Thus, in 1949, Robey founded Peacock Records, named after the Bronze Peacock, his nightclub in Houston's Fifth Ward.

Duke-Peacock became the second significant black owned record company to influence the music landscape. The first was Atlantic Records, founded in 1947. The third was Motown Records, founded by Berry Gordy in 1959.

In the 1950's, the Peacock roster, in addition to Brown, included Memphis Slim, Marie Adams, Floyd Dixon, and Willie Mae "Big Mama" Thornton, whose 1953 recording of "Hound Dog" was covered in 1956 by Elvis Presley. In 1953, Robey acquired full control of the Duke label, founded by David J. Mattis and Bill Fitzgerald in Memphis in 1952, and with it the recording contracts of, among others, Bobby Bland, Junior Parker and Johnny Ace. Also in 1953 Robey moved his expanding record label operations from Lyons Avenue in northeastern

Houston to 2809 Erastus Street, the site of his now-closed Bronze Peacock. Robey used Houston's ACA Studios to cut many of his finished recordings, and he often sent out recordings for mastering to Bill Quinn's Gold Star Studios in the city.

Johnny Ace accidentally shot and killed himself backstage during a show at Houston's City Auditorium on Christmas Day 1954. He had eight Top 40 hits in his brief career, including "Pledging My Love," "The Clock" and "Cross My Heart," all of which reached the Number 1 spot on the R&B charts.

Bobby Bland had 46 songs on the R&B charts from 1957-1972, including "Farther On Up the Road" (1957), "I Pity the Fool" (1961), and "That's the Way Love Is" (1963). His recordings are considered exemplars of the Duke-Peacock Sound, a combination of gospel vocals and brass-heavy arrangements from Joe Scott and Bill Harvey. Musicians who played on those recordings included guitarists Clarence Hollimon and Wayne Bennett, pianist Teddy Reynolds, bassist Hamp Simmons and drummer Sonny Freeman.

Duke and Peacock benefited from the managerial talents of Evelyn Johnson, who filled roles at his nightclub, record labels, Buffalo Booking Agency and Lion Publishing Company, one of whose clients was blues star B. B. King.

Peacock released gospel records by the Bells of Joy, Dixie Hummingbirds, Sensational Nightingales, Mighty Clouds of Joy and Inez Andrews. Robey's also owned the Back Beat and Song Bird labels. Back Beat's artists included the Original Casuals, whose "So Tough" reached Number 6 on the R&B charts in 1958; Joe Hinton, whose version of Willie Nelson's "Funny How Time Slips Away" hit Number 1 in 1964; Roy Head and the Traits, whose "Treat Her Right" reached Number 2 on both the pop and R&B charts in 1965; and O. V. Wright, whose "8 Men 4 Women" reached Number 4 on the R&B charts in 1967. Song Bird had a hit with "Lord Don't Move That Mountain" by Inez Andrews in 1972.

By then, however, the Duke-Peacock empire had yielded primacy in the R&B/soul field to the Motown and Stax labels, which had superior promotion and distribution networks. In 1973, Robey agreed to sell his Duke-Peacock holdings, which included some 2,700 song copyrights, contracts with approximately 100 artists, and 2,000 unreleased master recordings, to New York-based ABC-Dunhill Records. The last major hiot was "Everlasting Love" by Carl Carlton in 1974. Robey reportedly was to receive $25,000 a year for four years and reimbursement of the cost of leasing a new Cadillac for his personal use. He died just over two years later. Shortly thereafter, ABC closed the old Duke-Peacock offices on Erastus Street.

On April 16, 2011, the Harris County Historical Commission dedicated a Texas Historical Marker to Peacock Records at its original offices, now the Louis Robey Professional Building on Lyons Avenue.

Nightclubs

Although clubs like Taylor Hall, Teen Hall, Love Street Light Circus and the Catacombs became legendary, they had short life-spans.

Dome Shadows opened in 1963. The address was 9218 Buffalo Speedway. It was owned by Marshall Stewart. One of the headliners was Johnny Williams, whose biggest hit record was "Long Black Veil" in 1965. Band members included Bobby Beason-trumpet, Dennis Dyer-drums, Larry Webb-guitar, Leo O'Neil–trombone, Bill Hershey-saxophone, Tommy Cashwell-vocals-organ, Ron Hobbs-bass and Dean Stipp-trumpet-valve trombone-vocals. The Houston Oilers held private parties at the Dome Shadows on Monday nights when the club was closed. There is a great website recalling the club: http://domeshadows.com/Dome_Shadows.php

Van's Ballroom was a country and western club in Montrose, owned in the 1960's and 1970's by Van Bevill. Band members included Edgar Winter-saxophone, Bert Fanette-organ, Walter Boenig-trombone, Glen Spreen-saxophone, Buddy Wright-bass and vocals, Raul Cuesta-saxophone, Luis Cardenas-trumpet, Randall Dolahan-guitar, Kit Reid-trumpet and Willie Ornelas-drums.

Cooter's was a fashionable club at the intersection of Richmond and Sage. In the 1970's and 1980's, it boasted goodtime bands like Johnny Dee and the Rocket 88's. Studebaker's was an early 1950's nostalgia-themed bar and grill. It's parent company, Entertainment One, evolved into a food managing agent group at Houston Intercontinental Airport.

Other memorable nightspots from days past include the Lizard Lounge, Gallant Knight, Ale House, Theodore's 19th Century Fox, La Carafe, Prufrock's, the Cellar Door, Numbers, Turtle Club, Orchid Lounge, the Red Door, Crush Bar and Market Square venues.

Liberty Hall

On March 4, 1971, Liberty Hall opened at 1610 Chenevert Street, downtown near where the Toyota Center is today. While Liberty Hall would last only seven years, it became a legendary venue. The owners were Mike Condray, Ryan Trimble and Lynda Herrera. Built in the 1940s, it was originally a church, but later became an American Legion hall.

Liberty Hall opened with a rock opera, then featured blues shows with Freddie King, Big Mama Thornton, Lightnin' Hopkins and John Lee Hooker. One of the memorable events was having ZZ Top open for Willie Dixon and the Chess Records session band.

Then came the national touring acts. Bruce Springsteen played his first Texas shows at Liberty Hall in 1974. Springsteen later commemorated the venue in "This Hard Land," which appears on his 1995 Greatest Hits CD and 1998 box set. Sample lyrics: "Hey frank, won't you pack your bags. And meet me tonight down at Liberty Hall. Just one kiss from you my brother. And well ride until we fall. We'll sleep in the fields. We'll sleep by the rivers and in the morning. We'll make a plan. And meet me in a dream of this hard land."

Others who played the hall and then soared to international fame included Billy Joel, Jimmy Buffet, Jerry Jeff Walker, Townes Van Zandt and Cheech & Chong, when tickets were $2 each.

Liberty Hall covered every musical genre, hosting acts like the Velvet Underground, Waylon Jennings, Ted Nugent, Tim Buckley, Roy Buchanan, Rory Gallagher and Bonnie Raitt. Jimmy Reed once joined Johnny Winter and his band for a show. Zydeco king Clifton Chenier played holiday dances and parties. In 1973, Neil Young and Linda Ronstadt sat in with Gram Parsons and Emmylou Harris. The hall closed in 1978 with a concert by Chicago bluesman Muddy Waters.

There is a website recalling posters for concerts at Liberty Hall: http://people.missouristate.edu/dennishickey/libertyhall.htm

Music Legends from Houston

Nancy Ames is a folk and pop singer who burst into fame on the 1960's NBC-TV series, "That Was the Week That Was." She recorded albums of eclectic songs and even wrote the theme song to CBS-TV's "Smothers Brothers Comedy Hour." She moved to Houston and hosted a noontime variety show on KPRC-TV. From there, she evolved into producing shows, convention extravaganzas, gala balls and other events.

Baby Bash was born Ronnie Ray Bryant. He is a Mexican-American rapper. He has collaborated with numerous other artists during his career, such as West Coast rappers B-Legit, C-Bo, Coolio- Da'unda'dogg, E-40 and Mac Dre, R&B singers like Akon, Avant, Natalie, Mario, and Nate Dogg, plus other Latino rappers such as Fat Joe, Nino Brown, Doll-E Girl, Frost and Pitbull.

Allen Becker founded PACE Concerts. He was an insurance salesman when he partnered with Sidney Shlenker to produce a boat show for the newly opened Astrodome. The company debuted in 1966, producing trade and thrill shows for the Astrodome. Pace Entertainment is credited with firsts in the sports and entertainment industry, including being the first to produce exhibitions for domed stadiums, first to build a chain of amphitheaters, first to take motor-sports to stadiums and first to take theater to smaller communities, developing an industry that thrives around its core concert promotion firm.

Archie Bell and the Drells emerged in the East End." Their signature hit "Tighten Up" in 1968 immortalized Houston in the lyrics. In a follow-up hit, "Showdown," he encouraged party-goers to participate in dance contests down on Market Street.

Clint Black is a popular country music singer, songwriter and record producer. He has had 30+ singles on the Billboard charts, of which 15 have gone to #1. He is married to actress Lisa Hartman, a graduate of Lamar High School.

Danielle Bradbery from Cypress was the season 4 winner on NBC-TV's "The Voice."

Buddy Brock was a prominent band leader at dances, weddings, proms and elegant galas. Clarence L. "Buddy" Brock Jr. was born in Houston, where his father, Clarence Sr., was Houston's superintendent of parks and instrumental in the effort to plant oak trees along South Main near Hermann Park and Rice University. After graduating from the University of Houston, Buddy taught physics and then gravitated toward music.

William Butler was born in California and raised in The Woodlands. He is an American multi-instrumentalist and composer who is best known as a member of the band Arcade Fire. William plays synthesizer, bass, guitar and percussion. He is the brother of Arcade Fire leader Win Butler.

Chamillionaire (born Hakeem Seriki) is a hip-hop rapper. He began his career independently with local releases, including the collaboration album Get Ya Mind Correct with fellow Houston rapper and childhood friend Paul Wall. He signed to Universal Records in 2005 and released The Sound of Revenge, including the hit singles "Turn It Up" featuring Lil' Flip and the number-one, Grammy-winning hit "Ridin'" featuring Krayzie Bone of Bone Thugs-n-Harmony. Ultimate Victory followed in 2007, which was notable for not containing any profanity.

Rodney Crowell is a Grammy Award-winning American musician, known primarily for his work as a singer and songwriter in country music. Crowell had five number one singles on Hot Country Songs, all from his 1988 album Diamonds & Dirt. He has also written songs and produced for other artists. Crowell was born in Crosby and played in various garage rock bands in Houston. He was influenced by songwriters Guy Clark and Townes Van Zandt. Crowell played guitar and sang for three years in Emmylou Harris' "Hot Band."

Terry Ellis is a singer and member of the R&B girl group En Vogue. She is a graduate of Prairie View A&M University.

Kelly Emberg was a model best known for her appearances in the Sports Illustrated Swimsuit Issue and in advertisements for companies like Cover Girl. She was born in Houston and attended Stratford High School, where she was a member of the school's female drill team, the Spartanaires. She modeled part-time during high school, discovered by Alan Martin, a local photographer in Houston who introduced her to Elite Model Management, where her print career took off. She appeared on the covers of Vogue, Harper's Bazaar, Glamour and Cosmopolitan magazines. She also appeared in the Sports Illustrated Swimsuit Issue and in advertisements for Cover Girl cosmetics, Napier Jewelry and Calvin Klein.

Roky Erickson was a rock pioneer with the Thirteenth Floor Elevators. The 1960's psychedelic band served to inspire punk music and its mellower cousin new wave.

Blue October is an American alternative rock band originally from Houston. The band was formed in 1995 and currently consists of Justin Furstenfeld (lead vocals, guitar), Jeremy Furstenfeld (drums, percussion), Ryan Delahoussaye (violin/viola, mandolin, piano, backing vocals), C.B. Hudson (lead guitar, backing vocals) and Matt Noveskey (bass guitar, backing vocals).

Ed Gerlach was a prominent band leader at dances, weddings, proms and elegant galas. As a child, he played saxophone, studying music at Texas A&M and Sam Houston State University. During World War II, he conducted a dance band. During his years at Ellington Field, his band performed weekly at The Rice Hotel. On furlough, he befriended Milton Larkin and Arnett Cobb while frequenting music venues in Houston's Fourth Ward. Mr. Gerlach developed a deep admiration for these fellow-musicians, and was asked to join them in playing on occasion. He was hired to play with the Hal McIntyre Band, followed by the Glenn Miller Orchestra.

In 1953, Gerlach returned home. He taught music history and orchestration at the University of Houston, while teaching private music lessons and performing. Thereafter, the Ed Gerlach Orchestra began performing locally, primarily at the Shamrock Hotel and the River Oaks Country Club. The group played with such performers as Tony Bennett, Bob Hope and the Manhattan Transfer. He operated a successful booking agency for performing artists.

The Geto Boys is a rap group from Houston, consisting of Scarface, Willie D and Bushwick Bill. The Geto Boys have earned notoriety for their lyrics which cover controversial topics. About.com ranked them No. 10 on its list of the 25 Best Rap Groups of All-Time, describing them as "southern rap pioneers who paved the way for future southern hip-hop acts."

Billy Gibbons is a guitarist and singer, a member of the legendary rock band ZZ Top.

Roy Head was born in Three Rivers and has worked the nightclub circuit for 50 years. His biggest national hit was "Treat Her Right" in 1965, with a steady output of country and rock recordings since. His group was called The Traits.

Don Janicek ran the popular Don's Record Shop in Bellaire. He produced many local recording artists, including all the Houston Oilers spirit songs.

Mickey Jones is a musician. His career as a drummer had him backing up such artists and bands as Trini Lopez, Johnny Rivers, Bob Dylan and The First Edition with Kenny Rogers. Mickey has 17 gold records from his musical career of over two decades. After the break-up of The First Edition in 1976, Mickey concentrated on his career as a character actor, where he has made many appearances on film and television.

Bradley Jordan, better known by his stage name Scarface, is an American rapper. He hails from Houston, Texas and a member of the Geto Boys. In 2012, The Source ranked him #16 on their list of the Top 50 Lyricists of All Time. About. com ranked him #10 on its list of Greatest MCs.

Robert Earl Keen is a singer-songwriter and entertainer living in the central Texas hill country. Debuting with 1984's No Kinda Dancer, the Houston native has recorded 18 full-length albums for both independent and major record labels, while his songs have also been covered by several different artists from the country, folk and Texas country music scenes (including George Strait, Joe Ely, Lyle Lovett, The Highwaymen, Nanci Griffith, and the Dixie Chicks). He has been heralded as one of the state's most acclaimed musical ambassadors, leading to his induction into the Texas Heritage Songwriters Hall of Fame in 2012, along with Lovett and Townes Van Zandt.

Johnny Lee hails from Texas City and is nationally known for hit records and his association with the Gilley's nightclub, immortalized in the movie "Urban Cowboy." Lee worked 10 years with Mickey Gilley both on tour and at Gilley's Club in Pasadena, Texas. His hits include "Lookin' For Love," "One in a Million," "Bet Your Heart on Me," "The Yellow Rose," "Pickin' Up Strangers," "Prisoner of Hope," "Cherokee Fiddle," "Sounds Like Love" and "Hey Bartender." He is now based out of Branson, MO.

Lyle Lovett was born in Houston and is a country music singer and songwriter. He has recorded 13 albums and released 21 singles to date, including his highest entry, the number 10 chart hit on the U.S. Billboard Hot Country Songs chart, "Cowboy Man." Lovett has won four Grammy Awards, including Best Male Country Vocal Performance and Best Country Album.

Mark Lowry is a Christian comedian, songwriter and singer, best known for co-writing the song "Mary, Did You Know?" Lowry performed with the Gaither Vocal Band from 1988–2001 and, in 2009, re-joined the group along with other "GVB" alumni Michael English and David Phelps. Lowry has recorded 12 albums, both music and comedy.

LeToya Luckett was an original member of the R&B group Destiny's Child, with whom she won two Grammy Awards and released many successful commercial recordings. She began a solo career with Capitol Records. Her solo debut album, LeToya (2006), topped the albums chart and was certified platinum by the RIAA.

The single, "Torn", achieved records on BET's top ten countdown show 106 & Park. She was named one of the Best New Artists of 2006 by AOL and the Top Songwriter by ASCAP. Luckett released a second solo album, Lady Love, which debuted at No. 1 on the U.S. Top R&B/Hip-Hop Albums chart and No. 12 on the U.S. Billboard chart.

Barbara Mandrell shines in country music and, with her sisters, headlined a weekly music variety series on NBC-TV. She is known for a series of Top 10 hits and TV shows in the 1970's and 1980's that helped her become one of country's most successful female vocalists. She was inducted into the Country Music Hall of Fame in 2009. She was the first performer to win the Country Music Association's "Entertainer of the Year" award twice. She also won twice the Country Music Association's "Female Vocalist of the Year" in 1979 and 1981.

Larry Moore is a veteran, musician, architect and painting artist. He and his twin brother Garry were a popular band from the 1960's-1980's. They had a great Everly Brothers harmony and performed pop, rockabilly, country and oldies in local clubs. From 1980-1982, they performed several radio jingles for me, as I was a radio DJ with an oldies show. Larry moved to Branson, MO, where he performed with all the headliner acts. In recent years, he has concentrated on paintings and has been exhibited in leading art galleries nationally.

Bill Nash is a pop and country singer, as well as an ordained minister. For years, he has operated Champions Kids Camp, a non-profit organization serving children in need. His son Jimmy Nash is a popular recording and concert star.

Johnny Nash is a singer from Houston whose catchy "I Can See Clearly Now" reached Number 1 in 1972. In the 1950's, he recorded for ABC Paramount Records, positioning him as a pop teen idol. He then added reggae influences to his music, recording for JAD and Epic Records. He also enjoyed success as an actor, appearing in the screen version of playwright Louis S. Peterson's "Take a Giant Step." Nash won a Silver Sail Award for his performance from the Locarno International Film Festival.

Mickey Newbury was a 1958 graduate of Jeff Davis High School. He moved to Nashville and worked as a staff writer for Acuff-Rose Publishing Co. His biggest hit was "An American Trilogy," popularized by Elvis Presley.

Billy Preston was born in Houston and performed with Mahalia Jackson at an early age. He played piano in the movie "St. Louis Blues" and was a regular on the "Shindig" TV show. He played keyboards on The Beatles' hit "Get Back" and toured with The Rolling Stones. Throughout the 1970's, he had top chart hits on the Apple and A&M labels.

P.J. Proby was born James Marcus Smith in Houston. He moved to Los Angeles in 1957, performing as Jet Smith. As P.J. Proby, he achieved greater popularity in England, with "Niki Hoeky" in 1967 as his biggest hit record.

Kenny Rogers was a 1956 graduate of Jeff Davis High School. He began his musical career in 1958 as a member of The Scholars. In 1960, he became the bass player with the Bobby Doyle Trio, performing at the Tidelands Club. His first recorded as Kenneth Rogers, later becoming a member of such groups as the Kirby Stone Four and the New Christy Minstrels. Kenny expanded his singing skills to include pop, folk and country. In 1967, he formed Kenny Rogers & the First Edition, composed of former Minstrels members. He left the group in 1973 and became a major solo entertainer. His autobiography was called "Making It With Music."

Kelly Rowland was a founding member of Destiny's Child, one of the world's best-selling girl groups of all time. Rowland released her debut solo album Simply Deep (2002), which produced the number-one single "Dilemma" and the international top-ten hit "Stole." Rowland ventured into acting, with guest appearances in television sitcoms, and starring roles in Freddy vs. Jason (2003) and The Seat Filler (2004). In 2005, she released a second album, Ms. Kelly (2007), including "Like This" and "Work." In 2009, Rowland was a host on The Fashion Show. Her third album Here I Am (2011) spawned the hits "Commander" and "Motivation." In 2011, she returned to TV as a judge on the The X Factor.

Joe Sample was a pianist, keyboard player and composer. As a student at Texas Southern University, he was one of the founding members of the Crusaders, remaining a part of the group until its final album in 1991 and 2003 reunion album. He enjoyed a successful solo career and appeared on recordings by Miles Davis, George Benson, Jimmy Witherspoon, B. B. King, Eric Clapton, Steely Dan and The Supremes. Sample incorporated jazz, gospel, blues, Latin and classical forms into his music.

Tommy Sands began his career singing on Channel 2. As a teen pop singer, he had hit records on the Capitol label and appeared in movies. He married Nancy Sinatra and appeared in film dramatic roles.

DJ Screw (born Robert Earl Davis, Jr.) was a hip hop DJ. He was recognized for his albums mostly on a regional level, until after his death. His legacy was discovered by a wider audience when Houston hip-hop began reaching a national audience in 2005.

Terri Sharp was Houston's answer to Lesley Gore, with a 1966 hit record called "A Love That Will Last." At the time, she was a student at Memorial High School.

B. J. Thomas began his career singing with the Triumphs in Houston venues, before moving on to pop and country stardom with such hits as "Hooked on a Feeling," "New York Woman," "I Just Can't Help Believing" and "Raindrops Keep Fallin' on My Head."

Gene Thomas recorded some memorable pop songs in the 1960's, including "Sometimes," "Baby's Gone Away" and "The Last Song."

The Triumphs were the group that worked with B.J. Thomas on his early Houston-recorded hits. The Triumphs had their own hit record in 1965 with "Garner State Park," honoring the tourist venue of 60's Texas youths.

Jaci Velasquez is a Contemporary Christian and Latin pop singer and songwriter—in both English and Spanish languages. She has sold almost five million albums around the world,[1] recorded three Platinum and three Gold albums, and recorded 16 singles that hit No. 1 plus six more that hit the top 10. She has received seven Dove Awards including Best New Artist and Female Vocalist of the Year.

Wesley Weston Jr., better known by his stage name Lil' Flip, is a rapper. He is best known for his singles "Sunshine", "Game Over", "The Way We Ball", "I Can Do Dat" and "Rollin on 20's" from the 2 Fast 2 Furious Soundtrack.

Barry White hailed from Galveston, Texas. He was a music writer, arranger and conductor extraordinaire. His deep rich voice was a mainstay of 1970's disco in his recordings with the Love Unlimited Orchestra and under the Barry White moniker.

Musical history was made in 1974 when Bruce Springsteen performed at Liberty Hall. He later immortalized that watershed in his career for a tribute song.

Apartment impresario Harold Farb recorded a series of record albums featuring him singing the music classics.

Chapter 11

MEDICAL, SCIENCE
AND TECHNOLOGY

Medical Institutions

T he Baylor College of Medicine was the first institution to locate in the Texas Medical Center in Houston. It was founded in Dallas in 1900, when Texas had only two other schools of medicine, the University of Texas Medicine Branch, which started in Galveston in 1891, and the Fort Worth School of Medicine, which began in 1894. BCM was the first of eight medical schools to be organized in Dallas during the first decade of the 20th Century.

With three physicians as incorporator, the school enrolled 81 students for its opening on Nov. 19, 1900. At the first commencement, April 18, 1901, 15 diplomas were bestowed. From 1903-1943, Baylor awarded M.D. degrees to 1,670 graduates.

In 1943, BCM accepted an invitation from the M. D. Anderson Foundation and other Houston benefactors to move to Houston. On July 12, 1943, BCM began its Houston era in a former Sears, Roebuck and Company building on Buffalo Drive. These renovated quarters housed the college until the Cullen Building was ready for occupancy in 1947. Ties to Baylor University ended officially in 1969. Despite its status as a private school Baylor, since 1971, has annually received state appropriations from the Texas legislature to subsidize the medical education of Texas residents.

Since its founding Baylor has trained more than 11,251 physicians and residents. Baylor's graduate school enrolls 237 students in 13 Ph.D. programs in the biomedical sciences and an M.S. program in nurse anesthesiology. About 835 resident physicians receive training in 22 medical specialties offered jointly by Baylor and its eight primary affiliated teaching hospitals. Another 443 students are postdoctoral fellows or students in allied health programs, where they learn nuclear medicine technology, nurse midwifery and similar skills. In 1972, Baylor and the Houston Independent School District started the nation's first high school for health professions program.

Since occupying the Roy and Lillie Cullen Building in 1947, Baylor has expanded its physical plant with Jesse H. Jones Hall (1964), M. D. Anderson Hall (1964), Jewish Institute for Medical Research (1964), Michael E. DeBakey Center for Biomedical Education (1980), Family Practice Center (1983), Ben Taub Research Center (1986) and the Vivian and Bob Smith Medical Research Building (1989). With Methodist Hospital it has administered the Neurosensory Center of Houston since 1977, and with Texas Children's Hospital and the U.S. Department of Agriculture it has operated the Children's Nutrition Research Center since 1988. The Woodlands campus is the site of the Baylor Center for Biotechnology, marketing commercially viable products from laboratory research done by Baylor scientists.

The M.D. Anderson Cancer Center began in 1941, established by the Texas Legislature as the Texas State Cancer Hospital and the Division of Cancer Research. In 1942, it was renamed MD Anderson Hospital for Cancer Research of The University of Texas to honor support from the M.D. Anderson Foundation. Its temporary quarters were on the James A. Baker estate at 2310 Baldwin Street downtown, with Ernst William Bertner, M.D., as acting director.

In 1946, the first full-time president, Randolph Lee Clark, M.D., took charge. He served 32 years until retirement in 1978 and was followed by Charles A. LeMaistre, M.D., who retired in 1996. The third full-time president was John Mendelsohn, M.D. (1996-2011). In 2011, Ronald DePinho, M.D., became the fourth full-time president.

In 1955, the name changed to The University of Texas M.D. Anderson Hospital and Tumor Institute at Houston. In 1972, the UT System reorganization led to the establishment of The University of Texas System Cancer Center, including both the hospital and research facility in Houston and the Science Park in Smithville. In 1988, the name was changed to The University of Texas M.D. Anderson Cancer Center.

It is one of the original three comprehensive cancer centers in the U.S., established by the National Cancer Act of 1971. It is a degree-granting academic institution and a cancer treatment and research center located at the Texas Medical Center. For 10 of the past 12 years, M.D. Anderson ranked No. 1 in cancer care in the "Best Hospitals" survey published in U.S. News & World Report. The center provides care for 115,000 patients annually and employs 19,000 people.

The Texas Medical Center was created by trustees of the Anderson Foundation in the early 1940's, envisioning the first units of the center to be the University of Texas Hospital for Cancer Research and the Baylor College of Medicine. A 134-acre site of city-owned property adjacent to the Hermann Hospital grounds passed to the foundation from the city in 1944, via vote authorization. The Texas Medical Center was organized and received title to the land in 1945.

TMC attracted institutions related to health education, research and patient care, the center assembled staffs, provided facilities, and developed programs necessary to assure the highest standards of attainment in medicine. From 1951-1955 facilities were completed for University of Texas M.D. Anderson Cancer Center, Methodist Hospital, Shriner's Hospital for Crippled Children, Jesse H. Jones Library Building, Texas Children's Hospital, St. Luke's Episcopal Hospital and the University of Texas Dental Branch. Expansion in 1959-1960 included the Texas Institute for Rehabilitation and Research, Houston Speech and Hearing Institute, Houston State Psychiatric Institute for Research and Training, Texas Woman's University, Houston Center and the Institute of Religion. Added 1962-

1965 were Ben Taub General Hospital, Texas Heart Institute and the Houston Department of Health and Human Services.

In 1972, the University of Texas Houston Health Science Center joined the Texas Medical Center, including eight operating units: the Dental Branch, Graduate School of Biomedical Sciences, Division of Continuing Education, Harris County Psychiatric Center, Medical School, School of Allied Health Sciences, School of Nursing and the School of Public Health.

UTHSC is also affiliated with 196 area and state hospitals and facilities, the major Houston hospital affiliations being Hermann Hospital, Lyndon B. Johnson General Hospital, the University of Texas M. D. Anderson Cancer Center, St. Joseph Hospital and the Memorial Healthcare System. The Harris County Psychiatric Center joined UT-Houston, as it is commonly called, in 1989.

TMC established the nation's first High School for Health Professionals in 1971 and the Life Flight helicopter rescue program at Hermann Hospital in 1976. In the 1980's, TMC added the University of Houston College of Pharmacy, Veterans Affairs Medical Center, LifeGift Organ Donation Center, Lyndon B. Johnson General Hospital and the Albert B. Alkek Institute of Biosciences and Technology, Texas A&M University.

The Texas Medical Center is the largest medical center in the world, with more than 675 acres and 100 permanent buildings housing 41 member institutions, which including 14 hospitals, two medical schools, four colleges of nursing and six university systems. Dr. Robert Robbins is president of TMC.

Medical Legends

Dr. Michael DeBakey was a world-renowned American cardiac surgeon, innovator, scientist, medical educator, and international medical statesman. He was the chancellor emeritus of Baylor College of Medicine, director of The Methodist DeBakey Heart and Vascular Center and senior attending surgeon of The Methodist Hospital in Houston.

DeBakey received his BS and M.D. degrees from Tulane University. He completed his surgical fellowships at the University of Strasbourg, France, and at the University of Heidelberg, Germany. He served on the Tulane faculty from 1937-1948. From 1942-1946, he was on military leave as a member of the Surgical Consultants' Division in the Office of the Surgeon General of the Army and in

1945 became its Director and received the Legion of Merit. Dr. DeBakey helped develop the Mobile Army Surgical Hospital (MASH) units and helped establish the Veteran's Administration Medical Center Research System.

He joined the faculty of Baylor College of Medicine in 1948, serving as Chairman of the Department of Surgery until 1993. DeBakey was president of the college from 1969-1979, served as Chancellor from 1979-1996 and was then named Chancellor Emeritus. He was also Olga Keith Wiess and Distinguished Service Professor in the Michael E. DeBakey Department of Surgery at Baylor College of Medicine and Director of the DeBakey Heart Center for research and public education at Baylor College of Medicine and The Methodist Hospital.

Dr. DeBakey was one of the first to perform coronary artery bypass surgery and in 1953 performed the first successful carotid endarterectomy. A pioneer in the development of an artificial heart, DeBakey was the first to use an external heart pump successfully in a patient. He pioneered the use of Dacron grafts to replace or repair blood vessels. He performed the first successful patch-graft angioplasty. This procedure involved patching the slit in the artery from an endarterectomy with a Dacron or vein graft. The patch widened the artery so that when it closed, the channel of the artery returned to normal size. The DeBakey artificial graft is now used around the world to replace or repair blood vessels. He and his team of surgeons were among the first to record surgeries on film. The Congressional Gold Medal awarded to Dr. DeBakey.

Dr. Denton Cooley is a heart surgeon famous for performing the first implantation of a total artificial heart. Cooley is founder and surgeon in-chief of The Texas Heart Institute, chief of Cardiovascular Surgery at St. Luke's Episcopal Hospital, consultant in Cardiovascular Surgery at Texas Children's Hospital and a clinical professor of Surgery at the University of Texas Health Science Center at Houston.

Cooley graduated in 1941 from the University of Texas and completed his medical degree and his surgical training at the Johns Hopkins School of Medicine in Baltimore, Maryland, where he also completed his internship. At Johns Hopkins, he worked with Dr. Alfred Blalock and assisted in the first procedure to correct an infant's congenital heart defect. In 1946, he was called to active duty with the Army Medical Corps, serving as chief of surgical services at the hospital in Linz, Austria. He completed residency at Johns Hopkins and remained an instructor in surgery. In 1950, he went to London to work with Lord Russell Brock.

In the 1950's, Dr. Cooley returned to Houston to become associate professor of surgery at Baylor College of Medicine and to work at its affiliate institution, The Methodist Hospital. He worked with Dr. Michael DeBakey, developing a new method of removing aortic aneurysms, the bulging weak spots that may develop in the wall of the artery.

In 1960, Dr. Cooley moved his practice to St. Luke's Episcopal Hospital while continuing to teach at Baylor. In 1962, he founded The Texas Heart Institute. He and colleagues worked on developing new artificial heart valves from 1962-1967. In 1970, he performed the first implantation of an artificial heart in a human when no heart replacement was immediately available. In 1984, he was awarded the Medal of Freedom by President Ronald Reagan. In 1998, he was awarded the National Medal of Technology by President Bill Clinton. Dr. Cooley has authored or co-authored more than 1,400 scientific articles and 12 books.

Dr. Red Duke is a trauma surgeon and professor at The University of Texas Health Science Center at Houston and Memorial Hermann-Texas Medical Center. James Henry "Red" Duke, Jr. was born in Ennis, graduated from Hillsboro High School and earned a bachelor's degree from Texas A&M University in 1950. At A&M, he served as a yell leader and was the first person to publicly deliver the poem "The Last Corps Trip." After a two-year tour of duty as a tank officer in the U.S. Army, he went on to earn a divinity degree from Southwestern Baptist Theological Seminary in 1955.

A lifelong desire to become a doctor resulted in studying at the University of Texas Southwestern Medical School in Dallas, from which he received his M.D. in 1960. Dr. Duke completed his internship in internal medicine and his residency in general surgery at Dallas' Parkland Memorial Hospital in 1965. During that residency on Nov. 22, 1963, Dr. Duke was the first surgeon to receive President John F. Kennedy after being shot and taken to Dallas Parkland Hospital. Dr. Duke also attended to the wounds of then Texas Governor John Connally, who was shot at the same time John F. Kennedy was assassinated.

His academic career began in 1966 as an assistant professor of surgery at UT Southwestern Medical School and later at the College of Physicians and Surgeons in New York. He pursued graduate studies in chemical engineering, biochemistry and computer sciences at Columbia University under the auspices of an NIH Special Fellowship. While Dr. Duke was an assistant professor of surgery in New York, he had the opportunity to move his family and career to Jalalabad, Afghanistan, as a visiting professor and from 1970-1972 was chairman of surgery at Nangarhar University School of Medicine.

In 1972, he joined the faculty of the University of Texas Medical School at Houston where he is a professor of surgery. Among his many responsibilities, Dr. Duke has served as special assistant to the president of the UT Health Science Center and holds the John B. Holmes Professor of Clinical Sciences. He established Houston's Hermann Hospital Life Flight operations in 1976 and remains the medical director of its trauma and emergency services.

He hosted the nationally syndicated "Dr. Red Duke's Health Reports," which aired for 15 years (locally on KTRK-TV). The segments educated millions about health-related topics, with his popular segment sign-off "For your health!" He hosted the former PBS-TV series "Bodywatch." He has been featured on such programs as PM Magazine, NBC Nightly News, The Today Show and the Buck James television series. The UT Medical School at Houston Department of Surgery sponsored a scholarship fund in honor of Dr. Red Duke, for students to research and train in the field of trauma.

The Kelsey-Seybold Clinic is a large multi-specialty clinic system located in Greater Houston with its administrative headquarters in the City of Houston.[1] The clinic system is a major provider of healthcare for NASA and a center for healthcare research.

Dr. Mavis P. Kelsey had the purpose of combining primary and specialty medical services in one location, patterned after the Mayo Clinic model. In 1949, Dr. Kelsey, an internal medicine specialist, leased space in the Hermann Professional Building and set up his practice. Two of his Mayo friends, Dr. William D. Seybold, a surgeon, and Dr. William V. Leary, another internist, joined the practice. In 1953, Dr. John R. Kelsey Jr., specialist in gastroenterology, joined the practice, and Clinic doctors began serving rotations at area hospitals, including Hermann Hospital, Baylor College of Medicine and M.D. Anderson Cancer Center. In 1956, the Kelsey and Leary Foundation for the Advancement of Medicine was established to provide scholarships and financial support for research in cancer, epilepsy, cardiology, diabetes and obstetrics.

During the 1960's, the Clinic added more specialists and more departments. The rapidly expanding Radiology Department added lab technicians, while the multi-specialty team continued to grow with the addition Pediatrics, Rheumatology, Dermatology, Urology, Ophthalmology and Dentistry. In 1965, the name was changed to Kelsey-Seybold Clinic. In 1966, the Clinic became the first contract medical service provider for NASA. In 1971, KSC opened its first neighborhood health center on Post Oak. The success of that health center resulted in other locations being operated in downtown Houston, Sugar Land, The Woodlands and by Intercontinental Airport. Today, KSC operates 20 neighborhood health centers. In 1999, KSC moved into its Main Campus at 2727 West Holcombe Blvd. KSC has 370 physicians in 50-plus medical specialties and sub-specialties and offers a full range of diagnostic testing services and treatments, serving more than 400,000patients.

Ben Taub, philanthropist and medical benefactor, was born in 1889 in Houston. His father immigrated from Hungary to Texas in 1882 and became a tobacco wholesaler. Taub expanded the family business, becoming a real estate developer. At one time he served on the boards of directors of 23 institutions, including an investment firm, two banks, an insurance company and four universities.

In 1936, Taub donated 35 acres for establishing the University of Houston. In 1943, he was instrumental in encouraging the Baylor College of Medicine to move to the Texas Medical Center in Houston. He helped guide the Harris County Hospital through affiliation with BCM, which in 1949 joined the city and county in providing care for indigent patients.

Taub never married and spent his time visiting patients in the county hospital. For years, he helped run the DePelchin Faith Home for homeless children. He was a director of the Texas Medical Center, headed the United Way, gave out scholarships and sponsored visiting medical professors. He served as chairman of the Jefferson Davis Hospital from 1935-1964. When Houston's new charity hospital opened in 1963, the hospital board, in recognition of his service, named it Ben Taub General Hospital. It became one of the nation's major trauma centers. In 1986, Baylor College of Medicine opened the ten-story Ben Taub Research Center.

Science Institutions

The Lyndon B. Johnson Space Center is the National Aeronautics and Space Administration's center for human spaceflight training, research and flight control is a complex of 100 buildings on 1,620 acres. The JSC is home to the U.S. astronaut corps and is responsible for training astronauts from both the U.S. and its international partners. It is often referred to by its central function during journeys into space, Mission Control.

The center, originally known as the Manned Spacecraft Center, grew out of the Space Task Group formed after the creation of NASA to co-ordinate the U.S. manned spaceflight program. The facility was constructed on land donated by Rice University and opened in 1963. The center was renamed in honor of the late U.S. president and Texas native, Lyndon B. Johnson in 1973. LBJ had shepherded the legislation creating NASA when he was Senate Majority Leader. JSC is one of 10 major NASA field centers.

In addition to housing NASA's astronaut operations, JSC is the site of the Lunar Receiving Laboratory, where the first astronauts returning from the moon were quarantined and where the majority of lunar samples are stored. The center's Landing and Recovery Division operated MV Retriever in the Gulf of Mexico for Gemini and Apollo astronauts to practice water egress after splashdown.

The JSC is home to the Christopher C. Kraft Jr. Mission Control Center, which coordinates and monitors all human spaceflight for the United States. MCC-H directs all Space Shuttle missions and activities aboard the International Space Station. The Apollo Mission Control Center, a National Historic Landmark, is in Building 30. From the moment a manned spacecraft clears its launch tower until it lands back on Earth, it is in the hands of Mission Control. The MCC houses several Flight Control Rooms, with computer resources to monitor, command and communicate with spacecraft. When a mission is underway, the rooms are staffed around the clock, usually in three shifts.

JSC handles most of the planning and training of the astronaut corps and houses training facilities such as the Sonny Carter Training Facility and the Neutral Buoyancy Laboratory. The facility provides pre-flight training in becoming familiar with crew activities and with the dynamics of body motion under weightless conditions. Building 31-N houses the Lunar Sample Laboratory Facility, which stores, analyzes and processes most of the samples returned from the moon during the Apollo program.

JSC is also responsible for direction of operations at White Sands Test Facility in New Mexico, which serves as a backup Shuttle landing site and would be the coordinating facility for the Constellation program, which was planned to replace the Space Shuttle program after 2010. The visitor center has been the adjacent Space Center Houston since 1994. The Johnson Space Center Heliport is located on the campus. JSC operates the National Space Biomedical Research Institute at Baylor College of Medicine to study the health risks related to long-duration space flight. The Prebreathe Reduction Program is a research program at JSC to improve the safety and efficiency of space walks from the International Space Station. The Overset Grid-Flow software was developed at JSC in collaboration with NASA Ames Research Center.

The Harris County Institute of Forensic Sciences provides forensic investigation and analysis through the Medical Examiner Service and the Forensic Crime Laboratory Service. HCIFS has been a member institution of the Texas Medical Center since 1983.

The Methodist Hospital Research Institute encompasses 90 principal investigators, core facilities to enhance interdisciplinary research and two Good Manufacturing Practice facilities to prepare clinical-grade radio-pharmaceuticals, biological agents and small molecules. Also included is a surgical simulation training facility.

The Methodist DeBakey Heart and Vascular Center provides cardiovascular care through research in cardiology and cardiovascular surgery, education and patient services. The Methodist Neurological Institute research leader teams are developing new treatments, therapies, drugs and clinical trials for stroke, Parkinson's disease, Alzheimer's disease, ALS, brain and spinal tumors, aneurysms, disc disease and other disorders.

The Methodist Hospital, University of Houston and Weill Cornell Medical College of Cornell University jointly founded the Institute for Biomedical Imaging Science, with interdisciplinary programs in biomedical imaging and training programs to produce basic and applied scientists.

Technology Legends

Red Adair was an oil well firefighter. He became world notable as an innovator in the highly specialized and extremely hazardous profession of extinguishing and capping blazing, erupting oil well blowouts on land and offshore. He was born in Houston and attended Reagan High School. He began fighting oil well fires after returning from serving in a bomb disposal unit during World War II. He started his career working with Myron Kinley, the blowout/oil firefighting pioneer.

In 1959, he founded Red Adair Co., Inc. During his career, Adair battled more than 2,000 land and offshore oil well, natural gas well and similar spectacular fires. In 1962, he gained global attention by tackling a fire at the Gassi Touil gas field in the Algerian Sahara, a 450-foot pillar of flame that burned for five months. In 1977, he and his crew contributed to the capping of the biggest oil well blowout in the North Sea. In 1988, he was again in the North Sea where he helped to put out the UK sector Piper Alpha oil platform fire. At age 75, Adair took part in extinguishing the oil well fires in Kuwait set by retreating Iraqi troops after the Gulf War in 1991. John Wayne's 1968 movie "The Hellfighters" was based upon the feats of Adair during the 1962 Sahara Desert fire.

Baker Hughes Center for Technology Innovation is a research and engineering center in Houston. Opened in 2009 and located on a 14-acre campus, CTI continuously develops approaches to the industry's toughest completions and production challenges. These include extreme high-pressure/high-temperature (XHPHT), deepwater, production optimization and big-bore completions. 600 scientists, engineers, and technicians research and test these new solutions applying a systems approach. Test cells, metallurgy, composites, electronics research labs, visualization centers and rapid prototyping are studied.

Barrios Technologies was founded in 1980 by Emyre "Emy" Barrios Robinson. It started with a contract to train and manage flight design and mission integration specialists for the Space Shuttle Program. Barrios has fulfilled contracts supporting Johnson Space Center, NASA Headquarters, and the Department of Defense. Services expanded to include Aerospace Engineering & Science, Program Planning & Control, Mission Integration & Operations and Software Engineering & Integration. In 1993, Sandra G. Johnson, one of the original founder, purchased majority interest in the company. Barrios has a subcontractor relationship with other major aerospace contractors including Alliant Techsystems,

Boeing Company, Jacobs Technology, Lockheed Martin, Science Applications International Corporation, Teledyne Brown Engineering, United Space Alliance and Wyle Integrated Science and Engineering.

BMC Software, Inc. is a Houston company specializing in business service management (BSM) software. BMC develops, markets and sells software used for multiple functions, including IT service management, data center automation, performance management, virtualization lifecycle management and cloud computing management. The name BMC was taken from the surnames of its three founders, Scott Boulette, John Moores and Dan Cloer.

Rod Canion was a co-founder of Compaq Computer Corporation where he served as its first President and CEO. He and other co-founders had been senior managers at Texas Instruments. Venture capitalist Benjamin M. Rosen became chairman of the board of Compaq. In 1992, Canion founded Insource Technology Group with Jim Harris and Ronald L. Fischer and served as chairman until Sept. 2006. He is Director Emeritus of the Houston Technology Center.

Dr. Paul Chu is a Chinese-born American physicist specializing in superconductivity, magnetism and dielectrics. He took an appointment as Professor of Physics at the University of Houston in 1979. Subsequently, the title expanded to T.L.L. Temple Chair of Science in the College of Natural Sciences and Mathematics at the University of Houston. In 1987 he was one of the first scientists to demonstrate high-temperature superconductivity. Dr. Chu and Maw-Kuen Wu announced the historic discovery of superconductivity above 77 K in YBCO, touching off a frenzy of scientific discussion. He was appointed director of the Texas Center for Superconductivity. He also has served as a consultant and visiting staff member at Bell Laboratories, Los Alamos Scientific Laboratory, the Marshall Space Flight Center, Argonne National Laboratory and DuPont.

Cooper Industries began in 1833 when Charles and Elias Cooper established a foundry in Mt. Vernon, Ohio. It produced steam engines in 1869 and entered the production of natural gas internal combustion engines in 1900. In 1965, it branched into electrical, automotive tools and hardware industries. In 1967, its headquarters moved to Houston. In 1989, Cooper acquired Cameron Iron Works, which had started in Houston in 1920 by Harry Cameron and James S. Abercombie. In 2006, Cooper Cameron Corporation officially changed its name to Cameron International Corporation.

Michael Holthouse founded and ran a computer network services firm, Paranet Inc. He sold it to Sprint Corp. for $375 million in cash. He took the proceeds from the Paranet sale and created the Holthouse Foundation for Kids, a non-profit organization that aims to help at-risk children learn critical life skills. He devised "Lemonade Day," an annual community event that champions entrepreneurship for children.

The Houston Technology Center is a Technology Accelerator and Incubator. The HTC creates economic wealth in the region by supporting technology businesses in the sectors of Energy, Information Technology, Life Sciences, and NASA based space technologies with business guidance, access to capital and professional services and education. HTC was named among Forbes Magazine's "Ten Technology Incubators Changing the World."

Robert C. "Bob" McNair was born in Tampa, FL, and moved to Houston in 1960 and ran a trucking business. In 1983, he founded Cogen Technologies. Cogen grew by selling steam first, and then using the profits to increase its electricity business. Cogen started out as an innovator and a leader in the electricity cogeneration industry and today remains the largest non-utility electricity generator in the U.S. He now owns the Houston Texans football team, which will be discussed in Chapter 12.

On Nov. 18, 1837, Charles Morgan's steamship Columbia arrived at New Orleans in the first recorded voyage of Morgan Lines, the first steamship company in Texas. The Columbia made its inaugural voyage to Galveston a week later. Originated by shipping and railroad magnate Charles Morgan, the company introduced his economic influence into the Gulf region. In 1858, the Morgan Lines had three sailings a week from Galveston and two from New Orleans, and by 1860 the company had a monopoly on coastal shipping.

The Morgan Steamship Company took an active part in building railroads to feed the ship lines. In the 1870's, pooling agreements were made among Morgan's Louisiana and Texas Railroad and Steamship Company, the Louisiana Western Railroad Company, and the Texas and New Orleans Railroad. In the late 1870's, Morgan worked with E. W. Cave to make Houston an inland port with better facilities for the line. In the early 1880's, the Morgan Lines were sold to C. P. Huntington of the Southern Pacific Railroad. The fleet was sold to the United States Maritime Commission in 1941. The community Morgan's

Point is named for Charles Morgan, an early advocate and shipper for the Port of Houston.

Schlumberger was founded in 1926 by French brothers Conrad and Marcel Schlumberger as the Société de prospection électrique (French: Electric Prospecting Company). The company recorded the first-ever electrical resistivity well log in Merkwiller-Pechelbronn, France, in 1927. Schlumberger supplies the petroleum industry with services such as seismic acquisition and processing, formation evaluation, well testing and directional drilling, well cementing and stimulation, artificial lift, well completions, flow assurance and consulting, and software and information management. The company is also involved in the groundwater extraction and carbon capture and storage industries. In the 1970s, the company's top executives in North America were relocated to New York City. In 2005, Schlumberger relocated its U.S. corporate offices from New York to Houston.

Harry K. Smith started as a teenager in 1926 in the family business, working on oil tankers, welding pipelines and selling welding equipment. Smith took the reins of the business in 1948 after the death of his father, Benjamin K. Smith, who co-founded Big Three in 1920. During his 38 years at the helm of that company, Smith took it from a $6 million regional oxygen and nitrogen distribution company to a billion-dollar behemoth that, among other things, supplied all the liquid nitrogen to NASA and the space program.

Smith met a man who had developed a tool that would send nitrogen to oil wells beneath the surface. To take advantage of the offshore drilling boom in the 1960s, Smith expanded his business internationally into Scotland, Venezuela, Mexico and Canada. After selling Big Three to L'Air Liquide for more than $1 billion in 1986, Smith and his brother Albert founded Smith Development Corp. and started investing in South Texas oil and gas wells.

*Dr. Michael DeBakey,
famed heart surgeon.*

*One of the many NASA
astronauts who have called
Houston their home,
Donald H. Peterson.*

Chapter 12

SPORTS

Houston is the home to teams in every major professional sport except the National Hockey League. Sports powerhouses include the Houston Astros (MLB), Houston Texans (NFL), Houston Rockets (NBA), and Houston Dynamo (MLS).

Baseball

From 1888-1961, Houston's professional baseball club was the minor league Houston Buffaloes. They were the first minor league team to be affiliated with a Major League franchise, which was the St. Louis Cardinals. Dizzy Dean played for the Buffs, leading his path to later play for the Cardinals. The club was founded in 1888, and played in the Texas League. From 1959 through 1961, the team played in the American Association at the Triple-A level as an affiliate of the Chicago Cubs. The Buffaloes derived their nickname from Buffalo Bayou, the principal waterway through Houston. The team's last home was Buffalo Stadium, built in 1928. Before that, they played at West End Park from 1905-1928 and at League Park prior to that. Although expansion from the National League eventually brought a Major League team to Texas in 1962, Houston officials had made efforts to do so for years.

In 1961, Houston Sports Association, headed by Judge Roy Hofheinz, purchased The Houston Buffaloes, in order to obtain Houston-area territorial rights for the Major League Houston Colt .45s. Several of those associated with the Buffaloes continued with the major league team including manager Harry Craft.

The Houston Astros were established as the Houston Colt .45s in 1962. The Colt .45s began playing at Colt Stadium. Colt Stadium, a temporary field until the domed stadium could be built. The current name was adopted three years later when they moved into the Astrodome, the world's first domed sports stadium. The name reflects Houston's role as the center of the U.S. space program.

The Houston Astros are a professional baseball team, a member of the Western Division of Major League Baseball's American League, having moved in 2013 after spending their first 51 seasons in the National League. The Astros played their home games at The Astrodome from 1965-1999 and Minute Maid Park since 2000. The Astros have one World Series appearance, in 2005 against the Chicago White Sox.

The Sugar Land Skeeters are a professional baseball team based in Sugar Land, Texas. They are a member of the Atlantic League of Professional Baseball, an independent league not affiliated with Major League Baseball. In 2008, Sugar Land residents voted for the allocation of civic revenues toward the construction of a new baseball park. Beginning in the 2012 season, the team played its home games at Constellation Field.

The Skeeters are the first Atlantic League team to play outside of the Northeast. The team is the first of a planned Western division to include up to six other teams. The Skeeters are also the first independent league baseball team in the Greater Houston metropolitan area since the Houston Buffaloes' final season in 1961. The name Skeeters is a Southern slang word for mosquito, the result of a team-sponsored fan poll.

Football

The Houston Oilers began playing in 1960 as a charter member of the American Football League. The Oilers won two AFL championships before joining the NFL as part of a merger. The Oilers competed in the East Division (along with Buffalo,

New York and Boston) of the AFL before the merger, after which they joined the newly formed AFC Central. The Oilers throughout their existence were owned by Bud Adams and played its home games at the Astrodome for the majority of its time. The first years were played at Jeppesen Stadium and Rice Stadium.

The Oilers were the first champions of the American Football League, winning the 1960 and 1961 contests. The Oilers were a consistent playoff team from 1987-1993, an era that included both of the Oilers' only division titles (1991 and 1993). The Oilers' main colors were Columbia blue and white, with red trim, while their logo was a simple derrick. Oilers jerseys were always Columbia blue for home and white for away.

Owner Bud Adams relocated the Oilers to Nashville, Tennessee, where they were known as the Tennessee Oilers for the 1997 and 1998 seasons. In 1999, Adams changed the team name to the Tennessee Titans, and the color scheme from Columbia Blue, Red and White to Titans Blue, Navy, and White. The new Titans franchise retained the Oilers' team history and records, while the team name and colors were officially retired.

The Houston Texans are a professional football team, a member of the South Division of the American Football Conference (AFC) in the National Football League (NFL). The Texans joined the NFL in 2002 as an expansion team, playing at the newly founded Reliant Stadium. Houston's previous NFL franchise, the Houston Oilers, had moved to Nashville, where they are now the Tennessee Titans. The team majority owner is Bob McNair. The team clinched its first playoff berth during the 2011 season as champions of the AFC South. The Texans repeated as AFC South champions in 2012. More on Bob McNair appears in his profile later in this chapter.

Basketball

The Houston Rockets are a professional basketball team, playing in the Southwest Division of the Western Conference in the National Basketball Association (NBA). The team was established in 1967, and played in San Diego, California, for four years, before moving to Houston. After signing Elvin Hayes in the 1969 NBA Draft, they made their first appearance in the playoffs in that year. After Hayes was traded, Moses Malone was later acquired to replace him. Malone won the MVP award twice and lead Houston to the conference finals in his first year with the team. He took the Rockets to the NBA finals in 1981, but they were defeated in six games by Larry Bird's Boston Celtics which also featured the Rockets current head coach, Kevin McHale.

In 1984, the Rockets drafted Hakeem Olajuwon who, paired with Ralph Sampson and both collectively known as the "Twin Towers," led them to 1986 NBA finals. In 1993, they battled the Seattle SuperSonics to the end before falling short in an overtime Game 7. Inspired by the tough playoff defeat, Olajuwon famously proclaimed to the team "We go from here."

The Rockets stormed all the way to the 1994 NBA Finals, where Olajuwon led them to the franchise's first championship against his rival Patrick Ewing and the New York Knicks. The team repeated as champions in 1995 with a memorable run as the 6th seed in the West and sweeping the favored Orlando Magic led by a young Shaquille O'Neal and Penny Hardaway.

Soccer

The Houston Dynamo is a Major League Soccer club, founded in 2005. The club began play in the MLS in 2006, and originally played its home games at Robertson Stadium on the University of Houston campus before moving to the BBVA Compass Stadium during the 2012 season. The team won the 2006 and 2007 MLS Cups in their first two years, following player and coaching staff relocation of the San Jose Earthquakes. In 2008, the Houston Dynamo became the first Major League Soccer club to secure a point on Mexican soil in the CONCACAF Champions League era. The Dynamo is owned by majority owners Anschutz Entertainment Group (AEG) in partnership with Brener International Group (headed by Gabriel Brener) and world and Olympic boxing champion Oscar De La Hoya. The team's head coach is Dominic Kinnear.

The sports landscape in Houston is further illuminated by golf, tennis, soccer, running, college sports, high school sports and community sports programs.

Houston hosts annual sporting events such as the PGA Tour's Shell Houston Open, the college football Texas Bowl and college baseball's Houston College Classic. Since 1971, Houston's two NCAA Division/FBS football teams, the Rice Owls and Houston Cougars, have played in the annual Bayou Bucket Classic. The U.S. national rugby team is played an international match against a top European team at BBVA Compass Stadium.

Runners from all over the world participate in the Houston Marathon, held on city streets each January.

The Houston Livestock Show and Rodeo is held in late-February and early-March at Reliant Stadium.

The U.S. Men's Clay Court Tennis Championships are held each April at River Oaks Country Club.

Former sports teams

H-Town Cyclones, women's football.

Houston Aeros of the American Hockey League existed in Houston from 1994-2013, when they were moved to become the Iowa Wild.

Houston Comets, women's basketball. The Comets won four consecutive WNBA Championships, which is still the most championships of any sports team in Houston.

Houston Dash, soccer.

Houston Energy, women's football.

Houston Gamblers, football.

Houston Lightning, football.

Houston Power, women's football.

Houston Takers, basketball.

Houston Wranglers, tennis.

Several annual sporting events are no longer held in Houston. The final official event of the LPGA golf season, the LPGA Tour Championship, was held in Houston in 2009, but moved to Orlando, Florida in 2010. From 1998-2001, old CART auto racing series held the Grand Prix of Houston on downtown streets. The CART program's successor series, Champ Car, revived the race for 2006 and 2007 on the streets surrounding Reliant Park. The race was discontinued again in 2008, following Champ Car's merger with the rival Indy Racing League.

Sports Legends

Kenneth Stanley "Bud" Adams Jr. was the owner of the Houston Oilers and Tennessee Titans. He was instrumental in the founding and establishment of the American Football League. Adams became a charter AFL owner with the establishment of the Oilers. He was the senior owner (by time) with his team in the National Football League, a few months ahead of Buffalo Bills' owner Ralph Wilson. Adams was an owner of the Houston Mavericks of the American Basketball Association and the second Nashville Kats franchise of the Arena Football League. Adams had many business interests in the Houston area. He was chairman and CEO of Adams Resources & Energy Inc., a wholesale supplier of oil and natural gas. He also owned several Lincoln-Mercury automobile dealerships.

Cyclone Anaya, began his wrestling career at age 17, subsequently becoming the Champion of Mexico. He then came to the United States and was active on the professional wrestling circuit. Cyclone Anaya won numerous awards and thrilled the hearts of millions of fans. Here he met his wife, Carolina, a former Miss Houston. After many championship titles and five children, Cyclone and his family entered the restaurant business in Houston. After 40 years Cyclone Anaya's remains a popular spot.

Bob Aspromonte was a former utility player who had a 13-year career in 1956 and from 1960 to 1971. He played for the Brooklyn/Los Angeles Dodgers, Houston Colt 45's/Houston Astros, Atlanta Braves and New York Mets, all in the National League. Aspromonte played first base, second base, shortstop, third base and outfield. In 1971, he was the last Brooklyn Dodger player to retire. He appeared in 1,324 games, and came to bat 4,369 times.

Paul Boesch was a professional wrestling promoter. He hosted broadcast wrestling matches, the earliest hit show on Houston's first TV station, Channel 2, and later on Channel 39. During the time of professional wrestling nationalizing in the 1980s, Boesch was a leader in the organization. The now-WWE hosted a sell-out retirement party in his honor in 1987.

Earl Campbell, nicknamed The Tyler Rose, is a former professional American football running back. He, Paul Hornung and O. J. Simpson are the only Heisman Trophy winners to have also been first overall National Football League draft picks and members of both the Pro Football Hall of Fame and College Football Hall of Fame. He began playing football in fifth grade as a kicker, but moved to linebacker and then to running back in sixth grade. In 1973, he led the Corky Nelson-coached John Tyler High School to the Texas 4A State Championship.

As a collegiate football player at the University of Texas at Austin, he won the Heisman Trophy in 1977 and led the nation in rushing with 1,744 yards. In 1977, he became the first recipient of the Davey O'Brien Memorial Trophy which was awarded to the most outstanding player in the now-defunct Southwest Conference. Campbell was the first draft pick overall in the 1978 NFL Draft by the Houston Oilers, who signed him to a six-year contract. The Luv Ya Blue era in Houston was due mostly to Campbell's running ability and Coach Bum Phillips' personality. Campbell possessed a rare combination of speed and power, and was a prolific running back from 1978-1985. In 1984, he was traded to the New Orleans Saints, reuniting him with his former Oilers coach O.A. "Bum" Phillips. Campbell retired in 1986 and in 1991 was inducted into the Pro Football Hall of Fame.

Roger Clemens played baseball at Spring Woods High School, then began his college career pitching for San Jacinto College North in 1981. He then attended the University of Texas at Austin, compiling a 25-7 record in two All-American seasons and was on the mound when the Longhorns won the 1983 College World Series. He became the first player to have his baseball uniform number retired at UT. In 1983, he was drafted by the Boston Red Sox in 1983 and quickly rose through the minor league system, making his major league debut on May 15, 1984. In 1986, he also won the first of his seven Cy Young Awards.

He played for the Boston Red Sox from 1984-1996. On April 29, 1986, Roger Clemens became the first pitcher in history to strike out 20 batters in a major league game, against the Seattle Mariners at Fenway Park. He played for the Toronto Blue Jays from 1997-1998 and the New York Yankees from 1999-2003. Clemens left for the Houston Astros in 2004, where he spent three seasons and won his seventh Cy Young Award. He rejoined the Yankees in 2007 for one last season. In 2012, he pitched for the Sugar Land Skeeters.

Clyde Drexler lived in the South Park area in Houston and attended Ross Sterling High School, where he was a classmate of tennis player Zina Garrison. After a high school basketball career, he was recruited by the University of Houston. Drexler majored in finance and worked at a bank during the summer. At UH, Drexler performed a slam dunk as a member of the Houston Cougars men's basketball team, including Michael Young, Larry Micheaux and Hakeem Olajuwon. They were known as the "Phi Slama Jama" basketball fraternity that gained national attention for its acrobatic, above-the-rim play.

In 1983, Clyde Drexler was drafted by the Portland Trail Blazers. In 1995, he was traded to the Houston Rockets. He was a basketball shooting guard and small forward. A 10-time All-Star and member of the Basketball Hall of Fame, the NBA named him one of basketball's 50 greatest players as of 1996. Drexler won an Olympic gold medal in 1992 as part of the Dream Team and an NBA championship in 1995 with the Houston Rockets. He is now the color commentator for Rockets home games.

A sports celebrity opened a Chevrolet dealership on South Post Oak. He was A.J. Foyt, the champion race car driver. Anthony Joseph Foyt, Jr. raced in motorsports. His open wheel racing includes USAC Champ cars and midget cars. He raced stock cars in NASCAR and USAC. He holds the all-time USAC career wins record with 159 victories and the all-time American championship racing career wins record with 67.

A.J. Foyt was the only driver to win the Indianapolis 500 (four times), Daytona 500, 24 Hours of Daytona and the 24 Hours of Le Mans. Foyt won the International Race of Champions all-star racing series in 1976 and 1977. In the NASCAR stock car circuit, he won the 1964 Firecracker 400 and the 1972 Daytona 500. He survived three spectacular crashes and narrowly escaped a fourth with skillful driving. Foyt's success has led to induction in numerous motor-sports halls of fame. Since his retirement from active racing, he has owned A. J. Foyt Enterprises, which has fielded teams in the CART, IRL and NASCAR associations.

Tara Lipinski won the ladies' singles Olympic gold medal in figure skating at the 1998 Winter Olympics. She remains the youngest individual gold medalist in the history of the Olympic Winter Games (15 at the time). In 1991, her father's job required the family move to Sugar Land, where she trained. After the Olympics, she toured withy Stars on Ice for four seasons. In 2006, Lipinski was the youngest ever inductee into the United States Figure Skating Hall of Fame. She made several television appearances, including Are You Afraid of the Dark?, Touched by an Angel, Sabrina the Teenage Witch, Malcolm in the Middle, Veronica's Closet, Early Edition, 7th Heaven, Still Standing, The Young and the Restless, Ice Angel and the CBS-TV special "Tara Lipinski: From This Moment On." In 2014, she was a commentator and analyst for NBC Sports during the Sochi Winter Games.

Robert C. "Bob" McNair was born in Tampa, FL, and moved to Houston in 1960 and ran a trucking business. In 1983, he founded the cogeneration company Cogen Technologies in 1983. Cogen grew by selling steam first, and then using the profits to increase its electricity business. Cogen started out as an innovator and a leader in the electricity cogeneration industry and today remains the largest non-utility electricity generator in the country.

McNair always had interests in sports. He co-owned Strodes Creek, the 1994 Kentucky Derby runner-up. He is part owner of Stonerside Farm in Paris, Kentucky, where Touch Gold (winner of the 1997 Belmont Stakes) is the attraction. In 1997, Bob McNair's attempted to bring a National Hockey League team to Houston. The fourth-largest city in the U.S. found itself without professional football for the first time since 1959, as Houston Oilers owner Bud Adams got the final approval to move his team to Tennessee.

McNair founded Houston NFL Holdings, for purposes of bringing a new football team to town. The NFL Stadium Committee reported to Commissioner Paul Tagliabue on the attractiveness of Cleveland, Los Angeles and Houston. Two days later, Houston Livestock Show and Rodeo (HLS&R) officials announced they would push for a domed stadium to lure the NFL back to Houston. In 1998, the NFL granted a new franchise to Cleveland. On Oct. 6, 1999, the NFL owners voted 29-0 to award the 32nd franchise and the 2004 Super Bowl to Houston. The Texans launched their inaugural season on Sept. 8, 2002 against the Dallas Cowboys at Reliant Stadium.

The Robert and Janice McNair Foundation makes grants to organizations and programs that benefit the education of children in low-income and needy neighborhoods from elementary school to high school. Robert McNair has served on the Boards of Trustees of Rice University, Baylor College of Medicine, Houston Grand Opera and the Museum of Fine Arts. McNair retains ownership in power plants in New York and West Virginia. He is Chairman and Chief Executive Officer of The McNair Group, a financial and real estate firm that is headquartered in Houston, Texas. He owns Palmetto Partners, Ltd., a private investment company that manages the McNairs' public and private equity investments.

Gifford Nielsen grew up in Provo, Utah, and attended Provo High School, playing as the school's quarterback. He began attending Brigham Young University, where he was an All-American quarterback, under head coach LaVell Edwards, for which he was inducted into the College Football Hall of Fame in 1994. Nielsen was selected in the third round of the 1978 NFL draft by the Houston Oilers, the team with which he spent his entire NFL career. Nielsen played six seasons as backup quarterback to Dan Pastorini in 1978-79 and to Ken Stabler in 1980-81. He played the most games in his last two seasons, 1982–83, when he shared quarterbacking duties with Archie Manning and Oliver Luck. From 1984-87, he served as a color commentator on Oilers radio broadcasts. He was sports director for KHOU-TV for many years. He has served in the Church of Jesus Christ of Latter-day Saints (LDS Church) in many capacities, including elders quorum president, bishop, president of the Houston Texas South Stake and mission president's counselor. He was released as an area seventy on April 6, 2013, and called as a general authority and member of the First Quorum of the Seventy.

Hakeem Ojajuwon is a retired Nigerian-American professional basketball player. From 1984-2002, he played the center position in the National Basketball Association (NBA) for the Houston Rockets and Toronto Raptors. He led the Rockets to back-to-back NBA championships in 1994 and 1995. In 2008, he was inducted into the Basketball Hall of Fame. Listed at 7 ft 0 in, Olajuwon is considered one of the greatest centers ever to play the game. Olajuwon was a member of the Olympic gold-medal-winning United States national team, and was selected as one of the 50 Greatest Players in NBA History. He ended his career as the league's all-time leader in blocks, with 3,830.

Dan Pastorini was a football quarterback in the National Football League for the Houston Oilers, Oakland Raiders, Los Angeles Rams and Philadelphia Eagles and was also a winning NHRA Top Fuel Dragster driver. Pastorini was drafted by the Houston Oilers in the first round of the 1971 NFL Draft out of Santa Clara University. By 1978, the Oilers had a running game with the drafting of future Hall-of-Famer Earl Campbell. Pastorini was also named to the 1975 AFC Pro Bowl Team. Pastorini's best season came in 1978 when he threw for a career high 2,473 yards and 16 touchdowns. In the 1978 playoffs, Pastorini fared very well, helping lead the Oilers to wins over the Miami Dolphins and AFC East division champion New England Patriots. Pastorini's last game as a Houston Oiler was the 1979 AFC championship game against the Pittsburgh Steelers.

Oail Andrew "Bum" Phillips was an American football coach and the father of Wade Phillips, the interim head coach of the Houston Texans. Bum Phillips coached at the high school, college and professional levels. He played football at Lamar University and served in the U.S. Marine Corps in World War II. After he returned from the war, Phillips completed his education at Stephen F. Austin State University. He coached high school football in various Texas cities, including Nederland, Jacksonville, Amarillo High School, and Port Neches–Groves. His college coaching stints included serving as an assistant coach at Texas A&M University (for Bear Bryant), the University of Houston (for Bill Yeoman), Southern Methodist University (for Hayden Fry) and Oklahoma State University (for Jim Stanley). He was head coach at the University of Texas at El Paso for one season in 1962.

Phillips was hired by Sid Gillman to serve as a defensive assistant coach for the San Diego Chargers. In 1973, Gillman became head coach of the Houston Oilers and brought Phillips with him as his defensive coordinator. In 1975, Phillips was named head coach and general manager of the Oilers, serving in that capacity through 1980. He became the highest-winning coach in Oiler history (59-38 record). He was known for his trademark cowboy hat on the sidelines, except when the Oilers played in the Astrodome or other domed stadiums.

From 1981 through the first 12 games of the 1985 season, Phillips was head coach of the New Orleans Saints. He later was a football color analyst for television and radio. Phillips served as commercial spokesman for Spectrum Scoreboards, Texas State Optical, Hearing Aid Express, Blue Ribbon Sausage and GLO CPA's. In 2010, he published his memoirs, "Bum Phillips: Coach, Cowboy, Christian."

Allen Russell, the 1946-1952 President of the Houston Buffaloes, put the city on the map for major league baseball expansion.

Nolan Ryan is a former Major League Baseball pitcher and chief executive officer (CEO) of the Texas Rangers. During a major league record 27-year baseball career, he pitched in 1966 and from 1968-1993 for the New York Mets, California Angels, Houston Astros and Texas Rangers. He was inducted into the Baseball Hall of Fame in 1999. Ryan, a hard-throwing, right-handed pitcher, threw pitches that were regularly recorded above 100 miles per hour. The high velocity remained throughout his career, even into his 40s. Ryan was also known to throw a devastating 12–6 curve ball at exceptional velocity. He has done numerous commercial endorsements over the years.

Rudy Tomjanovich, nicknamed Rudy T., is an American retired basketball player and coach who coached the Houston Rockets to two consecutive NBA championships. He was an All-Star forward for the Rockets during his playing career.

He was selected in the 1970 NBA Draft as the second overall pick by the San Diego Rockets (the franchise relocated to Houston in 1971), for whom he would play the entirety of his NBA career. He was the third-leading scorer in Rockets history behind Hall of Famers Calvin Murphy and Hakeem Olajuwon. The Rockets retired his #45 jersey upon the conclusion of his playing career.

Tomjanovich retired in 1981 and became a scout for two years before being named an assistant coach in 1983. He served as an assistant under Bill Fitch and Don Chaney. He was named the Rockets' interim head coach in February, 1992 after Chaney's resignation. He served as head coach from 1992-2003. He is currently a scout for the Los Angeles Lakers.

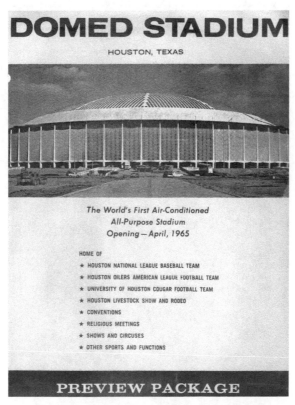

This is the original press kit for the opening of The Astrodome in 1965.

The very first Houston Astros baseball team lineup, from 1965.

The author of this book, Hank Moore (left) is posed in 1985 with Mary Lou Retton, five-time medalist at the 1984 Olympic Games.

Chapter 13

COMMUNITY SERVICE AND QUALITY OF LIFE LEGENDS

T his is the crossroads chapter of the book. All of the legends came together in support of the community, worthwhile causes, meaningful programs and the pursuit of a better quality of life for all.

I knew and worked with virtually everybody in this chapter. That's the power of non-profit volunteerism and community stewardship.

That's how I got to know other legends profiled in other chapters of this book, including George R. Brown, George Bush, Robert Finger, Oveta Culp Hobby, Ima Hogg, Ninfa Laurenzo, Ben Love, Carroll Masterson, George Strake, Lynn Wyatt and Marvin Zindler.

I worked with several Houston Mayors in community betterment projects, including Louie Welch, Fred Hofheinz, Jim McConn, Kathy Whitmire, Bob Lanier, Bill White, Lee Brown and Annise Parker. I advised city council members, state officials and national public figures.

It's all about giving back to the city in which we live and pockets of service where each of us can contribute. I believe that a good leader is also a community leader. Most companies want and need to give back to the communities in which they do business. The most successful ones realize that everyone wins by such activities. They also know that executives who serve on community boards will improve their leadership skills through the process, thus making them more valuable to the company.

By recognizing and praising corporate organizations, entrepreneurs, and company rising stars, they will try even harder to do better. Community stewardship programs are opportunities for involvement, achievement and commitment to the wider scope of business.

Ima Hogg was a philanthropist and patron of the arts. She was named for the heroine of a Civil War poem written by her uncle Thomas Elisha. She was affectionately known as Miss Ima for most of her long life. She was eight years old when her father was elected Governor of Texas. After her mother died of tuberculosis in 1895, Ima attended the Coronal Institute in San Marcos and in 1899 entered the University of Texas.

She started playing the piano at age three and in 1901 went to New York to study music. Her father's illness drew her back to Texas in 1905. After his death in 1906 she continued her music studies in Berlin and Vienna from 1907 to 1909. She then moved to Houston, where she gave piano lessons to a select group of pupils and helped found the Houston Symphony Orchestra, which played its first concert in June, 1913.

Miss Ima served as the first vice president of the Houston Symphony Society and became president in 1917. In the meantime, oil had been struck on the Hogg property near West Columbia, Texas, and by the late 1920's Miss Ima was involved in a wide range of philanthropic projects. In 1929, she founded the Houston Child Guidance Center, an agency to provide therapy and counseling for disturbed children and their families. In 1940, with a bequest from her brother Will, who had died in 1930, she established the Hogg Foundation for Mental Health at the University of Texas.

In 1943, Miss Hogg, a lifelong Democrat, won an election to the Houston school board, where she worked to establish symphony concerts for school children, to get equal pay for teachers regardless of sex or race, and to set up a painting-to-music program in the public schools.

In 1946, she again became president of the Houston Symphony Society, a post she held until 1956, and in 1948 she became the first woman president of the Philosophical Society of Texas. Since the 1920s, she had been studying and collecting early American art and antiques, and in 1966 presented her collection and Bayou Bend, the River Oaks mansion she and her brothers had built in 1927, to the Museum of Fine Arts in Houston. The Bayou Bend Collection, recognized as one of the finest of its kind, draws thousands of visitors each year.

In the 1950s Miss Ima restored the Hogg family home at Varner Plantation near West Columbia and in 1958 presented it to the state of Texas. It became Varner-Hogg Plantation State Historical Site. In the 1960s, she restored the Winedale Inn, a 19th Century stagecoach stop at Round Top, Texas, which she gave to the University of Texas. The Winedale Historical Center now serves as a center for the study of Texas history and is also the site of a widely acclaimed annual fine arts festival. Miss Hogg also restored her parents' home at Quitman, Texas, and in 1969 the town of Quitman established the Ima Hogg Museum in her honor.

In 1953, Texas Governor Allan Shivers appointed her to the State Historical Survey Committee (later the Texas Historical Commission), and in 1967 that body gave her an award for "meritorious service in historic preservation." In 1960 she served on a committee appointed by President Dwight D. Eisenhower for the planning of the National Cultural Center (now Kennedy Center) in Washington, D.C. In 1962, at the request of Jacqueline Kennedy, Ima Hogg served on an advisory panel to aid in the search for historic furniture for the White House.

In 1968 Miss Hogg was the first recipient of the Santa Rita Award, given by the University of Texas System to recognize contributions to the university and to higher education. In 1969 she, Oveta Culp Hobby, and Lady Bird Johnson became the first three women members of the Academy of Texas, an organization founded to honor persons who "enrich, enlarge, or enlighten" knowledge in any field. In 1971, Southwestern University gave Miss Hogg an honorary doctorate in fine arts, and in 1972 the National Society of Interior Designers gave her its Thomas Jefferson Award for outstanding contributions to America's cultural heritage.

Lyndall Wortham, civic leader and benefactor, was born in Sherman. After receiving a bachelor of arts degree and teaching certificate from the University of Texas in 1912, she taught in Galveston and New York City. She married Gus Wortham, whom she had known during their days at UT, on October 4, 1926, just after he organized American General Insurance Company. The couple made their home in Houston and had two daughters. Gus Wortham grew his company into a multi-million dollar business.

Lyndall Wortham devoted her energy to serving the Houston community. She volunteered in local hospitals and served the Harris County Cancer Society, Houston Speech and Hearing Center and Girlstown U.S.A.. She supported Theater under the Stars, Houston Grand Opera, Ballet Foundation of Houston, Miller Memorial Theater, and the Society for Performing Arts. Gus and Lyndall established the Wortham Foundation, through which they funded a fountain on Allen Parkway, plans for a Buffalo Bayou park and the Wortham IMAX theater at the Houston Museum of Natural Science. The foundation supported the Wortham Theater Center, a $72 million opera and ballet facility.

From 1963-1979, Mrs. Wortham served on the University of Houston's board of regents. She was also active in the YWCA, Houston Garden Club, Galveston Historical Foundation, Colonial Dames of America, Harris County Heritage Society, UT Ex-Students' Association and the American Foundation of Religion and Psychiatry in New York City. She died in 1980.

In 1907, an East End school teacher named Sybil Campbell enlisted the help of Alice Graham Baker to address an immediate need for an affordable nursery and kindergarten. Along with the Second Ward Women's Club, Mrs. Baker founded the Houston Settlement Association and served as the organization's first president. the Association's stated purpose was to extend "educational, industrial, social and friendly aid to all those within reach." The organization is now known as Neighborhood Centers Inc., with economic and social development programs serving 400,000 each year.

The Houston Livestock Show and Rodeo is the world's largest live entertainment and livestock exhibition. It has been held at NRG Stadium since 2003, previously held in the Astrodome. The rodeo has drawn some of the world's biggest recording artists, including Gene Autry, Roy Rogers & Dale Evans, Elvis Presley, Bob Dylan, Brooks & Dunn, George Strait, Garth Brooks,

Willie Nelson, Selena, Bon Jovi, ZZ Top, Taylor Swift and Lynyrd Skynyrd, among others.

Community Service Legends

Dr. J. Don Boney was an educator who served as an administrator in the Houston Independent School District, president of Houston Community College System and president of the University of Houston–Downtown. He served on Lieutenant Governor Bill Hobby's Special Committee on Human Services Delivery. He was on the Board of Directors of Entex, Inc., Riverside National Bank and the Better Business Bureau. His son, the Rev. Jew Don Boney, was a Houston City Council member.

Barbara Bush served as First Lady of the United States from 1989 to 1993. She is the mother of the 43rd President, George W. Bush, and of the 43rd Governor of Florida, Jeb Bush. Barbara Bush has supported and worked to advance the cause of universal literacy. She founded the Barbara Bush Foundation for Family Literacy while First Lady. Since leaving the White House, she has continued to advance this cause.

Kirbyjon Caldwell is pastor of Windsor Village United Methodist Church, a 14,000-member congregation. He was one of President George W. Bush's spiritual advisors.

John Connally was born in Floresville and graduated from the University of Texas. He served in the U.S. Navy during World War II. On his release from the Navy, he practiced law, until Lyndon Baines Johnson persuaded him to return to Washington, D.C. to serve as a key aide. At Johnson's request, in 1961, President Kennedy named Connally as Secretary of the Navy. He resigned 11 months later to run for the Texas governorship.

Connally ran as a conservative Democrat. I had an office at his headquarters, working for the campaign. He taught me one of the great lessons at that time. "Always put stamps on the envelopes correctly," Connally stated. "Everything that you do is symbolic of the thorough way that you handle important assignments. Consistency and quality matter." A masterful campaigner, he was elected in 1962. He served as Governor of Texas from 1963–1969. He signed into law the creation of the Texas Higher Education Coordinating Board. He appointed regents who backed the entry of women into previously all-male Texas A&M University in

College Station. He championed travel and tourism, including HemisFair '68, the world's fair held in San Antonio.

On Nov. 22, 1963, Connally was seriously wounded while riding in President Kennedy's car in Dallas when the president was assassinated. He recovered from wounds in his chest, wrist and thigh. In 1971, President Nixon appointed Connally as Treasury Secretary. Connally switched political parties in 1973.

Interstate 410 in San Antonio is named the Connally Loop in his honor. The Connally Memorial Medical Center in Floresville is named for John and his brothers Wayne and Merrill. The John Connally Unit of the Texas Corrections Department in Karnes County is named for him. There is also a Connally Plaza, with a life-sized statue in downtown Houston. The Texas A&M University System Offices, located in College Station, are housed in a building named for him. John B. Connally High School in Austin is named in his honor.

Nellie Connally was the First Lady of Texas from 1963-1969. She was the wife of John Connally, who served as Governor of Texas and later as Secretary of the Treasury. She was born in Austin and attended the University of Texas, where she was named "Sweetheart of the University" in 1938. Studying drama, she considered becoming an actress but gave up those plans after meeting John Connally, while attending UT in 1937. They married in 1940.

During her tenure as First Lady, Mrs. Connally created the gardens at the Texas Governor's Mansion and also collected the state silver. She and her husband were passengers in the presidential limousine carrying President John F. Kennedy when he was assassinated in Dallas on Nov. 22, 1963. While riding in the car, she said, "Mr. President, you can't say Dallas doesn't love you." Within a few seconds, she heard the first of what she later concluded were three gunshots in quick succession.

After serving as First Lady of Texas, Nellie Connally supported the Children's Miracle Network Telethon for Hermann Children's Hospital. She served on the University of Texas M.D. Anderson Cancer Center Board of Visitors, and a fund in her name raised millions for research and patient programs. She was named Woman of Distinction by the Crohn's & Colitis Foundation. She was a member of the Texas Historical Commission and helped to complete Tranquility Park.

Robert J. Cruikshank was managing partner at Deloitte Haskins & Sells. He served on the governing boards of the American Heart Association, Texas Children's

Hospital, the Institute of Religion, Fish Foundation, Museum of Science, the M.D. Anderson Board of Visitors and the University of Texas System.

Carolyn Farb is a social leader who has raised more than 35 million dollars for numerous charitable causes. She was the first Texan to raise a million dollars in a single gala, helped to raise more than $3 million in one campaign for the University of Houston and worked with other notable Houston celebrities to raise more than half a million dollars for tsunami relief. In 2011, she published her first children's book, "Lucas Comes to America."

Joseph Anthony Fiorenza is a prelate of the Catholic Church. He was the seventh Bishop and the first Archbishop of Galveston-Houston, serving from 1985-2006. He previously served as Bishop of San Angelo from 1979-1984.

Felix Fraga was the first of his brothers to graduate from high school. He got a scholarship to the University of Houston, where he played baseball. After that, he earned a master's degree in social work. He became one in the East End. For many years, he was the director of Ripley House, a community center where he used to play as a child. Felix served two terms on the HISD school board, then was elected to three terms on the Houston City Council, where he served three terms.

Dr. Norman Hackerman started his academic career in 1945 as a chemistry instructor at the University of Texas. I knew him in the 1960's, when he was president at UT. From 1970-1985, he was president of Rice University. In all of his executive years, Dr. Hackerman continued teaching freshman chemistry, believing that beginning students needed the best possible instruction.

In 2002, the Rice Board of Trustees established the Norman Hackerman Fellowship in Chemistry. In 2008, the original Experimental Science Building at the UT Austin campus was demolished and rebuilt as the Norman Hackerman Experimental Science Building in his honor. The main building at the J. Erik Jonsson Center of the National Academy of Sciences is Hackerman House, named in his honor. Hackerman House overlooks Quissett Harbor in Woods Hole, MA, on Cape Cod.

George Henry Hermann, oilman and philanthropist, was born in Houston on August 6, 1843. He served in the Texas Cavalry during the Civil War. He operated a sawmill in what is now Hermann Park, sold cordwood, cattle business and real estate. The discovery of oil at Humble in 1903 made him a millionaire. Afterward, he traveled extensively in America and Europe visiting physicians and hospitals.

Before his death, he donated Hermann Park to the city of Houston. The bulk of his estate, evaluated at $2.6 million, was willed to the city of Houston for the erection and maintenance of Hermann Hospital.

Joanne King Herring is a Houston socialite, political activist and businesswoman. Her second book, "Diplomacy and Diamonds: My Wars from the Ballroom to the Battlefield," was published in 2011. She was known as Joanne King when hosting a talk show on KHOU-TV, later on KPRC-TV. After marrying Robert Herring, she was active on the Houston social circuit, raising funds for worthwhile causes. She served as honorary consul to Pakistan and Morocco. In the 2007 movie "Charlie Wilson's War," Herring was portrayed by actress Julia Roberts. In 2009, Herring founded Marshall Plan Charities, which unites the efforts of various NGO's concerned with the Afghan people in hopes of providing villages with clean water, food, health care, schools and jobs, helping villages reduce reliance upon the Taliban.

John Hill was the only person to have served as Secretary of State of Texas, Texas Attorney General, and Chief Justice of the Texas Supreme Court. Hill went to work for a small law firm in Houston which gave him invaluable experience in trial work. In 1951, he founded his own Houston-based firm specializing in plaintiff's trial work. He was considered one of the top lawyers in Texas.

Hill's career in politics started as a county campaign manager for John Connally in Harris County during the 1964 gubernatorial campaign. In 1966, Connally appointed him Secretary of State. In 1968, he ran for governor. In 1972, Hill was elected as Attorney General. His most significant achievement was in consumer affairs, persuading the legislature to support a deceptive trade practices act providing triple damages for victims of unfair trade practices. In 1978, he again ran for governor.

Hill practiced law in Houston until 1984, when he was elected as Texas Supreme Court Chief Justice to succeed the retiring Jack Pope. Hill championed reform of the partisan election of judges and argued that judges should be selected based on merit, similar to the system used at the federal level. In 1997, Texas Governor George W. Bush called Hill from retirement, asking him to become a member of the Texas Lottery Commission following a scandal. His son Graham Hill is an attorney. His daughter Martha Hill Jamison is a judge. His daughter Melinda Hill Perrin is a member of the Texas Coalition for Excellence in Higher Education.

Dr. Phillip G. Hoffman was the fifth president of the University of Houston and the first chancellor of the University of Houston System. At UH, he was instrumental in obtaining state affiliation, transitioning to a racially integrated status and expanding enrollment in multiple locations. Upon retirement from the UH System, he served as President of the Texas Medical Center from 1981-1984.

Lyndon B. Johnson was a distinguished member of the U.S. House of Representatives, then the U.S. Senate, serving as Senate Majority Leader. He served as Vice President of the United States, then President. What many do not know is that, prior to his political career, LBJ was a school teacher in Houston. In the 1930-31 school year, LBJ taught public speaking at Sam Houston High School, coaching the student debate team to a state championship.

Barbara Jordan was the first African American to be elected to the Texas Senate after Reconstruction, the first southern black female elected to the United States House of Representatives and the first African-American woman to deliver the keynote address at a Democratic National Convention.

In 1974, Jordan made an influential, televised speech before the House Judiciary Committee supporting the process of impeachment of Richard Nixon as President. In 1975, she was appointed by Carl Albert, then Speaker of the United States House of Representatives, to the Democratic Steering and Policy Committee. Jordan retired from politics in 1979 and became an adjunct professor teaching ethics at the University of Texas at Austin Lyndon B. Johnson School of Public Affairs. She again was a keynote speaker at the Democratic National Convention in 1992. In 1994, Jordan was awarded the Presidential Medal of Freedom. On her death, Jordan became the first African-American woman to be buried in the Texas State Cemetery.

James Ketelsen was a CEO who put his retirement wealth to good purpose. As Chairman and CEO of Tenneco, he supported many causes, including being the founding name sponsor of the Houston Marathon. Tenneco supported educational initiatives, one of them being Communities in Schools, a scholarship program began in 1989 at Jeff Davis High School. That program spawned his non-profit foundation, Project GRAD. With his wife Kathryn, Jim spearheaded approaches to the challenges facing Houston's inner city schools.

Working with Jeff Davis, Ketelsen learned that one needed to reach kids long before high school, in order to encourage them to stay in school and become good citizens. His foundation realized that every school in the feeder pattern needed to benefit from Project GRAD (Graduation Really Achieves Dreams). The result is a system of curricular, methodological, and student and family support programs that help build academic skills, improve student behavior, address family needs and set children on the road to college. The foundation provides training and support to classroom teachers, along with reading, math and classroom management (leadership) curricula.

William A. Lawson taught bible studies at Texas Southern University, also becoming director of Upward Bound, a pre-college program for high school students. During his TSU years, residents persuaded him to establish a church near the university. Wheeler Avenue Baptist Church was opened in 1962. The congregation grew to 5,000 members and is much respected in the community. In 1996, a non-profit organization was named in his honor, the William A. Lawson Institute for Peace and Prosperity.

Mickey Leland was an effective spokesman for hungry people in the United States and throughout the world. During six terms in the Congress, six years as a Texas state legislator and, Democratic National Committee official, he gave attention on issues of health and hunger, marshaling support that resulted in public and private action. Leland died on a 1989 mission to an isolated refugee camp, Fugnido, in Ethiopia, which sheltered thousands of unaccompanied children fleeing the civil conflict in neighboring Sudan.

Harris Masterson III, philanthropist and native Houstonian, attended San Jacinto High School, the New Mexico Military Institute and Rice Institute during the 1930's. He served as an intelligence officer in World War II and as an instructor during the Korean conflict. Carroll Sterling married Harris Masterson in 1951. She died in 1994.

Harris and Carroll Masterson were deeply involved in the culture and arts of their Houston community. Their philanthropic interests included the Wortham Center, Houston Grand Opera, Houston Museum of Natural Science, Houston Ballet, Houston Symphony, Alley Theatre, Houston area hospitals and the YWCA.

The Mastersons' relationship with the Museum of Fine Arts began in 1953. In addition to donations made to the MFAH over the years, the Mastersons gifted Rienzi, their River Oaks home, to the museum in 1991. Their collection of European decorative arts, including extensive holdings of Worcester porcelain, had been previously given to the museum. The museum assumed control of Rienzi following Mr. Masterson's death and opened it as a center for European decorative arts, now offering tours.

Cynthia Woods Mitchell was known as a patron of the arts, impassioned environmentalist and avid historical preservationist. Her other causes included Boy Scouts, Girl Scouts and Texas Children's Hospital. She and George Mitchell were married in 1943.

In the 1970's, Mitchell launched plans for The Woodlands, a planned community north of Houston. Cynthia Mitchell picked the new development's name. She and her husband breathed new life into economically bypassed Galveston, George Mitchell's hometown. She was instrumental in creating the University of Houston's Cynthia Woods Mitchell Center for the Arts.

Also named: the George and Cynthia Mitchell Center for Neurodegenerative Diseases at the University of Texas Medical Branch-Galveston and the George P. and Cynthia Mitchell Center for Research on Alzheimer's Disease and Related Brain Disorders at the University of Texas Health Science Center in Houston.

Hanni Orton was the wife of Stewart Orton, the long-time CEO of Foley's. She took plates of brownies to the Foley's parking lot attendants and made comparable gestures for other employees. She personally oversaw one of Foley's signature community activities, the Savvy Award, given each year to three top community leaders. I was one of the recipients of that awards on April 12, 1989, along with news anchor Ron Stone and social program leader Sister Helem Gay. Each year, she hosted a reunion party for past honorees at her River Oaks high-rise, and we welcomed in the next honorees. Her other causes included the Houston Symphony and Planned Parenthood.

John Osteen was the founder and first pastor of Lakewood Church in Houston, from its beginnings in 1959 until his death in 1999. Holding a doctorate from Oral Roberts University, he started what is now Lakewood Church in what was described as a "dusty, abandoned feed store" in northeast Houston. He hosted a weekly television program for 16 years, reaching millions in the U.S. and other countries with his interpretation of the Gospel. His books, cassettes and videotapes were widely distributed.

Joel Osteen succeeded his father as pastor in 1999. His ministry is seen by seven million broadcast viewers weekly and 20 million monthly in 100 nations around the world. His books include "Your Best Life Now," "Become a Better You," "It's Your Time," "Every Day a Friday" and "I Declare," #1 national bestsellers. In 2003, Lakewood Church acquired the Compaq Center, former home of the NBA Houston Rockets.

Dr. Rod Paige moved from classroom teacher to college dean and school superintendent to be the first African American to serve as the nation's education chief. From 1971-1975, Paige served as head football coach at Texas Southern University, and served as the university's athletic director. Dr. Paige was a teacher at TSU from 1980-1984 and became Dean of the College of Education.

Dr. Paige was a trustee and an officer of the Board of Education of Houston Independent School District (HISD) from 1989-1994 and was superintendent of HISD from 1994-2001. President George W. Bush appointed Dr. Paige as Secretary of Education, a post which he held from 2001-2004.

Judson Robinson Sr., was a founding member of the Houston Area Urban League, a nonprofit, community-based United Way agency with a mission to provide economic assistance and job resources to minorities.

Judson Robinson Jr. became the first African-American elected to Houston City Council in 1971. He was re-elected nine times and served twice as mayor pro tem. He fought for better working conditions for Sanitation Department employees, insisted that the Houston Fire Department and Police Department hire minorities and urged the city to build parks and libraries in disadvantaged neighborhoods. A Houston elementary school, library and community center bear his name.

Judson Robinson III was elected in 1990 to Houston City Council, where he served three terms. He is also the president and chief executive officer of the Houston Area Urban League.

George William Strake Jr. is a Houston businessman and philanthropist who served as Texas Secretary of State from January 16 1979-1981. He is chairman and president of Strake Energy, Inc. His activities include the Council for National Policy, Greater Houston Partnership's World Trade Supervisory Board, the Albert and Ethel Herzstein Foundation, Strake Foundation, Notre Dame College of Arts & Letters Advisory Council, Boy Scouts of America, San Jacinto Museum of History, Free Interprise Board, Nimitz Museum and restoration of the USS Cavalla (SS-244), which saw action during World War II in the Pacific theatre. In 1990, Strake was co-chairman of the host committee of the Houston Economic Summit of Industrialized Nations, held on the campus of Rice University.

Albert Thomas was a Congressman from Houston for 29 years and was responsible for bringing the Johnson Space Center to Houston. He moved to Houston in 1930 to become Assistant United States Attorney for the Southern District of Texas. In 1936, Thomas was elected to the U.S. House of Representatives.

He became chairman of the House Appropriations Committee's subcommittee on defense. In that capacity, he was able to steer projects to Texas including supporting Johnson's proposal to build the Corpus Christi Naval Air Station. Thomas served on the Joint Committee on Atomic Energy and was instrumental in securing the NASA's Manned Spacecraft Center in Houston in 1961. The center has served as mission control for every U.S. manned space flight.

On what turned out to be the last night of his life, President John F. Kennedy attended a dinner honoring the congressman on Nov. 21, 1963, with 3,200 attendees at the event. That night, Kennedy said, "Next month, when the United States of America fires the largest booster in the history of the world into space for the first time, giving us the lead, fires the largest, payload into space, giving us the lead. The United States next month will have a leadership in space, which wouldn't have without Albert Thomas. And so will this city." Thomas traveled with the Presidential party to Dallas, where the next day President Kennedy was assassinated. Thomas witnessed the swearing in of President Lyndon B. Johnson on Air Force One.

By the time of his death on Feb. 15, 1966, Thomas ranked eleventh in seniority in the House. In the fall of 1967, downtown Houston's Albert Thomas Convention and Exhibit Center was built and named in his honor.

Mark White practiced law in Houston, then served as the state's assistant attorney general. From 1973-1977, White was Texas Secretary of State. From 1979-81, he was Attorney General. From 1983-1987, he was Governor of Texas.

Dr. Martha Wong was the first Asian American woman to be elected to the Texas House of Representatives, representing Houston's District 134. In 1993, she became the Houston City Council's first elected Asian American Councilwoman, and was elected to three successive terms. A career educator, she was once served as principal at an elementary school in Meyerland. She walked door-to-door, re-acquainting residents of the value of a good public school education. She later served as an administrator with Houston Community College.

Lynn Wyatt is the daughter of Bernard Sakowitz and the sister of Robert T. Sakowitz. She is a Houston socialite, philanthropist and third-generation Texan. Her husband, Oscar Wyatt, is an energy executive, the founder of Houston's Coastal Corporation—now owned by El Paso Corporation—and current CEO of NuCoastal LLC.

In 1977, Lynn was inducted into the International Best Dressed List Hall of Fame. In 1982, the Government of France honored her with admission to the prestigious Order of Arts and Letters, rank of Chevalier, for her significant contribution to the enrichment of the French cultural inheritance. In 2007, the French government promoted her to the Order's rank of Officier. She received the Woodson Medal from the Houston Forum. To benefit the Red Cross and the American Hospital of Paris, she chaired the annual Bal de la Rose in Monaco. Prince Rainier asked her to be a Founding Trustee of the Princess Grace Foundation U.S.A. (on which Board she continues to serve). President Ronald Reagan appointed her to the Board of the U.S. Naval Academy, serving for eight years.

John Henry "Jack" Yates was an African-American slave and later minister who became influential in the community. Yates and his family moved to Houston in 1865. He later purchased an area in the Freedmen's Town area of the Fourth Ward.

In 1868, Yates became the pastor of Antioch Missionary Baptist Church, Houston's first African-American Baptist church. He established Houston Academy, a school for African-American children. He died in 1897. Yates High School in Houston was named after him. The house he occupied in the Fourth Ward was later moved to Sam Houston Park. At Antioch, the original pews, made by hand, are still being used.

Potlache

Potlache is the ultimate catalyst toward Customer Focused Management. It means extra gifts, beyond value-added, visionary mindset and the ultimate achievement of the organization.

The word "potlache" is a native American expression, meaning "to give." For American Indians, the potlache was an immensely important winter ceremony featuring dancing, food and gift giving. Potlache ceremonies were held to observe major life events. The native Americans would exchange gifts and properties to show wealth and status. Instead of the guests bringing gifts to the family, the family gave gifts to the guests.

Colonists settled and started doing things their own way, without first investigating local customs. They alienated many of the natives. Thus, the cultural differences widened. The more diverse we become, the more we really need to learn from and about others. The practice of doing so creates an understanding that spawns better loyalty.

When one gives ceremonial gifts, one gets extra value because of the spirit of the action. The more you give, the more you ultimately get back in return. Reciprocation becomes an esteemed social ceremony. It elevates the givers to higher levels of esteem in the eyes of the recipients.

Potlache is a higher level of understanding of the business that breeds loyalty and longer-term support. It leads to increased quality, better resource management, higher employee productivity, reduced operating costs, improved cash management, better management overall and enhanced customer loyalty and retention.

The Business Leader as Community Leader

In eras following downturns and scandals, it is incumbent upon good companies to go the extra distance to be ethical and set good examples. Demonstrating visible caring for communities by company executives is the ultimate form of potlache.

No matter the size of the organization, goodwill must be banked. Every company must make deposits for those inevitable times in which withdrawals will be made.

To say that business and its communities do not affect each other, is short-sighted...and will make business the loser every time. Business marries the community that it settles with. The community has to be given a reason to care for the business. Business owes its well-being and livelihood to its communities.

Business leaders have an obligation to serve on community boards and be very visible in the communities in which they do business. If done right, community stewardship builds executives into better leaders, as well as receiving deserved credit for the company. Civic service is the ultimate way to steer heir apparents toward the leadership track.

Communities are clusters of individuals, each with its own agenda. In order to be minimally successful, each company must know the components of its home community intimately. Each company has a business stake for doing its part. Community relations in reality is a function of self-interest, rather than just being a good citizen.

Companies should support off-duty involvement of employees in pro bono capacities but not take unfair credit. Volunteers are essential to community relations. Companies must show tangible evidence of supporting the community by assigning key executives to high-profile community assignments. Create a formal volunteer guild, and allow employees the latitude and creativity to contribute to the common good. Celebrate and reward their efforts.

Publicity and promotions should support effective community relations and not be the substitute or smokescreen for the process. Recognition is as desirable for the community as for the business. Good news shows progress and encourages others to participate.

The well-rounded community relations program embodies all elements: accessibility of company officials to citizens, participation by the company in business and civic activities, public service promotions, special events, plant communications materials and open houses, grassroots constituency building and good citizenry.

No entity can operate without affecting or being affected by its communities. Business must behave like a guest in its communities, never failing to give potlache or return courtesies.

Community acceptance for one project does not mean than the job of community relations has been completed. It is not "insurance" that can be bought overnight. It is tied to the bottom line and must be treated accordingly, with the resources and expertise to do it effectively. It is a bond of trust that, if violated, will haunt the business. If steadily built, the trust can be exponentially parlayed into successful long-term business relationships.

*The author of this book, Hank Moore (left) is posed in 1967
with Texas Governor John Connally at a gala ball.*

*The first reunion of Houston mayors took place in 1987 at
a charity fund raising event. Pictured (left to right) are Jim
McConn, Louie Welch, Kathy Whitmire and Neal Pickett.
Also participating was former Mayor Fred Hofheinz.*

Chapter 14

STREETS, BUILDINGS
AND PROGRAMS NAMED
FOR THE LEGENDS

There are about 50,000 streets in Harris County. Many of the street names give us some history of the area.

Some streets were named for heroes of Texas history, including Travis, Austin, Lamar, Milam, Houston, Pease, McKinney, Hamilton, Crockett, Deaf Smith, Preston, Walker, Franklin, Smith, Ruiz, Bissonnet, Bell, Dunlavy, Calhoun, Holman and Rusk.

Some streets were named for universities, including Cambridge, Harvard, Oxford, Yale, Marquette, Wakeforest, Amherst, Vanderbilt, Annapolis, Case, Oberlin, Southwestern, Northwestern, Rutgers, Villanova and Duke.

Some streets were named for writers, including Shakespeare, Longfellow, Browning, Chaucer, Byron, Wordsworth, Addison, Pemberton, Milton, Watts, Colleridge and Swift.

Some streets were named for states, including Alabama, California, Indiana, Texas, Carolina, Louisiana, Nevada, Michigan, Vermont and Missouri.

Some streets were named for heroes of U.S. history, including Thomas Jefferson, Ulysses S. Grant, Henry Clay, James K. Polk, Martin Luther King and Andrew Jackson.

Some streets were named for other cities, including Dallas, Austin, Portland, Fargo, Richmond, San Felipe, Katy, Pittsburg, Chevy Chase, Lubbock and Washington. The Katy Freeway connected to the city of Katy and ran parallel to the Missouri, Kansas and Texas railroad.

Stella Link was a road that ran parallel to a railroad line connecting the city of Bellaire with the Stella, Texas, station for the International-Great Northern and the Texas & New Orleans Railroads.

Streets Named for Legends

Business leaders have been remembered via street names. Ross Sterling and Walter Fondren were two founders of the Humble Oil & Refining Company.

Michael Louis Westheimer, was a German immigrant and flour mill operator, whose name is used for a major east-west thoroughfare.

Allen Parkway is named for Augustus Allen and John Kirby Allen, the land developers who originally settled Houston. They paid $1.40 per acre for 6,642 acres of land near Buffalo Bayou.

August Gessner moved from Germany 1886. He fought in the Spanish-American War with Teddy Roosevelt and later built a monument to the Rough Riders in Puerto Rico before coming to Houston and establishing himself in business as a cabinet-maker. When Harris County was building a north-south way on the west side, they needed a name. County Commissioner E.A. Squatty Lyons suggested: "I went to school with this nice guy named Gessner. We could name it for him."

Henry Frederick MacGregor, Houston businessman, moved to Houston in 1873 and for the next 50 years he was associated with a variety of Texas commercial ventures. He was general manager of the Houston Railroad System from 1883-

1903. After 1903, he was involved with real estate and other investments as well as State Land-Oil Company, The Houston Post, Bay and Bayou Company, South Texas Commercial

John Henry Kirby was a lumberman and capitalist. Because of Kirby, early professional baseball in Houston survived and set all in motion for the long banner life of the Houston Buffalos through 1961.

Oscar Holcombe was an engineer who developed the three-light traffic signal. He later served as Mayor of Houston. Mayor Oscar Holcombe was a politician who stood up to the Ku Klux Klan back in the 1920's, loosening their hate-mongering control of things and freeing Houston for future growth.

Tom Tellepsen led an industrial building contractor firm that is still active after 105 years.

Zindler Street was named for Benjamin Zindler, who founded a men and boys clothing store in 1888. His grandson was Marvin Zindler, the iconic media figure.

Hiram Clarke was an employee of Houston Lighting and Power.

Streets were named for retail merchants, including Cornelius Ennis, B.A. Shepherd, W.J. Hutchins, Thomas Bagby and Samuel McIlhenney.

Rice Boulevard was named after Rice University, which was named for William Marsh Rice.

David Underwood Boulevard is named for the chairman of the Texas Medical Center board.

Richard J.V. Johnson Street, also in the Medical Center, was named for the long-time president of The Houston Chronicle.

John H. Freeman was the original chairman of the board of the Texas Medical Center, when it was founded in 1945.

Bertner Avenue is named for Ernst William Bertner, M.D., the first president of the MD Anderson Cancer Center and the Texas Medical Center.

Ezekiel Wimberly Cullen was an early legislator, jurist and lawyer. He moved from Georgia to Texas in 1835 and settled at San Augustine, where he established a law practice. In 1835, he joined the Texas revolutionary forces and participated in the siege of Bexar. While representing San Augustine County in the House of Representatives of the Third Congress of the Republic (1838–39), where he was chairman of the education committee, he sponsored the Cullen Act, which started land endowments for public schools and universities, thus laying the basis for an eventual Texas public-education system.

In 1839, President Mirabeau B. Lamar appointed Cullen to a judgeship, vacant after the death of Shelby Corzine. Cullen practiced law in San Augustine until 1850, when he was appointed purser in the United States Navy. He lived for a time in Pensacola, Florida, and later in Washington, D.C. Noted oilman and philanthropist Hugh Roy Cullen was his grandson. The Ezekiel Cullen Building on the University of Houston campus, constructed in 1950, was named in his honor.

Cullen Boulevard by the University of Houston was named for Hugh Roy Cullen, Quintana Petroleum Company, the wildly successful oil man who gave millions to Houston charities over the years, especially to the University of Houston, Baylor University and most of Houston's major hospitals.

Mykawa Road was named for the Japanese farmer who introduced rice farming to the area. Texmatti Drive in Katy is named after Texmati rice, a blend of Indian basmati and Texas long grain rice.

Community leaders have been remembered via street names. T.C. Jester was a minister. Mylie Durham was a physician in the Heights. Dick Dowling was a Civil War veteran.

Crawford Street was named for Joseph Tucker Crawford, a British agent who was sent to Houston in 1837 to evaluate the developing situation in the newly formed Republic of Texas.

Will Clayton Parkway by Bush Intercontinental Airport was named for Will Clayton, a founder of the Anderson Clayton Company.

Staff Sergeant Macario Garcia Street (formerly 75th Street) is named for a World War II hero who captured German machine gun nest. Garcia earned a Purple Heart, a Bronze Star and a Combat Infantryman Badge.

Unique Name Choices

Developer and former mayor Bob Lanier used to name streets in one of his subdivisions to commemorate his love of roses. Those streets included American Beauty, Summer Snow, King's Ransom, Tropicana and Carrousel. Lanier has a boat named for him, part of the fleet of ferries from Galveston island.

Names of land developers appeared. Winrock Street was named for Winthrop Rockefeller, who served as the Governor of Arkansas. The south Texas town Weslaco was named for the W.E. Stewart Land Company.

Edloe Street is an abbreviation for the name of real estate developer Edward Lilo Crane.

Some streets in a Pasadena neighborhood were named for Kentucky Derby winners.

Inwood Street is named after the Inwood Country Club in Long Island, New York.

Lyons Avenue was named after John Lyons, a saloon owner. It was previously named Odin Street, after John Mary Odin, the first Catholic bishop in the Diocese of Galveston.

Rankin Road is named for George Clark Rankin, a Methodist minister who saved souls in the saloons and gambling halls of early boomtown Houston.

T.C. Jester was named for the pastor of the Baptist Temple, corner of 20th Street and Rutland in the Heights.

La Rue Street was named for La Rue Sachs, a resident of freedman's town who was run over by a streetcar.

Neighborhoods around the Johnson Space Center reflect its mission with streets named Saturn, Gemini, Jupiter and Mercury.

A couple of streets survived from the era in which Texas had pari-mutuel betting and a horse track. There is a street called Epsom. There is a street called Downs. But there is no trace of the stadium or stables where Epsom Downs was located.

There are a few street names that are no longer used. In 1954, my family came to Houston to visit with my aunt and uncle. They lived on Danville Street. Aunt Cele and Uncle Byron told us that the next visit would be at a new house because they were asked to leave the property. The city had exercised its right of eminent domain and needed to clear Danville Street (running between Lexington and Vassar) to build something new called a freeway.

Danville Street and part of Vassar were scooped out to build the Southwest Freeway. That's why the section of Vassar between Woodhead and Shepherd is half a street. Their home was located where the Hazard overpass crosses the freeway. There is only one block where the Danville Street sign is posted, and it is by Buffalo Speedway and Highway 59.

In 1907, the community of Peck was renamed Tomball in honor of local congressman Thomas Henry Ball, who had a major role in the development of the Port of Houston.

Buildings Named for Legends

Niels Esperson came from Denmark and went into the oil business. The Humble field made him millions, which he diversified. A skyscraper with a six-story Grecian top was built by his wife Mellie in 1927, named in his honor. A companion structure, the Mellie Esperson Building, was added in 1941.

Houston's first airport was named in honor of former Governor William P. Hobby. It opened in 1927 as a private landing field in a 600-acre pasture known as W.T. Carter Field. The airfield was served by Braniff and Eastern Airlines. It was acquired by the city of Houston and named Houston Municipal Airport in 1937. It was renamed Howard R. Hughes Airport in 1938. The city of Houston opened a new terminal and hangar in 1940. In 1967 the airport was renamed after former Texas governor William P. Hobby. Intercontinental Airport opened in 1969, and all airlines at Hobby moved there. Airline flights resumed at Hobby in 1971. Hobby has steadily grown from regional airport to international status.

Houston's second airport, Intercontinental (IAH), was re-named in honor of former President George H.W. Bush. The land was purchased in 1957 and named Jetero. The City of Houston annexed the area in 1965.

Houston Intercontinental Airport opened in 1969. In 1988, Terminal D was renamed for Congressman Mickey Leland. In 1997, the Houston City Council voted unanimously to rename the airport after George H. W. Bush, the 41st President of the United States.

The third airport is Ellington Field, which has the distinction of having all five military branches of the U.S. Department of Defense, the Army, Navy and Marine Reserve units, Army and Air National Guard, in addition Coast Guard and NASA operations, on one base. It was built in 1917 and named after Lt. Eric Lamar Ellington, an Army pilot killed four years earlier in a plane crash in San Diego.

During World War I, Ellington served as an advanced flight training base. As of 1918, Ellington had its own gunnery and bombing range on a small peninsula in the Gulf of Mexico near San Leon. World War II helped re-establish Ellington Field as an active facility. It was the site for advanced flight training for bomber pilots and the USAAC Bombardier School, also known as "the Bombardment Academy of the Air." Ellington Field was officially inactivated by the Air Force in 1976 and all Air Force Reserve squadrons were transferred to other military facilities. Still maintaining a presence at Ellington are the Texas Air National Guard, Texas Army National Guard, U.S. Army Reserve, U.S. Navy Reserve, U.S. Marine Corps Reserve and the U.S. Coast Guard. In 1984, the City of Houston purchased Ellington to use as a third civil airport and was renamed Ellington Airport, while the military cantonment area is known as Ellington Field Joint Reserve Base and Coast Guard Air Station Houston.

NASA's space center in Clear Lake was named in honor of former President Lyndon B. Johnson. Also named in his honor was Lyndon B. Johnson General Hospital, located in the Texas Medical Center.

Sylvan Rodriguez Elementary School was named for the late Channel 11 news anchor.

Jones Hall, the performing arts auditorium, is named for Jesse H. Jones, as is the Jones Library at the Texas Medical Center.

Yates High School in Houston was named after Jack Yates, pastor of Antioch Missionary Baptist Church.

Barbara Jordan High School was named in tribute of the distinguished member of Congress.

A federal building is named for the late Congressman Mickey Leland.

The Albert Thomas Convention Center was named for the member of Congress who served the area for 29 years. Thomas was instrumental in bringing NASA to the area.

The George R. Brown Convention Center was named to remember an engineering and building leader. It was named for George R. Brown of Brown & Root.

Hofheinz Pavilion on the University of Houston campus is named for Roy M. Hofheinz, former Houston mayor and Harris County Judge.

The Cynthia Woods Mitchell Pavilion is named for the arts patron.

Frank Sharp named his planned community Sharpstown.

Gus Wortham was chairman of the board and chief executive officer of American General Insurance Corporation from 1926-1976. He built civic support for cultural activities and parks through the Wortham Foundation.

Public places in Houston that are named for him include the Wortham Theater Center, Gus Wortham Park, Gus Wortham Memorial Fountain, Wortham Fountain at the Texas Medical Center, Wortham House (home of the University of Houston chancellor), Wortham IMAX Theater at the Museum of Natural Science, Wortham World of Primates at the Houston Zoo and Wortham Tower in the American General Center.

Houston's Carnegie Library was built on a grant from and named for steel tycoon Andrew Carnegie.

The Hobby Center for the Performing Arts is named for the entire Hobby family.

Programs Named for Legends

Harris County, originally called Harrisburg County, was named for John R. Harris. The New York native platted the town in 1826. He built a home and store and in 1829 began assembling a steam sawmill in partnership with others. He died of yellow fever, while in New Orleans on business. Harrisburg was absorbed by Houston in 1926,

Herman Brown Park sits on the city's northeast side. It was named for Herman Brown of Brown & Root.

Strake Jesuit College Preparatory is named for oil titan George Strake.

The M.D. Anderson Cancer Center is named for Monroe Dunaway Anderson, founder of the Anderson Clayton Company.

Bayou Bend was the residence of Miss Ima Hogg. It is now a museum.

The Hogg Foundation for Mental Health was named in honor of Miss Ima's father and brother.

The Blaffer Art Gallery is named for the family of Robert E. Blaffer, one of the founders of the Humble Oil & Refining Company.

MacGregor Park is named for Henry F. MacGregor. He was one of the organizers of the Houston Symphony and donated the land for St. Agnes Academy.

The John C. Freeman Weather Museum is named for a meteorologist who conducted research for several major companies and organizations. Some of his most notable work includes being a forecaster and researcher for the U.S. Army Air Force, U.S. Weather Bureau, Texas A&M University, Gulf Consultants, and the National Engineering Science Company. He has also conducted research at the University of Chicago, the Institute for Advanced Study. He was the founding Director of the Institute for Storm Research.

Miller Memorial Outdoor Theater was built in Hermann Park in the 1920's, named for Jesse Miller. It was opened and still operates as a free performing arts open-air venue, hosting a variety of concerts, plays, festivals and public events each year.

The Leonel Castillo Community Center is named for the first Hispanic to be elected to citywide office. In 1972, he was elected Houston City Controller. In 1977, President Jimmy Carter appointed Castillo to serve as Commissioner of the Immigration and Naturalization Service. He continued to accept appointments to several posts in city and county offices over the years while also mentoring as a social work instructor at the University of Houston.

Chapter 15

SCHOOLS WHICH THE LEGENDS ATTENDED

Austin High School
Harold Farb
Eva Guzman

Bellaire High School
Laurie Bricker
Richard Linklater
Randall Onstead
Dennis Quaid
Randy Quaid
Steve Radack
Brent Spiner

Jeff Davis High School
Felix Fraga
Gene Green
Mickey Newbury
Kenny Rogers
Gracie Saenz

Furr High School
Paula Arnold

High School for the Performing and Visual Arts
Lisa Hartman Black

Andre Hayward
Beyonce Knowles
Chandra Wilson

Sam Houston High School
John C. Freeman

Humble High School
R.E. "Bob" Smith

Jones High School
JoBeth Williams

Kashmere High School
Kirbyjon Caldwell

Katy High School
Renée Zellweger

Klein High School
Matt Bomer

Lamar High School
Lauren Anderson
Jack S. Blanton
Buddy Brock
Jonathan Day
Linda Ellerbee
Robert Foxworth
Johnny B. Holmes Jr.
Kelly Rowland
Tommy Sands
Jaclyn Smith
Tommy Tune

Mark White
Marvin Zindler

Lee High School
Billy Gibbons
Ron Stone Jr.

Memorial High School
Paul Bettencourt
Anne Clutterbuck
Michael Dell
Graham Hill
John Norris
Ted Poe
Dominique Sachse
Chase Untermeyer
David Weekley

Milby High School
Mike Barajas
Michael Berryhill
Fentress Bracewell
Gordon Quan

North Shore High School
Mary Gibbs

Reagan High School
Red Adair
Mary Kay Ash
Racehorse Haynes
Dan Rather
Martha Wong

San Jacinto High School
Walter Cronkite
Denton Cooley
A.J. Foyt
Richard J.V. Johnson
Harris Masterson
Glenn McCarthy
Kathy Whitmire

Sharpstown High School
Dr. Michael J. Reardon
Dr. Patrick R. Reardon
Margaret Spellings

St. John's School
Wes Anderson
Katherine Center
Molly Ivins
Peter Roussel

St. Thomas High School
Lupe Fraga
George Strake Jr.

Stafford High School
Clint Black
Marc Ostrovsky

Stephen F. Austin High School in Austin
Hank Moore
Jane Moore Taylor
Julie Moore

Sterling High School
Yolanda Adams
Clyde Drexler
Zina Garrison

Waltrip High School
Shelley Duvall
Patrick Swayze
John Whitmire

Washington High School
Jennifer Holliday
Westbury High School
Bob Allen
Joan Severance

Wheatley High School
Archie Bell
Harold V. Dutton
Al Edwards
Illinois Jacquet
Barbara Jordan
Hubert Laws
El Franco Lee
Mickey Leland
Joe Sample

Yates High School
Debbie Allen
Conrad Johnson
Phylicia Rashad

Baylor University
Crystal Bernard

Howard E. Butt Jr.
Price Daniel
Thomas W. Horton
Tom Kennedy
Drayton McLane
Willie Nelson
Ann Richards
Mark White

Blinn College
Dan Kubiak
Gus Mutscher
Cam Newton

Carleton College
Kirbyjon Caldwell

Colorado School of Mines
George R. Brown

Harvard University
Tony Chase
Tommy Lee Jones
Robert Sakowitz
George Strake Jr.
Jack Valenti

Hill's Business College
Jesse Jones

Houston Baptist University
Ron Stone
Ed Young

Howard University
Debbie Allen
Phylicia Rashad

Lon Morris College
Sandy Duncan

Massey Business College
Joseph Weingarten

Ohio State University
Dr. Phillip G. Hoffman

Pan American College
Donna Fujimoto Cole

Prairie View A&M University
J. Don Boney
Charles Brown
Emanuel Cleaver

Princeton University
Dudley C. Sharp
Harry Wiess

Purdue University
Gerald Hines

Rice University
Bill Archer
James Baker
Lance Berkman
George R. Brown
William Broyles Jr.

Jack Boyd Buckley
Candace Bushnell
Robert Cruikshank
Thomas H. Cruikshank
L. John Doerr
Charles Duncan
Lynn Eisenhans
John C. Freeman
Alberto Gonzales
William P. Hobby Jr.
Roy Hofheinz
Howard Hughes
John Kline
Fred C. Koch
James E. Lyon
Harris Masterson
Larry McMurtry
Seth Irwin Morris
Hermann Joseph Muller
Annise Parker
David Rhodes
Hector Ruiz
Albert Thomas
Jim Turley
Peggy Whitson

Sam Houston State University
Dana Andrews
Timothy Frank
Ed Gerlach
Gibson D. Lewis
Richard Linklater
Dan Rather
Charlie Wilson

Ralph Yarborough

Southern Methodist University
Kathy Bates
Powers Boothe
Laura Bush
William P. Clements
John Culberson
Kirbyjon Caldwell
Roy M. Huffington
Karen Hughes
Lamar Hunt
Jerry LeVias
Harriet Miers
Dennis Murphree
Lamar Smith
Aaron Spelling

Southwestern University
Pete Cawthon
J. Frank Dobie
Bill Engvall
Will Hogg
John Tower

St. Louis University
George W. Strake

Stephen F. Austin State University
O.A. "Bum" Phillips

Texas A&M University
A.D. Bruce
George H.W. Bush

Earle Cabell
Henry Cisneros
Ryan Crocker
James DeAnda
Dr. Red Duke
Lupe Fraga
Ed Garza
Phil Gramm
Patricia Gras
Gerald D. Griffin
Norman Hackerman
Michael T. Halbouty
Ty Hardin
Garry Mauro
Glenn McCarthy
Peyton McKnight
George P. Mitchell
Rick Noriega
Rick Perry
James Earl Rudder
Rip Torn
Frank Vandiver
Oscar Wyatt

Texas A&M University at Kingsville (A&I)
Buster Brown
Eva Longoria
Dwayne Nix
General Ricardo Sanchez

Texas Christian University
Kyle Bass
Betty Buckley

Bob Lilly
Winthrop Rockefeller
H.B. Zachry
Donald Zale

Texas Southern University
Yolanda Adams
Kenny Burrough
Rodney Ellis
Barbara Jordan
Mickey Leland
Senfronia Thompson

Texas State University (SWTSU)
Powers Boothe
Buster Brown
Lyndon B. Johnson
General Robert L. Rutherford
John Sharp
George Strait

Texas Tech University
Jerry Allison
Bob Bullock
Waggoner Carr
Richard E. Cavazos
John Denver
George Eads
Natalie Maines
Randall Onstead
Scott Pelley
Preston Smith
Charles "Tex" Thornton

University of Denver

Welcome Wilson Jr.

University of Houston

Edward Albee

Erik Barajas

Mike Barajas

Otis Birdsong

Peter C. Bishop

Larry Blyden

J. Don Boney

Joe Bowman

Peter Breck

Buddy Brock

A.D. Bruce

Tony Campise

Rod Canion

Hugh Roy Cullen

Clyde Drexler

Steve Edwards

Tilman Fertitta

Felix Fraga

Vanessa Gilmore

Alberto Gonzales

Elvin Hayes

Racehorse Haynes

Fred Hofheinz

Roy Hofheinz

Larry Hovis

Kevin James

Tom Jarriel

Star Jones

Tom Landry

Carl Lewis

Guy Lewis

Patricia Lykos

Dave Marr

Maxine Mesinger

John Moores

Barry Munitz

Richard W. Murray

Jim Nantz

Hakeem Olajuwon

John O'Quinn

Wade Phillips

Cindy Pickett

Ted Poe

Dennis Quaid

Randy Quaid

Dan Rather

Jennifer Reyna

Kenny Rogers

Clyde Roller

Peter Roussel

Dominique Sachse

Hyman Judah Schachtel

Kenneth Schnitzer

Margaret Spellings

Brent Spiner

Allen Stanford

Patsy Swayze

Henry Taub

Tom Tellez

Ron Trevino

Tommy Tune

Sylvester Turner

Jack Valenti

Richard Van Horn

Townes Van Zandt
John Whitmire
Kathryn J. Whitmire
Welcome Wilson Sr.
Gene Wolfe
Melvin Wolff
Martha Wong
Cynthia Woods Mitchell
Robert Wuhl
Bill Yeoman
Judith Zaffarini

University of North Texas
Dick Armey
Joan Blondell
Pat Boone
Thomas Haden Church
Phyllis George
Don Henley
Jim Hightower
Norah Jones
Dr. Phil McGraw
Larry McMurtry
Bill Moyers
Roy Orbison
Anne Rice
Ann Sheridan

University of Notre Dame
George Strake Jr.

University of Pennsylvania
Bernard Sakowitz

University of St. Thomas
Ken Bentsen
Garnet Coleman
Sean Patrick Flanery

University of Texas at Austin
James Baker
Alan Bean
Lloyd Bentsen
Jack Blanton
J. Don Boney
Dolph Briscoe
Jeb Bush
Jenna Bush
Laura Bush
Earl Campbell
Liz Carpenter
Waggoner Carr
John Chase
Lois Chiles
Ramsey Clark
Tom C. Clark
Roger Clemens
John Connally
Nellie Connally
Tom Connally
Walter Cronkite
Kathryn Grant Crosby
Gail Davis
Michael Dell
Lloyd Doggett
Bibb Falk
Farrah Fawcett
Jane Hall

Kent Hance

John Hill

Ima Hogg

Will Hogg

Susan Howard

Kay Bailey Hutchison

Joe Jamail

Lady Bird Johnson (Claudia A. Taylor)

Lynda Bird Johnson Robb

L.Q. Jones

Janis Joplin

W. Page Keaton

Tom Kite

Richard Kleberg

Bob Lanier

Allen Ludden

Jayne Mansfield

Crawford Martin

Leonard F. McCollum

Dan Moody

Hank Moore

Jane Moore Taylor

Julie Moore

Bill Moyers

Fess Parker

J.J. "Jake" Pickle

Gary Polland

Sam Rayburn

Mary Lou Retton

Ann Richards

Tex Ritter

Larry Sachnowitz

Barefoot Sanders

Liz Smith

Albert Thomas

Thomas Thompson

Homer Thornberry

Karen Tumulty

Tommy Tune

Eli Wallach

Sarah Weddington

Bill White

Martha Wong

Gus Wortham

Lyndall Wortham

Ralph Yarborough

Renee Zellweger

University of Texas at Arlington

General Tommy Franks

Lou Diamond Phillips

Ray Price

Bruce L. Tanner

Morgan Woodward

University of Texas at El Paso

Sam Donaldson

Wharton School of the University of Pennsylvania

Kirbyjon Caldwell

Dennis Murphree

Yale University

George H.W. Bush

George W. Bush

Bill Clinton

W. Edwards Deming

Chapter 16
WHAT IT TAKES TO BE A LEGEND
Leadership Advice From the Halls of Fame

Beacon to Your Business Success

D o you admire people who went the distance? Have you celebrated organizations that succeeded? I hope that you are and will continue to be distinctive.

This essay is to give insights into those who leave legacies. The secret to long-term success lies in mapping out the vision and building a body of work that supports it. The art with which we build our careers and our legacy is a journey that benefits many others along the way.

These are the ingredients that make a legend:

- Significant business contributions.
- Mature confidence and informed judgment.

- Courage and leadership.
- High performance standards.
- Professional innovation.
- Public responsibility.
- Ethics and integrity.
- Cultural contributions.
- Giving to community and charity.
- Visionary abilities.
- Commitment to persons affected (stakeholders).

I have been blessed by receiving several Legend honors. What I remember the most are the ceremonies and the nuggets of wisdom that flowed. The commonality was the zest of giving back the honors to others.

The first was a Rising Star Award, presented to me in 1967 by Governor John Connally. That was the first time that I was called Visionary, and that experience told me to live up to the accolades later. The governor whispered to me, "Get used to wearing a tuxedo. Live up to the honor by saluting others."

That same year (1967), I met singers Sonny and Cher, little knowing that 26 years later, I would be inducted into the Rock N' Roll Hall of Fame and that they would hand me the award. I remarked to Sonny that I often quoted his song "The Beat Goes On" as analogous to change management, and he was pleased. Cher recalled the 1971 occasion where she and I visited at a jewelry store on Rodeo Drive in Beverly Hills, California. I remembered that we drank champagne in a pewter cup. Her quote: "There are new ways to approach familiar experiences," and I have applied that to corporate turnarounds.

It was by being inducted into the U.S. Business Hall of Fame that I met Peter Drucker. We subsequently worked together, doing corporate retreats. You'll note his endorsement on the back cover of my signature book, The Business Tree™.

One year, I received several awards. I got a Savvy Award, for the top three community leaders. I was a Dewar's profile subject. I had gotten a standing ovation at the United Nations for volunteer work that was my honor to do (especially since it enabled me to work with my favorite actress, Audrey Hepburn).

Subsequently, I was judging a community stewardship awards program. I quizzed, "Why is it that the same old names keep popping up? There are great people to honor other that those of us from business, high society or other top-of-the-mind awareness. What this community needs is an awards program that people like us cannot win."

I was then challenged to come up with such a program, the result being the Leadership in Action Awards. At the banquet, the swell of pride from the winning organizations was heartening to see. These unsung heroes were finally getting their just recognition for community work well done.

One cannot seek awards just for glorification reasons. However, recognition programs are a balanced scorecard that involves the scrutiny of the company and its leaders by credible outside sources.

Awards inspire companies of all sizes to work harder and try more creative things. Good deeds in the community are not done for the awards; they just represent good business. Receiving recognition after the fact for works that were attempted for right and noble reasons is the icing on the cake that employees need. Good people aspire to higher goals. Every business leader needs to be groomed as a community leader.

Recognition for a track record of contributions represents more than "tooting one's own horn." It is indicative of the kind of organizations with whom you are honored to do business. The more that one is recognized and honored, the harder that one works to keep the luster and its integrity shiny. Always reframe the recognition back to the customers, as a recommitment toward serving them better and further.

Characteristics of a Legend

- Understands that careers evolve.
- Prepares for change, rather than becoming the victim of it.
- Realizes there are no quick fixes in life and business.
- Finds a blend of perception and reality, with heavy emphasis upon substance.
- Has grown as a person and professional and quests for more enlightenment.
- Has succeeded and failed and has learned from both.
- Was a good "will be" in the early years, steadily blossoming.
- Knows that one's dues paying accelerates, rather than decreases.

Best Advice to Future Legends

Fascinate yourself with the things you are passionate about. Be fascinated that you can still be fascinated. Be glad for people who mentored you. Be grateful for the opportunities that you have had. Be proud of yourself and your accomplishments. Do not let the fire burn out of your soul.

There comes a point when the pieces fit together. One becomes fully actualized and is able to approach their life's Body of Work. That moment comes after years of trial and error, experiences, insights, successes and failures.

As one matures, survives, life becomes a giant reflection. We appreciate the journey because we understand it much better. We know where we've gone because we know the twists and turns in the road there. Nobody, including ourselves, could have predicted every curve along the way.

However, some basic tenets charted our course. To understand those tenets is to make full value out of the years ahead. The best is usually yet to come. Your output should be greater than the sum of your inputs.

This is accomplished by reviewing the lessons of life, their contexts, their significance, their accountabilities, their shortcomings and their path toward charting your future.

Whatever measure you give will be the measure that you get back.

- There are no free lunches in life.
- The joy is in the journey, not in the final destination.
- The best destinations are not pre-determined in the beginning, but they evolve out of circumstances.
- You've got to give in order to get.
- Getting and having power are not the same thing.
- One cannot live entirely through work.
- One doesn't just work to live.
- As an integrated process of life skills, career has its place.
- A body of work doesn't just happen. It is the culmination of a thoughtful, dedicated process, carefully strategized from some point forward.

Chapter 17
QUOTES ABOUT HOUSTON

"The prosperity of Texas has been the object of my labors, the idol of my existence. It has assumed the character of a religion, for the guidance of my thoughts and actions for 15 years."

—Stephen F. Austin

"These, I may be permitted to hope, you will attend in person, that all the essential functionaries of the government may deliberate, and adopt some course that will redeem our country from a state of deplorable anarchy. Manly and bold decision alone can save us from ruin. I only require orders, and they shall be obeyed. If the government now yields to the unholy dictation of speculators and marauders upon human rights, it were better that we had yielded to the despotism of a single man, whose ambition might have been satisfied by out unconditional submission to his authority, and a pronouncement, for which we were asked, in favor of his power."

—**Sam Houston**, Jan. 15, 1836

"Since you have chosen to elect a man with a timber toe to succeed me, you may all go to hell, and I will go to Texas. Remember these words when I am dead. First be sure you're right and then go ahead."

—**Davy Crockett**

"Houston is merely a city in embryo."

—The Telegraph & Texas Register, May 1, 1836

Houston was first viewed as "a mud-hole, a graveyard, an abominable Place."

—**Ezekiel Cullen**, 1836

"We move anything. We ship to all parts of the world."

—**Sid Westheimer**, whose company was Westheimer Transfer and Storage

"I knew that at last I was a real Houstonian because Miss Ima Hogg's name no longer seemed odd to me."

—**Citizen**

"One of the greatest disservices you can do to a man is to lend him money that he can't pay back."

—**Jesse H. Jones**

"Politics are not unlike war. Sometimes it is necessary to shoot from the hip. Hopefully, we can develop something that everybody will agree is a pretty good way to run a tournament. It will be a standard that everybody will want to replicate. When we have standardized rules, everybody will benefit from it. There really is no uniformity right now and one of the problems with poker is that it has exploded to the point where more and more of these tournaments are sprouting up. We need to get them all on the same page."

—**Jesse H. Jones**

Quotes about Jesse Jones:

"Jones is the only man in Washington who can say yes and no intelligently 24 hours a day,"

—President Franklin D. Roosevelt.

"I get all my money information from Jesse Jones,"

—Will Rogers, humorist.

"You do your best work for free."

—Seymour Cohen

"I don't think there is any better part of the country a man could have come to in post-World War II. What a wonderful opportunity Texas provided. Texas came out much faster than other parts of the country and will continue its preferential position."

—Gerald Hines

"What we need to do is always lean into the future; when the world changes around you and when it changes against you. What used to be a tail wind is now a head wind. You have to lean into that and figure out what to do because complaining isn't a strategy."

—Jeff Bezos

"A real man can take a hammer to the knees without changing expression. When two William Marsh Rice's meet, it either means we will team up to destroy some even greater evil, team up to perpetrate some even greater evil, or battle to the death on top of the tallest mountain."

—William Marsh Rice

"As the old Texas expression goes, 'The gun kicks as hard as it shoots.' There's a plus and minus to being in the fishbowl. The plus is that it helps your business. The minus is that you're a public persona, and you're always subject to scrutiny. You don't necessarily have a life of your own. Still, I do get recognized sometimes, and I appreciate it. I had this call the other day, 'You don't happen to be that Mr. Sakowitz? I miss your store, the quality.' It was so nice. I have really nice memories."

—**Robert Sakowitz**

"When I was a kid in Houston, we were so poor we couldn't afford the last two letters, so we called ourselves po'."

—**George Foreman**

"I still take failure very seriously, but I've found that the only way I could overcome the feeling is to keep on working, and trying to benefit from failures or disappointments. There are always some lessons to be learned. So I keep on working."

—**Dr. Denton A. Cooley**

"So much goes into doing a transplant operation. All the way from preparing the patient to procuring the donor. It's like being an astronaut. The astronaut gets all the credit, he gets the trip to the moon, but he had nothing to do with the creation of the rocket, or navigating the ship. He's the privileged one who gets to drive to the moon. I feel that way in some of these more difficult operations, like the heart transplant."

—**Dr. Denton A. Cooley**

"I wanted to be an astronaut when I was a kid. I grew up in Houston. Gordon Cooper was my favorite astronaut."

—**Dennis Quaid**, actor

"Houston, we've had a problem."

—**James A. Lovell**, astronaut

"Be thankful for problems. If they were less difficult, someone with less ability might have your job. I was only a hero by default. The flights were few and far between. There weren't that many astronauts. The moon flights were so interesting and exciting."

—**James A. Lovell**, astronaut

"People worry so much what they think about them. If they knew how little they thought, they wouldn't worry."

—**Adie Marks**

"Women who stepped up were measured as citizens of the nation, not as women. This was a people's war, and everyone was in it."

—**Oveta Culp Hobby**, on the role of women during World War II

"When I went to Houston, they had a conditioning coach by the name of Gene Coleman. And that was the first time I had gone to an organization that had a program with a weight room and designed specifically for pitchers."

—**Nolan Ryan**, baseball great

"I have this theory about performers who last for a long time, and that is, if you break it down, music is not as big a part of it as personality and who you are. I think that we are all 3 people. I am who I think I am, I am who you think I am, and I am who I really am. The closer those 3 people are together, the longer your career's gonna last. 'Cause people don't like to be fooled. Don't be afraid to give up the good for the great. You gotta know when to hold 'em, know when to fold 'em, know when to walk away, know when to run."

—**Kenny Rogers**

"I grew up in a very nice house in Houston, went to private school all my life and I've never even been to the 'hood. Not that there's anything wrong with the 'hood."

—**Beyonce Knowles**

"It's not so much how you begin a business relationship that counts. It's how you end it."

—**Larry Sachnowitz**

"Don't taunt the alligator until after you've crossed the creek. A tough lesson in life that one has to learn is that not everybody wishes you well. If all difficulties were known at the outset of a long journey, most of us would never start out at all. Only votes talk, everything else walks. Americans will put up with anything provided it doesn't block traffic. I'd much rather wear out than rust out."

—Dan Rather

Songs About and Mentioning Houston

"The Midnight Special" was a folk song written about the prison farm on Highway 90 in Sugar Land. The Midnight Special was a train, and its shining light was the beacon for prisoners to escape, if they were to do so. The sheriff in Houston was a reference to T.A. Binford.

"Well, you wake up in the morning, you hear the work bell ring. And they march you to the table to see the same old thing. Ain't no food upon the table, and no pork up in the pan. But you better not complain, boy, you get in trouble with the man. Let the Midnight Special shine her ever-loving light on me."

"If you're ever in Houston, well, you better do right. You better not gamble, there, you better not fight. Or the sheriff will grab you and the boys will bring you down. The next thing you know, boy. You're Sugar Land bound. Let the Midnight Special shine her ever-loving light on me."

"Let me tell you about my home town, largest in the great Southwest. It ain't bragging when you're the best. Houston, that's my home town."

"Where do the Astronauts and NASA people all call home. Where there's 8th wonder of the world, the mighty Astrodome. Where do the Astros, Oilers, Apollos, Owls and Cougars roam."

"At San Jacinto, men of Houston fought to set us free. We built the tallest monument to mark their victory. And KNUZ in Houston serves my home town." 1962 radio jingle from the PAMS recording factory. PAMS is further described in Chapter 18.

"Somebody help me get out of Louisiana. Just help me get to Houston Town. There are people there who care a little about me. And they won't let the poor boy down. Tell the folks back home this is the promised land calling. And the poor boy is on the line." 1964 song hit by Chuck Berry (later recorded by Elvis Presley).

"Well it's lonesome in this old town. Everybody puts me down. I'm a face without a name. Just walking in the rain. Goin' back to Houston." 1965 song hit by Dean Martin. Written by Lee Hazlewood.

"Hi, everybody. I'm Archie Bell of the Drells, from Houston, Texas. In Houston, we don't only sing but we dance just as good as we walk. In Houston, we just started a new dance called the Tighten Up." 1968 song hit by Archie Bell and the Drells.

"Hey frank, won't you pack your bags. And meet me tonight down at Liberty Hall. Just one kiss from you my brother. And well ride until we fall. We'll sleep in the fields. We'll sleep by the rivers and in the morning. We'll make a plan. And meet me in a dream of this hard land." Song hit by Bruce Springsteen, in tribute to the venue where he played his first Texas shows in 1974 at Liberty Hall.

"Luv Ya Blue. You know that we do. We'll always be true. Luv ya when you're passing, on the run, scoring touchdowns. The pride and joy of Texas. Oilers, you're the best." 1978 football spirit song hit by Mack Hayes. To the tune of "Love Me Do" by The Beatles.

"We take the ball from goal to goal like no one's ever seen. We're in the air, we're on the ground. We've got the offense, the defense. We give the other team no hope. Cause we're the Houston Oilers, you know we're gonna hold the rope." 1979 football spirit song hit by Lee Ofman.

"I love what I do for a living, I do . But, Houston means that I'm one day closer to you,"1983 song hit by Larry Gatlin and the Gatlin Brothers Band. Written by Larry Gatlin, who was born in Seminole, TX, graduated from Odessa High School and attended the University of Houston.

Interesting websites to recommend

http://houstonhistory.com/

http://people.missouristate.edu/dennishickey/libertyhall.htm

http://forwardtimesonline.com/index.php?option=com_content&view=article&id=1641:black-business-is-black-history-the-houston-forward-times-highlights-three-history-making-houston-businesses&catid=69:local-and-state&Itemid=126

http://abt-unk.blogspot.com/2011/02/kitirik-and-cadet-don-radio-tv-52-weeks.html

http://bill37mccurdy.wordpress.com/2010/08/21/early-houston-tv-programs-personalities/

Chapter 18

SLOGANS

Attraction Points of Houston

The entire history of Houston has been viewed in this book through the prism of business, growth and entrepreneurial spirit. An appropriate Executive Summary of the contents is to recapitulate the history as a listing of slogans.

In my estimation, here is the emphasis of 200 years of the growth of a dynamic city for commerce, entrepreneurship and opportunity. I summarize this book with my own slogans.

- Born out of revolution.
- Grown on Independence.
- Texas fever.
- Spirit of adventure.

- Magnet of opportunities.
- Celebrating the victories.
- Built by immigrants, seeking better lives for themselves and children.
- Modern city, no matter which era.
- Destination center.
- Reasons for being here.
- Put together winning teams.
- Let the world come top us.
- Let us do business all over the globe.
- Forerunner of the 20th Century boom.
- Gracious living on the frontier.
- Impressed by the quality of life.
- Not just for show.
- Lively activity.
- Exponential growth.
- Business at every juncture.
- Dreaming all the time.
- We're all immigrants. We're all natives. Diversity personified.
- Spreading oil on the streets to keep down the dust.
- Oil migration from Beaumont to Houston.
- No matter what the price per barrel might be, they buy it and refine it.
- Measured by the strength of each one's resolve.
- Always ahead of the national economy.
- Beginning each decade optimistically.
- Doors open for success.
- Building a city where bayous used to run.
- The future brighter than imagined.
- Forerunner of the 21st Century boom.
- Salad bowl of flavors.
- Maximizing the "good old days."
- The "good old days" are always here.
- Citizens of the world.
- Don't interrupt the dream.

Chapter 19
AMERICAN BUSINESS LEGENDS

PAMS, Texas Business Legend

One of the great lines in pop culture is attributed to an imaginative business enterprise from Texas. It is "More Music," sung in happy, grandiose tones. This column is a tribute to PAMS, based in Dallas. It was the premier jingle producer for radio stations. During its three-decade run, PAMS created on-air identity music for radio stations worldwide. The dominance of jingles helped to define the radio formats, distinguish stations from each other and fed compatibly into the mix of recorded music of the era.

In the 1940's, radio stations featured live local variety shows. Stations employed house orchestras. Bill Meeks was a musician in the band at stations WRR and WFAA. In 1947, Gordon McLendon opened a new station in Dallas (KLIF), with Bill and his band hired to perform live. House bands backed singers on the variety shows, and they performed on live advertising jingles. The station ID jingles were happy, peppy and equivalent to the upbeat advertising spots. Meeks also sold advertising time.

In 1951, Meeks opened his own company, PAMS. It stood for Production Advertising Merchandising Service. They began recording advertising for a variety of clients, distributing beyond KLIF and to stations throughout Texas. The barter deal was that if stations aired clusters of PAMS client ads, then they would also get PAMS-produced ID jingles for each local station.

By the late 1950's, Top 40 radio formats were the trend, with disc jockeys playing the latest hits, and the jingles augmented local "house ads" (also known as "talking breaks"), giving the stations discernable image, which translated to higher ratings.

By the mid-1960's, the company's total focus was on generating new, annual, creative jingle packages. They were supplying stations all over the world. In the early days, PAMS served one station per market. Eventually, they serviced multiple stations in some markets due to differing jingle packages. Their jingle practice expanded to country, easy listening and soul music stations. They even produced jingle packages for TV stations.

PAMS experimented with sounds and concepts. There was the talking guitar. There were holiday-themed jingles. There were high school sports salutes in jingle form. There were even jingles for the weather, sports and public service announcements (integral in the good old days of regulated radio). The tone of the jingles was listener appreciation, community salute and a familial city culture.

In 1961, PAMS innovated its "My Home Town" concept (part of PAMS Series 16). Song length jingles were recorded about each city where PAMS supplied jingles. Their client radio stations partnered with local sponsors, pressed the jingles onto 45RPM records and promoted this hot release throughout their communities. The success of "My Home Town" spawned a second PAMS community appreciation package, 1962's "Having a Ball in (City-name)." There was even a hit record, "The Frito Twist," recorded by Bill Meeks, accompanied by the PAMS house band.

PAMS hit its peak in the late 1960's. The client list included WABC, WIL, KFWB, WLS, WXYZ and the BBC. Most major Texas radio stations bought and aired PAMS jingles, including KLIF, KBOX, KNUZ, KILT, KNOW, KCRS,

WACO, KWKC, KOGY, KNIN, KBWD, KSPL, KGRI, WTAW, KEYS, KDLK and KDOK.

By the mid 1970's, the marketplace for PAMS jingles shrunk drastically. That was the time that groups began acquiring local radio stations and began automating the program, with generic jingles. As a result, the jingle industry shrank radically. PAMS suspended business in 1978. Other jingle companies picked up the remaining marketplace.

PAMS client stations were unique, and the trend toward homogenizing radio broadcasting did the listeners a disservice. The listeners of today do not remember the glory days of Top 40 radio, personality formats and unique jingle identities. Today's listeners do not know how much they lost from the powerhouse days, as punctuated by PAMS jingles.

The success of PAMS spawned a large colony of advertising, music production, film production and creative services companies in Dallas. Other jingle companies (notably TM Productions and JAM Productions) resulted from the PAMS influence. In turn, recording companies in Houston, Austin and San Antonio bore the fruit of the market for localized products and services. The prominence of PAMS in the 1960's had a powerful impact on broadcasting empires.

Back Stories of the Legends

No matter how much planning one does (which I strongly advocate and facilitate for clients), many things just happen. Accidents that work are called strokes of genius.

Daily business is shaped by eccentricities, external influences and chance occurrences. By studying some of them, we gain insight into what modern business could be.

During a visit to the United States in the 1960's, Soviet Premier Nikita Khrushchev placed his hand on the tail fin of a Cadillac limousine. With seeming innocence, he asked, "What does this thing do?"

Eliot and Ruth Handler founded a toy company known as Mattel, Inc. They had a daughter named Barbie, who played with paper dolls, pretending that she was a mommy. Ruth watched her child play and got the idea for a doll with accessories, pretending to be an independent adult. Thus was born the largest selling doll in the history of the world, the Barbie Doll.

For those wondering the practical applications of outer space technology and research, look to items now normally found in the home, notably pocket calculators and microwave ovens.

So many odd-but-true happenings created the lifestyle that the populace embraced. Pop art, inventions, fashions, fads, and natural obsessions have contributed more to molding a society than textbook lessons. Historians continue to ponder the effects of pop culture.

As times change, the nature of nostalgia changes. While it is fun to remember the old days, we realize that pop art and culture set the rules by which we live as adults. Each generation relates to different phases of pop culture.

In 1965, a young woman in New York suggested to her boyfriend, a printer, that he make posters with Humphrey Bogart's picture. He acquired a negative for free, bought some cheap paper, and printed a batch of posters. Next, he ran a few ads to promote the pop-art posters.

Some kids came into a Greenwich Village bookstore, inquiring about the Bogart posters. The owner found the printer and bought his supply. The printer left town for a long weekend. When he returned, the phone was ringing. The bookstore had sold more than 1,000 Bogart posters, and could they have more. Realizing they were sitting on a goldmine, the printer and the bookstore owner formed Personality Posters. Thus, the celebrity poster boom began.

The atomic bomb is responsible for many societal reactions and phenomena... the most surprising being the bikini bathing suit. Rumors spread during post-World War II research that the world would end soon.

Fashion designers scheduled the "ultimate" show with the most daring styles. One model shocked the world by wearing a skimpy two-piece suit. The costume—now accepted swimwear—was named for Bikini Atoll, location of bomb testing.

President John F. Kennedy was asked by a reporter from Life Magazine for a list of his favorite books. Kennedy was a known intellectual who reportedly read one book every day. When the list included the Ian Fleming novel, From Russia With Love, the James Bond spy story craze hit America and the rest of the world.

Hungarian design professor Erno Rubik devised a multi-colored puzzle in the mid-1970's. Each of six sides has nine squares, with each row able to rotate around its center. When solved, each side is one color. There are 43 quintillion possible positions. Least possible moves to solve is 20. Rubik's Cube sold billions of units in its heyday. Knowledge of group theory and algorithms is useful.

Witness these fabulous firsts:

- The first product to carry the union seal was the cigar (1874).
- Franz Schubert wrote 1,000 musical works but left only one symphony unfinished.
- The Beatles used to write all their hit songs within a two-hour window.
- Ohio is the birth state of the most U.S. Presidents (seven).
- The last teenager to rule England was Queen Victoria.

Thomas Edison in the Recording Industry

Thomas Alva Edison was perhaps America's most prolific inventor. In 1877, at age 30, he invented the phonograph unintentionally. At the time, Edison was trying to devise a high-speed telegraph machine as a counterpart to the telephone that Alexander Graham Bell had invented a year before.

For his contributions to the telephone, Edison had already become quite wealthy. Edison thought he heard sounds and sought out to track down the phenomena. It occurred top him that he could devise a low-cost machine that would record voices. On a metal cylinder, a needle would move. Once that apparatus was completed, Edison shouted a child's nursery rhyme into the mouthpiece, "Mary had a little lamb." He admittedly was shocked when it reproduced his voice.

Edison received his patent on the cylinder style phonograph in 1878. From 1879-1887, Edison dropped the idea of developing the phonograph and concentrated his energies on developing the electric light.

Meantime, a young German immigrant named Emile Berliner developed the gramophone, which played discs. It was patented in 1887 and involved the making of a reverse metal matrix from the original acid-etched recording. He then used the negative master to stamp positive duplicates. The record player became a huge success.

In 1888, Edison took note of Berliner's invention and retooled his cylinder technology for commercial recording. The first releases also recited poetry. The U.S. Marine Band recorded marches over and over again, as each consumer cylinder was a master. Only the wealthy could afford cylinders, priced in 1890 at $10 each. The machine on which they played sold for $200.

By the end of the 19th Century, Berliner's record machine process was out-distancing Edison's cylinder machine. This was similar to the manner in which VHS tapes out-distanced beta-max tapes in the early 1980's, becoming the dominant technology. By 1900, Edison had gotten into the commercial recording business but kept putting out cylinders until 1911, well past the time that Berliner's phonograph record had become the industry standard. The cylinders had more disc space to contain longer performances, but the phonograph records were the preferred media. In 1919, experimentation began on electrical recording and reproduction. Until then, the phonographs were cranked by hand. Those developments came from companies other than Edison.

On Nov. 1, 1929, the Edison company announced that they would cease the production of phonographs and records. The announced reason was so that they could concentrate on the manufacture of radios and dictating machines, which is what Edison's talking horn started out to be in the first place. Thomas Alva Edison was then 82 years old, and had long since ceased to be active in the business.

The two oldest record companies, Columbia (founded in 1898) and RCA Victor (founded in 1901) are still with us today. The two oldest record companies developed the next technologies as alternatives to the breakable 78RPM recordings. Though both companies started research and development in 1931, Columbia introduced the long playing record (LP) in 1948, and RCA Victor introduced the 45RPM single in 1949.

The fortunes and electrical recording techniques of Columbia, RCA Victor, Brunswick and others had years earlier shoved Edison's recording empire into nostalgia. One can still find Edison cylinders in antique shops.

The genius (Thomas Alva Edison) died in 1931. By that time, the recording industry had left its infancy and was experiencing the growing pains of youth. Edison saw it all and fathered it all, the industry that he started back in 1877.

By the way, the compact disc (CD) is an updated version of Emile Berliner's phonograph record, developed in 1877. CD's were developed by Sony and Philips in the late 1970's. Both companies started the research independently of each other but, learning from Edison's demise, combined as a joint effort in 1979. CDs had their first commercial releases in 1982. Both the original record and the CD play at the same speed, 78RPM.

Business Narrative by the Author

People possess and vigorously demonstrate a passion for trivia. Stored nuggets of information may burst from the memory banks at any given time.

We can recite lyrics to golden oldies on the radio, yet the tenets of business etiquette are not so familiar. We remember movie dialog and old TV advertising jingles, yet policies and procedures are a little foreign. Futurism and cutting edge philosophies have a basis in the familiar.

There are four ways to grow a business: (1) Sell more customers. (2) Cross-sell your existing customers. (3) Create new products and services. (4) Create additional opportunities by collaborating with other companies. PAMS did all four, and that's why they sustained over three decades.

If more companies would pay attention to creating new industries, then they will partner sooner, rather than later. Creative marketplaces come about when you look beyond today's business and focus toward the future.

Rather than keep doing more of the same things that you have done in the past, try to focus on new strategies. Employ a business mentor.

Develop and keep the talent that you have as loyal holders of the company mission. Develop new opportunities by expanding markets. Also, know when enough growth is enough, in order to keep creatively handling the business that you have.

There is nothing on this earth that does not change. Nothing is "made possible by technology." Thought processes, creativity, thinking, reasoning and commitments to action make things possible. Technology tools of the trade are utilized on a per-task basis, as evidenced when Thomas Edison allowed the sound recording marketplace to surpass him.

Every business or organization goes through cycles in its life. At any point, each program is in a different phase from others. The astute organization assesses the status of each program and orients its team members to meet constant change and fluctuation. Understanding where one has been provides disciplined thinking about the organization, its environment and its future.

Chapter 20
YESTERDAYISM

Learning from the Past, to Plan for the Future

People are interesting combinations of the old, the new, the tried and the true. Individuals and organizations are more resilient than they tend to believe. They've changed more than they wish to acknowledge. They embrace innovations, while keeping the best traditions.

When one reflects at changes, he-she sees directions for the future. Change is innovative. Customs come and go...some should pass and others might well have stayed with us.

There's nothing more permanent than change. For everything that changes, many things stay the same. The quest of life is to interpret and adapt that mixture of the old and new. People who fight change have really changed more than they think.

The past is an excellent barometer for the future. This is a concept which I call Yesterdayism. One can always learn from the past, dust it off and reapply it. I call that Lessons Learned but Not Soon Forgotten. Living in the past is not good, nor is living in the present without wisdom of the past.

Trends come and go...the latest is not necessarily the best. Some of the old ways really work better...and should not be dismissed just because they are old or some fashionable trend of the moment looks better.

When we see how far we have come, it gives further direction for the future. Ideas make the future happen. Technology is but one tool of the trade. Futurism is about people, ideas and societal evolution, not fads and gimmicks. The marketplace tells us what they want, if we listen carefully. We also have an obligation to give them what they need.

In olden times, people learned to improvise and "make do." In modern times of instantaneous disposability, we must remember the practicalities and flexibilities of the simple things and concepts.

Fond Remembrances of the Past

- Drugstore soda fountains.
- Driving into the gas station and saying, "fill 'er up"
- Dialog: "Fill 'er up." Response: "Regular or ethyl?"
- Gas station attendants, in uniform, cleaning windshields.
- One phone book that encompassed all listings.
- Chinese laundries (local family operated).
- Black and white movies and TV shows.
- Newscasts that contained actual news.
- Cream on top of milk delivered to your door in bottles.
- Schools broadcasting radio coverage of space launches over PA system.
- Quilting bees.
- Homemade bread.
- Ice cream socials.
- 4-poster bedposts.
- Laundry was hung out to dry on clotheslines in the backyard.
- Aluminum foil was called "tin foil."
- An umbrella was called a "parasol."

- Trash and garbage were called "debris, refuse, rubbish."
- A bathroom was called a "water closet."
- Records were played to hear music.
- One filled out business forms in triplicate, with carbon paper.
- Ironing boards were built into the wall of the kitchen (accessed by a door).
- Salt, pepper, sugar and other spices kept in a cupboard in the kitchen.
- The primary source of home or office building cooling was a ceiling fan.
- All office buildings had ledges.
- Milk came in glass bottles...delivered to your door.
- All hotels were located downtown.
- Suburban and rural hotels were called tourist courts...later motels.
- One opened beer or soft drink cans with a "church key."
- All movies and novels had happy endings.

Do You Remember When

- The entire family would take Sunday drives and hold picnics on the weekends.
- The entire family would gather around the 78-RPM record changer (a new invention) to enjoy new releases by such contemporary artists as Bing Crosby, Glenn Miller, Rudy Vallee, Tommy Dorsey, Duke Ellington, Gene Austin, Paul Whiteman, Benny Goodman, Guy Lombardo, Enrico Caruso, Artie Shaw, Russ Columbo, The Andrews Sisters, The Mills Brothers, Kate Smith, Vaughn Monroe, Harry James, Count Basie, Al Jolson.
- The entire family would gather around the radio (a new invention) to enjoy family-oriented programs such as "Fibber McGee and Molly," "The Shadow," "Edgar Bergen and Charlie McCarthy," "H.V. Kaltenborn With the News," "Suspense," "The Great Gildersleeve," "The March of Time," "Lux Radio Theatre" and "Bing Crosby's Kraft Music Hall."
- The entire family would gather around the three-speed record changer (a new invention) to enjoy new releases by such contemporary artists as Perry Como, Doris Day, Frankie Laine, Teresa Brewer, Nat "King" Cole, Rosemary Clooney, Eddie Fisher, Dinah Shore, Tony Bennett,

Jo Stafford, Dean Martin, Patti Page, Frank Sinatra, Eartha Kitt, Vic Damone, The McGuire Sisters, Kay Starr, The Four Aces, Joni James and Peggy Lee.

- The entire family would gather around the TV set (a new invention) to enjoy family-oriented programs such as "The Ed Sullivan Show," "What's My Line," "Wagon Train," "George Burns and Gracie Allen Show," "The Life and Times of Wyatt Earp," "Dragnet," "The Milton Berle Show," "Four Star Playhouse," "Disneyland" and "Gunsmoke."
- The entire family would gather around the Atari video machine (a new invention) to enjoy family-oriented games such as Pac Man and Donkey Kong.

Signs, Trends and Fads of Their Times
- Judges wearing powdered wigs and robes
- Car hops at drive-in restaurants
- Pizza parlors (in-store dining only)
- Jousting contests
- Dances: the Charleston, twist, etc.
- Married couples shown on TV sleeping in twin beds
- Short wave radios
- CB radios
- Mega Super Bowl parties
- Polio vaccinations
- Catholic church services entirely in Latin
- Pens and inkwells in schools and offices
- Slide rules as standard part of school supplies
- Choice of either a 2-ring or 3-ring binder
- Political messages printed on cardboard fans
- Advertising messages printed on school book covers

Automobiles: Trends, Fads and Technologies
- Hood ornaments and tail fins on cars
- All cars on the road being of the nation in which they were made
- Rumple seats and running boards on cars

- Regular gasoline
- Crank shafts
- Music via AM-only radio
- Spare tire mounted on the rear
- Running boards
- Visor over the windshield
- Small, framed front and back windshields
- Tail pipes
- Spark plugs

Things Which Made Comebacks

- Ceiling fans
- The jitterbug and swing music
- Hardwood floors
- Stained glass

Things the Economy Has Exempted

Penny arcades

Five-and-dime stores

Full-service gas stations

Free car washes at gas stations

Towels in boxes of detergent

Mom-and-pop stores

S&H Green Stamps and other redemption programs

Things which Technology Has Eclipsed

- Telegraphs (including operators, poles and stations to support them)
- The process of changing spark plugs in cars
- Eye patches
- Stagecoaches
- Monocles
- Horse-driven buggies
- Shooting horses when they go lame
- Muskets

- Blacksmiths
- Cobblestone streets
- Cows being milked by hand
- Fountain pen refills
- Cotton being picked by hand
- Wall-crank telephones
- Rotary dial telephones
- Telephone poles with glass conductors atop
- Placing long distance calls through a live operator sitting at a switchboard
- Fire places, which gave way to floor furnaces...which gave way to wall heaters, which gave way to space heaters, which gave way to central air and heat.
- Open-air vents above doors in office buildings, hotels and apartments (the oldest ones containing stained glass).
- Attic fans, which gave way to window fans, which gave way to water coolers, which gave way to window air conditioning units, which gave way to central air and heat.
- Ledges on high-rise office buildings
- Windows that open in high-rise office buildings
- Baseball games played outside in the sunlight
- Megaphones
- Wagon trains taking settlers westward as a group
- Steel coiled radiators
- Ledges on office buildings
- Check writing machines.
- Typewriters
- Typewriter paraphernalia (dust covers, stands, carbon paper, ribbons, liquid paper)
- Mimeograph machines while printed purple documents
- Office buildings with elevator operators and crank-turning mechanisms

Things which the Marketplace Has Eclipsed
- Ice delivered in blocks via a horse-driven carriage by the ice man
- Milk delivered in bottles via a horse-driven carriage by the milk man

- Going downtown to do all of your shopping
- Drive-in movies
- Stores closed on Sundays

Things that Ceased but Should Have Remained
- Locally produced children's TV shows
- Saturday matinees at the movies for children
- Neighborhoods coordinating Christmas decorations at the holiday season
- Community ice cream socials
- Frosted mugs of root beer
- Signs on public facilities stating, "inspected by Duncan Hines" (or some other objective third-party resource)
- Civil defense and community safety drills
- Getting dressed up to go to dignified places (church, theatre, business offices, etc.)
- Bookmobiles in the neighborhoods (i.e. formalized youth reading programs)
- Movie newsreels, cartoons and short subjects
- Regular immunizations against diseases administered in the schools, churches and community centers
- Charm schools
- Teaching formal ballroom dancing to children (and other social amenities that accompany it)
- Printed Top 40 music surveys
- Radio listeners being able to actually pick the songs that are played
- Reading books, magazines and newspapers on a regular basis. (37% of all high school graduates will never read a book the rest of their lives.)

The Old Became the New Again.
- The original speed for phonograph records, as invented in 1888, was 78-RPM, which engineers have determined to be the most ideal for sound quality. In the 1940s, technology brought us the 45-RPM and 33-1/3-RPM records, adding up to the "mother speed" of 78-RPM.

The 1980s brought us compact discs, which play at a speed of 78-RPM.

- Station wagons of the 1950s went out of style. They came back in the 1980s as sport utility vehicles.
- Midwives were widely utilized in previous centuries. In modern times, alternative health care concepts and practitioners have been embraced by all sectors of society. Herbal ingredients and home remedies have gained popularity, and cottage industries support them.
- Telephone party lines went out in the 1920s. They came back in the 1990s as internet chat rooms.
- Corporations have become extended families, embracing changes, modifications and learning curves.
- Schools started out as full-scope community centers. As the years passed, academic programs grew and became more specialized, covering many vital subject areas. Today, with parents and communities severely neglecting children and their life-skills education, schools have evolved back to being full-scope community centers.

Major Inventions that Have Impacted Our Lives
- Books, newspapers and magazines
- Frozen, packaged and instantly prepared foods
- Air conditioning, climate control
- Health care medication, aids, procedures and equipment
- Radio and television
- Computers
- Microwave ovens

Practical Extras that Have Impacted Our Lives
- Swizzle sticks
- Plastic spindles (couldn't play a 45-RPM record without one)
- Straws
- Sugar substitute
- Creamer in granules

Progressions of the Times

- Rabbit ears atop the TV set, to get better reception.
- TV antennas on the rooftops of our homes, to get better reception.
- Community television cable systems, to get better reception.
- Cable TV...to get more choices.
- Cutting off football games to begin the regularly scheduled show. (That was done for the last time in 1969, when NBC telecast "Heidi," and action in the un-televised last seconds altered the game's outcome. Through public outcry, games hence went their course and primetime programming ran in its entirety, just later.)

Fashion Trends, When Women Wore

- Pantaloons
- Corsets and bustles
- Hats with feathers
- Girdles
- Garters (used to hold up women's stockings)
- Petticoats with hoops
- Poodle skirts
- Wigs
- Hats
- Dresses, pearls and high heels while doing housework (icon of 1950s TV)

Fashion Trends, When Men Wore

- Loin cloths
- Buffalo skins
- Capes
- Starched high collars
- Arm garters (used to hold up men's sleeves)
- Chaps
- Handkerchief in front suit pocket
- Hats
- Vests and tie clasps as part of regular business attire

Brand Names that stuck as generic labels
- Xerox, for making photocopies.
- Kleenex, for any kind of tissue.
- Coke, for enjoying a soft drink.

Crime Waves of the Past
- Cattle rustling
- Bootlegging whiskey
- Horse theft

Punishment for Crimes in the Past
- Branded by a scarlet letter
- Execution by a firing squad
- Hanging
- Being put in the stockades
- Public thrashing
- Being fed only bread and water
- Debtors' prisons
- Blacklisting
- Internment camps for suspected aliens
- Having your name posted in the town square

Behaviors and Social Customs of Times Past
- Offering a social conversations by offering the other person a cigarette.
- Alcohol consumed at business lunches.
- Serving guests water directly from the tap.
- Opening school with both benedictions and the Pledge of Allegiance.
- Condoms available via machines in gas stations or under the counter at pharmacies.
- TV stations signing on and off with test patterns.
- The Solid South (predictable voting patterns).

Behaviors that Have Evolved

- Tossing soft drink cans out of the car. Through behavior modification and sensitivity to the environment, we now crush them and put them in recyclable containers.
- Mellowing out and absorbing culture on Sunday mornings, varying forms and habits.
- One set of water fountains and rest rooms for all. (It wasn't always that way.)

Descriptive Phrases

- Gay (for a person being happy and joyous)
- A real drag (something unpleasant)
- Twangy (a style of guitar playing)
- Twangy (nasal sound for country singers in the 1950's and 1960's)
- Sap (a person easily taken advantage of)
- Sap (substance coming out of a tree)

Expressions Not Heard Anymore

- The bee's knees
- The cat's meow
- Well, I'll be pickled in brine
- The cat's pajamas
- Well, dog my cat
- Heavens to Betsy
- If that doesn't take the cake
- Cock and bull
- Mum's the word
- Holy smokes
- Well, Doggie
- Snitch
- Golly gee
- Swell
- Fiddlesticks
- Well, I'll swannee

- Jeepers creepers
- Sunday go to meeting
- A month of Sundays
- Bust my britches

Fad Expressions, Hot at the Time
- Would you believe…(from "Get Smart")
- A silly millimeter longer (from a cigarette commercial)
- Let me make this perfectly clear (from Richard Nixon)
- Get while the getting's good
- Putting on the dog
- Heavens to Mergatroid
- See you later, alligator
- All dolled up
- That's the most
- Steppin' out
- What a drag
- Hot rod
- Gun moll
- Ain't that a groove
- What a bummer
- Heavens to Mergatroid
- Tell it like it is
- Groovy
- Rat fink
- Bitchin'
- Peace, Brother
- Right on
- Black is Beautiful
- Far out
- Have a nice day
- Time to rock and roll
- Keep on keepin' on
- Sooky (have mercy, baby)

- Tubular
- Make my day
- Shop till you drop
- Doofus (acting silly)
- Geek
- Biker babe
- Groupie
- Talk to the hand
- Good to go
- Don't go there

Nicknames for People

- Girlie
- Bucko
- Silly willy
- Little lady
- Buster
- Buckeroo
- Missy
- Sweet pea

Negative Labels for People

- Polecat
- Skunk
- Redneck
- You old buzzard
- Ethnic slurs too vile and repugnant to list here.

Perspectives, Depending Upon Your Vantage Point

- For most of us, the milk man brought products to your door. To farmers, the milk man was the delivery person who picked up the product.
- When dining, Europeans and Americans hold knives and forks in different patterns.

- Cherry coke in a drugstore soda fountain has a special meaning for consumers. It cannot be duplicated in consumable containers.
- Hot dogs in a ballpark have their own unique flavor, appeal and ambience. So do hot dogs bought from a street cart. So do those grilled over an open fire at a youth campout.
- The same commodity is seen differently, depending upon the circumstance.

The Winds of Change

- It takes many years to raise a person but only a few minutes to arrange for their burial.
- Society spends three times more on prisons than on public education.

Kinder Notions, We Need Them Now

- Heroes, role models.
- Fighting for the honor of a lady.
- Helping senior citizens across the street.
- Smiling at other people whom you pass on the street or in public places.
- Accountability by each person in their job.
- Humane treatment of people, as we confer upon animals.
- Voting for the man or woman, not the party.
- Saying "yes sir" and "yes ma'am" to our elders...or as in general to show respect to other adults.

7 Levels of Yesterdayism, Learning from the Past

1. Re-reading, reviewing and finding new nuggets in old files.
2. Applying pop culture to today.
3. Review case studies and their patterns for repeating themselves.
4. Discern the differences between trends and fads.
5. Learn from successes and three times more from failures.
6. Transition your focus from information to knowledge.
7. Apply thinking processes to be truly innovative.

The past repeats itself. History is not something boring that you once studied in school. It tracks both vision and blind spots for human beings. History can be a wise mentor and help you to avoid making critical mistakes.

7 Kinds of Reunions

1. **Pleasurable.** Seeing an old friend who has done well, moved in a new direction and is genuinely happy to see you too. These include chance meetings, reasons to reconnect and a concerted effort by one party to stay in the loop.

2. **Painful.** Talking to someone who has not moved forward. It's like the conversation you had with them 15 years ago simply resumed. They talk only about past matters and don't want to hear what you're doing now. These include people with whom you once worked, old romances, former neighbors and networkers who keep turning up like bad pennies and colleagues from another day and time.

3. **Mandated.** Meetings, receptions, etc. Sometimes, they're pleasurable, such as retirement parties, open houses, community service functions. Other times, they're painful, such as funerals or attending a bankruptcy creditors' meeting.

4. **Instructional.** See what has progressed and who have changed. Hear the success stories. High school reunions fit into this category, their value depending upon the mindset you take with you to the occasion.

5. **Reflect Upon the Past.** Reconnecting with old friends, former colleagues and citizens for whom you have great respect. This is an excellent way to share each other's progress and give understanding for courses of choice.

6. **Benchmarking.** Good opportunities to compare successes, case studies, methodologies, learning curves and insights. When "the best" connects with "the best," this is highly energizing.

7. **Goal Inspiring.** The synergy of your present and theirs inspires the future. Good thinkers are rare. Stay in contact with those whom you know, admire and respect. It will benefit all involved.

Appendix
OTHER WRITINGS BY HANK MOORE

Digest of excerpts from the author's other books

Books by Hank Moore:
- The Business Tree™. Published by major New York imprint, plus seven international editions.
- The High Cost of Doing Nothing. Why good businesses go bad.
- The Classic Television Reference.
- Power Stars to Light the Flame...The Business Visionaries and You.
- The Future Has Moved...and Left No Forwarding Address.
- The $50,000 Business Makeover.
- Two editions of the Chicken Soup books.
- Harvard Business Review Monograph Series.
- Library of Congress Archive Series.
- Strategy Driven Business Monograph Series.

- Articles in such other diverse media as Rolling Stone, Wall Street Journal, TV Guide, Wharton Business Review, the London Times, Huffington Post, Journal of Education, Training Magazine, Fast Company, Reader's Digest, TV-Radio Mirror, The Alcalde, the Washington Post and others.

From The Business Tree™

It seems so basic and so simple: Look at the whole of the organization, then at the parts as components of the whole and back to the bigger picture.

I advocate planning ahead and taking the widest possible view, very common-sense and utilizing a series of bite-sized chunks of business growth activity. This is the approach to clients that I have taken as a senior business advisor for 40 years. Even in times of crisis or when working on small projects, I use every opportunity to inspire clients look at their Big Pictures. The typical reaction is that my approach makes sense, and why haven't others taken it before.

The Big Picture can and does exist, though companies have not found it for their own applications very often. Organizations know that such a context is out there, but most search in vein for partial answers to a puzzling mosaic of business activity. The result, most often, is that organizations spin their wheels on inactivity, without crystallizing the right balance that might inspire success.

Obsession with certain pieces, comfort levels with other pieces and lack of artistic flair (business savvy) keep the work in progress but not resulting in a finished masterpiece.

Businesses rarely start the day with every intention of focusing upon the Big Picture. They don't get that far. It is too easy to get bogged down with minutia. This book and my advising activities are predicated upon educating the pitfalls of narrow focus and enlightening organizations on the rewards of widening the view.

Should every business become Big Picture focused? Yes. My job is to widen the frame of reference as much as possible. Under a health care model, I am the internist, a diagnostician who knows about the parts and makes informed judgments about the whole. This enables the specialists to then be more successful in their treatments, knowing that they stem from an accurate diagnosis and prescription.

Alas, the Big Picture of business is a continuing realignment of current conditions, diced with opportunities. The result will be creative new variations. Masterpieces can be continually evolving works in progress.

From Power Stars to Light the Flame

These are the stages in the evolution of ideas, concepts and philosophies:

1. Information, Data. There is more information available now than ever before. Most of it is biased and slanted by vendors with something to sell. There exists much data, without interpretation. Technology purveys information but cannot do the analytical thinking.
2. Perception. Appearance of data leads to initial perceptions, usually influenced by the media in which the information exists. To many people and organizations, perception is reality because they do not delve any further, and their learning stops at this point.
3. Opinion. Determined more by events-processes than words. Verbal statements are more important when people are suggestible and need interpretation from a credible source. Opinion does not anticipate emergencies, only reacts to them. Many perceptions and opinions are self-focused and affected by self-esteem. Once self-interest becomes involved, opinions do not change easily.
4. Ideas and Beliefs. Formulated ideas emerge, as people-organizations learn to hold their own outside their shells. Two-way communication ensues, whereby opinion inputs and outputs will craft ideas and beliefs. As people become more aware of their own learning, they tally their inventory of knowledge. Patterns of beliefs emerge, based upon education, experiences and environment.
5. Systems of Thought and Ideologies. Insights start emerging at this plateau. Connect beliefs with available resources and personal expertise. Measure results and evaluate outcomes of activities, using existing opinion, ideas and beliefs. Actions are taken which benchmark success and accountability to stakeholders.
6. Core value. Shaped by ideas, beliefs, systems of thought and ideologies. Becomes what the person or organization stands for. Leaders have conviction, commitment and ownership, able to change and adapt. Behavioral modification from the old ways of thinking has transpired.
7. Company-Career-Life Vision. This is an enlightened plateau that few achieve. They are able to disseminate information, perceptions and

opinions for what they really are. This level is wisdom focused, a quest to employ ideologies and core values for benefit of all in the organization. People are committed to thriving upon change.

From The High Cost of Doing Nothing

Each year, one-third of the U.S. Gross National Product goes toward cleaning up problems, damages and otherwise high costs of doing either nothing or doing the wrong things.

On the average, it costs six times the investment of preventive strategies to correct business problems (compounded per annum and exponentially increasing each year). In some industries, the figure is as high as 30 times...six is the mean average.

Human beings as we are, none of us do everything perfectly on the front end. There always must exist a learning curve. Research shows that we learn three times more from failures than from successes. The mark of a quality organization is how it corrects mistakes and prevents them from recurring.

Running a profitable and efficient organization means effectively reducing the potential for damage before it accrues. Processes and methodologies for researching, planning, executing and benchmarking activities will reduce that pile of costly coins from stacking up.

Doing nothing becomes a way of life. It's amazing how many individuals and companies live with their heads in the sand. Never mind planning for tomorrow... we'll just deal with problems as they occur. This mindset, of course, invites and tends to multiply trouble.

There are seven costly categories of doing nothing, doing far too little or doing the wrong things in business:

1. Waste, spoilage, poor controls, lack of employee motivation.
2. Rework, product recalls, make-good for inferior work, excess overhead.
3. 3.Poor controls on quality, under-capitalization, under-utilization of resources.
4. Damage control, crisis management mode.
5. Recovery, restoration, repairing wrong actions, turnover, damaged company reputation.

6. Retooling, restarting, inertia, anti-change philosophy, expenses caused by quick fixes.
7. Opportunity costs, diversifying beyond company expertise, lack of an articulated vision.

From The Classic Television Reference

Most of us have fantasized the possibility of our parents being other people. Sometimes, idolized parents were those who already were attached to our friends. Most often, role models were symbols of people we didn't know but wanted to be like.

Businesses operate the same way as individuals. What looks good on the outside is what we must have and become. Tactics are commonly devised to get what we perceive that someone else has and look like what we assume they appear to be. The process of chasing the perception becomes an obsession for businesses of all sizes until reality sets in.

With the advent of television in the 1950s, it was natural that TV families would be held up as ideals. We jokingly wonder how June Cleaver could do the housework in her fancy dress, high heels and pearls. We just knew that Harriet Nelson would make more delicious meals than our own mothers did.

The families on TV situation comedies were all white, middle-class, carried traditional family structures and were mostly based in mythical small towns.

The realities behind the facades now make for fascinating insights:

Harriet Nelson could not really cook. She had grown up in hotels and was accustomed to ordering room service.

Ozzie Nelson had no job on TV, and his wife didn't work outside the home. No explanation was ever made about their means of support. Though his character appeared light on screen, Ozzie Nelson was the true guru of that show. In my mind, he stands with Desi Arnaz and Dick Powell as one of the behind-the-scenes geniuses of TV.

There was dysfunctional behavior, even though we didn't recognize it as such. When Danny Thomas yelled at his kids and spit coffee on the living room floor, it was couched in wisecracks.

Women were stereotyped. Many TV wives appeared to be subservient... yet pursued their own pro-active courses. Laura Petrie always got her way. Lucy

Ricardo pursued hi-jinx. And mother did really "know best," though society would not quite position it that way in the 1950s. Nonetheless, women learned subtle ways to master the system, within the context of good humor.

While Western sheriffs won at the shootouts, the issues of good versus bad were overly simplistic. Life is mostly shades of gray, which tough strength does not work well against.

Behind the guns and action, the Westerns really did teach lessons of empowerment and team building. On "Wagon Train" and "Rawhide," people had no choice but to get along and work together. As a team, they fought the elements and usually won.

Gangsters always got their just deserves in movies and on cop TV shows. We were taught that crime does not pay and were shown the price for violating property and safety. Jack Webb, Broderick Crawford and other tough cops put the baddies in their place, in no uncertain terms.

Many of us wonder why values like these are not taught now. Where is society headed, we wonder. Where are the new heroes coming from?

We now realize that many of our childhood idols had demons of their own. Keeping up appearances and being interchangeably confused with their on-screen characters led many a performer toward personal abuse, career burnout and eventual ruin.

Not many taught us about going the distance. Too many actors and singers had short-term careers. That was the design of the system. In business, we must not follow pop culture and train ourselves to last, prosper and get better with age.

As we get older and more cynical, society tends to shoot down its media heroes and watches them stumble and fall, sometimes with interest and joy. We don't expect any of them to measure up to past pedestal status. When one falls from grace, we may either repudiate our past allegiance or justify unrealistic ways to keep them perched up on high.

Having met many major performers and media heroes, I know that raw talent does not directly translate to business savvy and people skills. The Paul McCartneys of the world who successfully embody it all are few and far between.

One of my first career idols was Dick Clark, another man who is smart and accomplished in many facets. He had just debuted on "American Bandstand." I was in the fifth grade and started working at a radio station, determined to be Texas' answer to Dick Clark.

A mentor reminded me that none of us should go through life as a carbon copy of someone else. We can admire and embody their qualities but must carve out a uniqueness all our own. Good advice from a 24-year-old Bill Moyers, who stands for me as an ever-contemporary role model.

Corporate executives do not get a rulebook when the job title is awarded. They are usually promoted on the basis technical expertise, team player status, loyalty and perceived long-term value to the company. They are told to assume a role and then draw upon their memory bank of role models.

Top executives have few role models in equivalent positions. Thus, they get bad advice from the wrong consultants. In the quest to be a top business leader, one quickly reviews how poorly corporate executives were portrayed to the mass culture.

J.R. Ewing ("Dallas") sold every member of his family and work force down the river. He is hardly a CEO role model, though many "good old boys" think how he operated was perfectly acceptable.

Alan Brady ("Dick Van Dyke Show") practiced nepotism with his brother-in-law, Mel Cooley. Brady yelled at everyone and was especially abusive to Mel, in front of others. Creativity was determined by his will. All were expected to parrot his "vision."

Lou Grant ("Mary Tyler Moore Show") was brash, threatened termination, asked pervasive questions and sometimes dated co-workers.

Charlie Townsend ("Charlie's Angels") was never around. He left his staff to their own devices and to supervise themselves. The reasons most employees do not perform as expected is that they are given insufficient direction and time with a mentor, not knowing what is expected of them.

It was never revealed where John Beresford Tipton ("The Millionaire") earned all that money that he gave away to total strangers.

Economic accountability was never a consideration in TV families. They lived well, but we rarely saw the relationship between workplace output to family quality of life. How did Mike Brady ("The Brady Bunch") afford to feed a family of eight, especially with his wife staying at home and not working? He seemed to stay at home much more than the average successful architect.

In reality, most TV lead characters were the employees of someone else. The boss was the brunt of the jokes. Fear of being disciplined was openly communicated to viewers as part of the territory in earning one's way in life.

Ralph Kramden ("The Honeymooners") was not considered to become a supervisor, nor a leader. He exhibited a defeatist attitude that probably kept him from being successful.

Certain characters did their jobs in such a way as that the bosses fell in love with them and eventually married them. Witness Katy Holstrum ("The Farmer's Daughter"), Agent 99 ("Get Smart") and Jeannie ("I Dream of Jeannie"). At one time, some women went into business with such an unrealistic view.

We never saw psychologist Bob Hartley ("Bob Newhart Show") conferring with colleagues, attending professional symposia, authoring academic papers or seeking professional help himself. When he wasn't in session, he was joking with the receptionist and the dentist.

Editor Perry White ("Superman") threatened young Jimmy Olsen, "Don't call me chief," when mentoring the eager reporter would have amplified Olsen's service to The Daily Planet. Alas, Olsen was always a tagalong and did not develop as a seasoned reporter, stalling his career.

Marshal Simon Cord (played by Henry Fonda) was always out of town. His "Deputy" (played by Allen Case) was a shopkeeper, who became the town's part-time law and order by default. Part-time jobs and careers are not the same thing.

Money was rarely an issue. We rarely saw families just scraping by, as were most Americans. "The Real McCoys" were farmers...with wealth in spirit and positive will.

There were unexplained quirks, showing insufficient resources necessary to do business. All the detectives on "77 Sunset Strip" drove the same car (a Ford convertible). How did the others get around and earn their livelihood, if a car was essential equipment?

Steve McGarrett ("Hawaii Five-0") drove the same car (a 1967 Mercury Monterey) year after year. With his arrest record, why didn't the department upgrade his equipment?

Jim Anderson was an insurance agent on "Father Knows Best." Yet, he never made evening calls...only working days. Thus, he couldn't sell that many policies and missed his marketplace...not being available at peak times that his customers were.

Ricky Ricardo worked in a nightclub and always went to work during the day, usually being home most evenings. Try to figure that one!

From Chicken Soup for the Non-Profit Soul

The successful volunteer leaves a mark, having done something in a way that others could not have done it. That's the way that I look at diversity...a concept that we must champion daily in our own unique ways.

One does not render pro-bono hours just to get acclaim. That's nice, after the fact. The real thrill was knowing that those few hours helped save lives.

The true heroes of our communities volunteer because it feels good and to help alleviate problems. We do not volunteer just to get awards. However, periodic recognition inspires the unsung heroes to chant a little more vibrantly the next time.

Community relations is action-oriented and should include one of these forms:

1. Creating something necessary that did not exist before.
2. Eliminating something that poses a problem.
3. Developing the means for self-determination.
4. Including citizens who are in need.
5. Sharing professional and technical expertise.
6. Tutoring, counseling and training.
7. Repairing, upgrading or restoring.
8. Promotion of the community to outside constituencies.
9. Moving others toward action.

The well-rounded community relations program embodies all elements: accessibility of company officials to citizens, participation by the company in business and civic activities, public service promotions, special events, plant communications materials and open houses, grassroots constituency building and good citizenry.

Community relations is not "insurance" that can be bought overnight. It is tied to the bottom line and must be treated accordingly...with resources and expertise to do it effectively. It is a bond of trust that, if violated, will haunt the business. If steadily built, the trust can be exponentially parlayed into successful long-term business relationships.

Successful people are products of mentorship. So are our communities. I've remembered and recorded most of the worthwhile advice that I've been given. We make and honor our commitments, nurtured by our responsibility to mentor others. If we're going to be called role models, we show it without fanfare and inspire others to lead.

From The $50,000 Business Makeover
Here are 14 sure-fire steps to begin putting this information to immediate use in your business.

1. Business cannot exist in a vacuum. You must put everything that you produce into a Big Picture context.
2. Recognize that there is a Big Picture, and be skeptical about niche consultants and vendors who purport that their approach is the only one.
3. Choose your advisors very carefully. Insist that they benchmark everything they do for you toward a Big Picture of your business.
4. You must have both a Sales Plan and a Marketing Plan as sub-sets of your Strategic Plan.
5. Advertising is a process, part of marketing and a cousin of sales. Running an ad here and there does not constitute advertising.
6. Have concurrent programs in your plan, including direct marketing, sales promotions, advertising, internet presence, specialty advertising, public relations and other marketplace presence.
7. Running a small business is tough. You cannot be a Lone Ranger. Develop a support system of friends and colleagues. Surrounding yourself with employees and consultants is not enough.
8. Always think about new products to create.
9. Never stop changing. Change is 90% positive. Every person and company changes 71% per year anyway. You might as well benefit from it, rather than become a victim of it.

10. Use my Business Tree as a way of always looking at the whole of any situation, then at the parts and back to the whole again.
11. You never stop paying dues. Opportunities create more successes.
12. Take ownership of planning programs, rather than abdicate them to human resources or accounting people.
13. Predict the biggest crises that can beset your company. 85% of the time, you'll prevent them from occurring.
14. Challenge yourself to succeed by taking a Big Picture look, while others are still thinking and acting small-time. Your biggest resource is a wide scope...and the daring to visualize success and then all of its components.

From The Future Has Moved...and Left No Forwarding Address

In moving forward, one must review those junctures where leaders and their companies recognize when a business is in trouble. These are the high costs of neglect, non-actions and wrong actions, per categories on The Business Tree™:

1. Product, Core Business. The product's former innovation and dominance has somehow missed the mark in today's business climate. The company does not have the marketplace demand that it once had. Others have streamlined their concepts, with greater success. Something newer has edged your company right out of first place.

2. Processes, Running the Company. Operations have become static, predictable and inefficient. Too much band-aid surgery has been applied, but the bleeding has still not been stopped. Other symptoms of trouble have continued to appear...often and without warning.

3. Financial Position. Dips in the cash flow have produced knee-jerk reactions to making changes. Cost cutting and downsizing were seemingly ready answers, though they took tolls on the rest of the company. The overt focus on profit and bean counter mentality has crippled the organizational effectiveness.

4. Employee Morale and Output. Those who produce the product-service and assure its quality, consistency and deliverability have not been given sufficient training, empowerment and recognition. They have not really

been in the decision making and leadership processes, as they should have been. Team members still have to fight the system and each other to get their voices heard, rather than function as a team.

5. Customer Service. Customers come and go...at great costs that are not tallied, noticed or heeded. After the percentages drop dramatically, management asks, "What happened?" Each link in the chain hasn't yet committed toward the building of long-term customer relationships. Thus, marketplace standing wavers.

6. Company Management. There was no definable style in place, backed by Vision, strategies, corporate sensitivities, goals and beliefs. Whims, egos and momentary needs most often guided company direction. Young and mid-executives never were adequately groomed for lasting leadership.

7. Corporate Standing. Things have happened for inexplicable reasons. Company vision never existed or ceased to spread. The organization is on a downslide, standing still and doing things as they always were done constitutes moving backward.

These situations are day-to-day realities for troubled companies. Yes, they brought many of the troubles upon themselves. Yes, they compounded problems by failing to take swift actions. And, yes, they further magnify the costs of "band-aid surgery" by failing to address the root causes of problems.

ABOUT THE AUTHOR

Hank Moore is an internationally known business advisor, speaker and author. He is a Big Picture strategist, with original, cutting-edge ideas for creating, implementing and sustaining corporate growth throughout every sector of the organization.

He is a Futurist and Corporate Strategist™, with four trademarked concepts of business, heralded for ways to remediate corporate damage, enhance productivity and facilitate better business.

Hank Moore is the highest level of business overview expert and is in that rarified circle of experts such as Peter Drucker, Tom Peters, Steven Covey, Peter Senge and W. Edwards Deming.

Hank Moore has presented Think Tanks for five U.S. Presidents. He has spoken at six Economic Summits. As a Corporate Strategist™, he speaks and advises companies about growth strategies, visioning, planning, executive-leadership development, futurism and the Big Picture issues affecting the business climate. He conducts independent performance reviews and Executive Think Tanks nationally, with the result being the companies' destinies being charted.

The Business Tree™ is his trademarked approach to growing, strengthening and evolving business, while mastering change. Business visionary Peter Drucker termed Hank Moore's Business Tree™ as the most original business model of the past 50 years.

Mr. Moore has provided senior level advising services for more than 5,000 client organizations (including 100 of the Fortune 500), companies in transition (startup, re-engineering, mergers, going public), public sector entities, professional associations and non-profit organizations. He has worked with all major industries over a 40-year career. He advises at the Executive Committee and board levels, providing Big Picture ideas.

He has overseen 400 strategic plans and corporate visioning processes. He has conducted 500+ performance reviews of organizations. He is a mentor to senior management. This scope of wisdom is utilized by CEOs and board members.

Types of speaking engagements which Hank Moore presents include:

- Conference opening Futurism keynote.
- Corporate planning retreats.
- Ethics and Corporate Responsibility speeches.
- University—college Commencement addresses.
- Business Think Tanks.
- International business conferences.
- Non-profit and public sector planning retreats.

In his speeches and in consulting, Hank Moore addresses aspects of business that only one who has overseen them for a living can address:

- Trends, challenges and opportunities for the future of business.
- Big Picture viewpoint.
- Creative idea generation.
- Ethics and corporate responsibility.
- Changing and refining corporate cultures.
- Strategic Planning.
- Marketplace repositioning.
- Community stewardship.

- Visioning.
- Crisis management and preparedness.
- Growth Strategies programs.
- Board of Directors development.
- Stakeholder accountability.
- Executive Think Tanks.
- Performance reviews.
- Non-profit consultation.
- Business trends which will affect the organization.
- Encouraging pockets of support and progress thus far.
- Inspiring attendees as to the importance of their public trust roles.
- Making pertinent recommendations on strategy development.

Additional materials may be found on Hank Moore's website:

www.hankmoore.com